# Public Sector Risk Management

# Public Sector Risk Management

# Martin Fone and Peter C. Young

OXFORD  AUCKLAND  BOSTON  JOHANNESBURG  MELBOURNE  NEW DELHI

Butterworth-Heinemann
Linacre House, Jordan Hill, Oxford OX2 8DP
225 Wildwood Avenue, Woburn, MA 01801-2041
A division of Reed Educational and Professional Publishing Ltd

℞ A member of the Reed Elsevier plc group

First published 2000

**British Library Cataloguing in Publication Data**
A catalogue record for this book is available from the British Library

ISBN 0 7506 5161 X

Printed and bound in Great Britain by Biddles Ltd, *www.biddles.co.uk*

FOR EVERY TITLE THAT WE PUBLISH, BUTTERWORTH-HEINEMANN
WILL PAY FOR BTCV TO PLANT AND CARE FOR A TREE.

# Contents

# Foreword by the Association of Local Authority Risk Managers

The Association of Local Authority Risk Managers (ALARM), which was formed in 1992, has been at the forefront of advocating and fostering a risk management culture in our public institutions in the United Kingdom. Today the Association has over 1,200 members and is widely recognised as the pre-eminent forum for the development and dissemination of issues that impact the management of public sector risk. A challenge our membership has set for the ALARM Council is to provide the skills and tools to enable members to do their job better and, more importantly, to help elevate risk management to senior management's agenda. ALARM sees this book as an important step in meeting this challenge.

Risk is dynamic and pervasive, nowhere more so than in the public sector. The challenges created by the imposition of a Best Value regime and the recognition of the need to embrace the corporate governance principles are just the latest two public sector risk managers have had to face. As this book illustrates, the management of risk is the responsibility of everyone involved in public institutions, from elected members to senior management to the rank-and-file employee.

Too many organisations inhibit imaginative risk taking because the process of risk management is not exercised. In order to change that, risk management has to become part of good management practice and culture. Indeed, no public sector organisation can meet best value expectations without a risk management culture, nor can a public sector organisation conform to corporate governance standards unless risk management is embedded in the processes and culture.

This book is about the processes, skills, techniques and information needed by public sector managers for whom risk management is a responsibility, irrespective of their title or job responsibilities. As such, ALARM endorses this book as both an introduction to risk management in the public sector and as a recommended text for the Institute of Risk Management syllabus for the IRM qualifications.

*Liz Taylor*                                                    *Kevin McGlone*
*Chief Executive*                                                    *Chairman*
*Association of Local*                            *Association of Local*
*Authority Risk*                                          *Authority Risk*
*Managers*                                                    *Managers*

# Foreword by the Institute of Risk Management

The Institute of Risk Management (IRM) is a professional and educational institute established in 1986 to provide a professional diploma qualification in Risk Management.

Public Sector Risk Management is one of five optional subjects that a successful candidate has to pass along with five core subjects to attain the Associateship qualification. The optional subject is an area whereby students can study their particular area of interest.

Public Sector Risk Management has been identified as being worthy of a separate examination in its own right owing to the fundamental differences in both the range and pervasiveness of public sector risk (relative to the private sector), but also because the management of public risk is precisely why public bodies exist. This book gives both a theoretical and practical framework for establishing the importance of public sector risk management as a subject in its own right and also provides a vital reference point for all who are involved in the management of our public institutions.

The formation of the Association of Local Authority Risk Managers (ALARM) in 1992 was a firm indication of the importance risk management holds in the public sector. The Institute of Risk Management was delighted to be involved with ALARM in this subject, thereby bringing it to a wider risk management audience.

The Institute is confident that with the revision of the public sector syllabus and the introduction of this new recommended text the topic area will be firmly established as an agenda item and will be instrumental in the promotion of a risk management culture within the decision making processes of all involved in managing and delivering front-line services.

*Maureen Gibbins*
*Chief Executive*
*Institute of Risk Management*

# *About the authors*

**Martin Fone** is a Vice-President of Munich-American Risk Partners in London with specific responsibility for developing public and not for profit business outside of the USA. He started his insurance career with Municipal Mutual, having previously worked for Price Waterhouse, and was Risk Management Services Manager at Zurich Municipal.

Martin is a Classics graduate from Trinity College, Cambridge as well as an Associate of the Chartered Insurance Institute and a member of the Institute of Risk Management.

Martin Fone has been at the forefront of developing integrated risk management programmes for the UK public sector and designing risk financing solutions aimed at maximising the financial efficiencies of risk retention and risk transfer strategies. He has written and spoken extensively on public sector risk management issues both in the UK and abroad and is an active supporter of the Association of Local Authority Risk Managers.

**Peter C. Young** is the E. W. Blanch Senior Chair in Insurance at the University of St Thomas Graduate School of Business, where he is responsible for the MBA concentration in risk and insurance management. Before joining the University of St Thomas, Dr Young was a professor of risk management in the College of Business at St Cloud State University.

Dr Young received his PhD in insurance and risk management from the University of Minnesota and his master's degree in public administration from the University of Nebraska-Omaha, where he specialised in state and local government.

Dr Young is considered one of the world's leading authorities on public sector risk management. He is the co-author of the most widely used risk management textbook in the world and has written numerous articles on organisation risk management theory and practice. He is active in advising businesses and government entities on insurance and risk management issues. He has served on the education committee for the Risk and Insurance Management Society, has been active in the Public Risk Management Association, serves on the advisory board of the State of Minnesota Risk Management Division and has been a visiting professor and adviser to City University-London and Aoyama Gakuin University in Tokyo.

# Acknowledgements

There are several people who deserve acknowledgement for the direct and indirect assistance and support they have provided us. Rich Vincelette of Munich-American RiskPartners has been a good friend and source of important information on public sector risk management. A similar comment could be made about Brad Johnson of Marsh, David Randle of Apex and J. C. Beckstrand of the E. W. Blanch Company. Equally, Ron Guilfoile, risk manager for the City of St Paul, and Fred Johnson, risk manager for the State of Minnesota, have been enormously important in demonstrating how effective risk management is practised. We would add to that group Taud Hoopingarner (risk manager and now deputy county administrator for Dakota County, Minnesota), who Peter Young had the pleasure of teaching nearly fifteen years ago. Steve Tippins of Roosevelt University has been a terrific professional and personal friend, as has Fiona Gilvey of Deloitte Touche in London. B. J. Reed, who heads the public administration programme at the University of Nebraska-Omaha, was a big influence on Peter Youngs life and professional development many years ago, and continues to exhibit an interest in his work, an interest that is greatly appreciated.

We should be remiss if we did not mention Michael Smith of the Ohio State University, with whom Peter Young co-authors a textbook on risk management. Mike is an extremely bright and able scholar, and we have learned much more from Mike than he has from us. Mike influenced a number of ideas in this book, so much so that we can only offer a general attribution and our sincerest thanks.

Specific thanks must go to John Riddell of Weightmans for his help and advice especially in relation to legal liability issues, Colette Dark of Gallagher Bassett, Liz Taylor, Chief Executive of the

Association of Local Authority Risk Managers, Ian Horwood of Wycombe District Council and Jackie Algar of Brighton and Hove Council. The authors are especially indebted to Shan Millie whose advice and encouragement was instrumental in ensuring that this book saw the light of day and to Mike Cash of Butterworth-Heinemann for backing this project.

On a personal note, the authors would like to thank their families for their support and patience. Martin Fone dedicates this book to his parents, Ray and Brenda, for their love, support and encouragement, and to his wonderful wife, Jenny, whose down-to-earth sense of realism kept his feet on the ground during this project.

Peter Young would like to thank his wife and daughters, Sian, Hannah and Mallory, for being the wonderful people that they are. They would say 'you are welcome', remind him that his more insufferable qualities invariably surface when writing, and observe that their patience and good humour definitely are more than he deserves. He would agree humbly, then make a shameless play for their affections by dedicating the book to them.

# How to use this book

The focus of this book is on practical management, specifically, the management of risks by public bodies. Within these pages, the guiding principle of content will be to help readers understand and apply risk management to their particular work circumstances. To that end, conceptual discussions will tend to be brief and the emphasis will be on observing concepts in action and, more importantly, providing readers with guidance in putting to use the concepts and practices discussed in the book.

While philosophy most decidedly is not a subject for treatment in this book, it is nevertheless important that readers understand the underlying premises that drive the book. These premises, or philosophical underpinnings, might be best summarised as follows:

- *Risk management is the management of all organisation risks.* Most scholars and practitioners in the field today would agree that risk management is moving beyond its insurance management roots and becoming more of a general management function. This book will address the particular aspects of traditional risk management in great detail, but the newer and broader interpretation of risk management will emerge persistently throughout the book.
- *A fundamental purpose of public institutions is risk management.* Although this statement could prompt a vigorous debate among political philosophers, it is practically true that in modern democratic societies, public institutions exist – at a fundamental level – to address risks that confront society (e.g., defence from outside attack, control of common threats to health, welfare and safety, maintenance of public order). The implications of this statement lie mainly in the observation that risk

management is not a peripheral or narrow technical function, but is central to the overall purposes of government.

- *Distinctions exist between public and private sector risks.* It could be argued that many distinctions made between the public and private sector are arbitrary; indeed, the past fifteen years have forced governments in many developed nations to reconsider what is properly the provenance of the public sector and what might better be undertaken by private or quasi-private institutions. However, this book will demonstrate that, while many risks confronted by public institutions are indistinguishable from those faced by private organisations, the nature of the exposure to risk exhibits fundamental differences. Further, significant number of public sector risks simply are different from private sector risks, and the differentiating elements in fact limit the private sector's ability to manage them.

- *The appropriate unit of analysis is the contract, the obligation, the commitment and the agreement.* Certain traditions in the study of politics and public institutions rely on an analysis of group and intergroup dynamics and the relationship of government to the populace. While not dismissing the appropriateness of this framework for many purposes, it is not one particularly well suited for understanding risk management in public sector institutions. The challenge of developing a comprehensive programme for managing all (or nearly all) organisational risks is a tall and complex order, and the only way to systematise such a programme is to break the exposure to risk into its smallest possible units. The concept and practice of risk management that are developed in this book arise from the idea that public institutions are collections of contracts, obligations, agreements and commitments made by the managers (or elected representatives) and the various stakeholders.

- *Risk management is more art than science.* There is a strong temptation to view risk management as a management function driven by a purely economics/finance/statistics-based model. While this has an element of truth to it, placing risk management in the domain of both general management and the public sector means that risk management policy and practice must be informed by a richer and more complicated understanding of how people and organisations deal with risk. Organisational risk assessment, for instance, will be demonstrated to have more in common with, say, a historian investigating the reasons for the outbreak of the First World War than it has in common with an analysis of the statistical incidence of mutations in tree frogs. An understanding of statistics is essential for risk managers, but arguably judgement, an ability to synthesise and reason, insight, intuition, an appreciation of human behaviour and effective communication skills probably are better predictors to effectiveness than is a narrower technical competence in mathematics-based modelling.

Since the purpose of this book is to translate ideas into action, each chapter will follow a relatively standardised structure. First, readers will be introduced to concepts and principles that are essential to understanding the particular subject in hand. Second, these concepts and principles will be demonstrated in the context of a public organisation. This will be accomplished through applications, which will expand on central themes of the chapter through an example. Third, readers will be given the means to actually apply the knowledge in a practical and usable way. Each chapter will conclude with a suitable presentation and commentary enabling readers to learn more about the particular topics and a chance to 'read more about it'.

# Abbreviations

| | |
|---|---|
| ABI | Association of British Insurers |
| ACII | Associate of the Chartered Insurance Institute |
| ACL | aggregate ceiling limit |
| AIRM | Associate of the Institute of Risk Management |
| AIRMIC | Association of Insurance and Risk Managers in Commerce |
| ALARM | Association of Local Authority Risk Managers |
| ASO | Administrative services only |
| BCCI | Bank of Credit and Commerce International |
| CBI | Confederation of British Industry |
| CGL | commercial general liability |
| CMT | crisis management team |
| COCA | contracts, obligations, commitments and agreements |
| CPM | Critical Path Method |
| CRO | chief risk officer |
| DETR | Department of Environment, Transport and the Regions |
| DTI | Department of Trade and Industry |
| EDP | Electronic Data Processing |
| EI | environmental impairment |
| EIL | environmental impairment liability |
| EU | European Union |
| FCII | Fellow of the Chartered Insurance Institute |
| FIRM | Fellow of the Institute of Risk Management |
| FSA | Financial Services Agency |
| GHQ | General Headquarters |
| GISC | General Insurance Standards Council |
| IOSH | Institute of Occupational Safety and Health |
| IRBC | Insurance Brokers Registration Council |
| IRM | Institute of Risk Management |
| MBA | Master of Business Administration |

| | |
|---|---|
| MEAT | most economically advantageous terms |
| NASA | National Aeronautics and Space Administration |
| NDR | non-domestic rate |
| *OJEC* | *Official Journal of the European Community* |
| ORM | organisation risk management |
| P & I | Protection and Indemnity Club |
| PCL | provision to meet credit liabilities |
| PERT | Programme Evaluation Review Technique |
| PIN | Prior Information Notice |
| PMP | performance management and planning |
| PRIMA | Public Risk Management Association |
| RIMS | Risk and Insurance Management Society, Inc. |
| RMIS | risk management information systems |
| RSG | Revenue Support Grant |
| SIR | self-insured retention |
| SRM | subjective risk matrix |
| SSA | standard spending assessment |
| SWOT | strengths, weaknesses, opportunities and threats |
| TEDIUM | time horizons, externalities, data credibility, interdependencies, uncertainty recognition and measurement of cost-benefits |

# Risk, uncertainty and the management of public sector risks

## EXECUTIVE SUMMARY

Risk exists whenever the future is not known with certainty, which means risk is ever present. In some respects risk is objectively measurable. We can measure the frequency with which accidents occur and the magnitude of the losses when they occur. However, risk is also a subjective concept, meaning we all have different attitudes towards risk. Many experts say the real challenge of risk management is to identify and manage attitudes and perceptions rather than the objective side of risk.

In some sense risks are risks, whether they are faced by public or private organisations. However, risks do have unique properties in a public sector environment. First, and most obviously, the organisations facing risk are unique; public bodies have numerous legal, social, and political attributes not seen in the private sector. Second, many of the public risks are unique and can be handled only by public institutions.

This book is about the management of risks in public bodies. In a broad and general sense, governments exist to manage risks (provide for the common defence, public safety, security and so on) and therefore risk management is a central function in public bodies. The focus of this book, however, is not on the broad philosophical basis of government as a risk management institution, but rather on the function of risk management within public bodies, a focus that will come to be known as organisation risk management.

# PRINCIPLES AND CONCEPTS

Risk appears to be a multifaceted, textured concept, so risk means (and may need to mean) different things in different situations.

The classic Indian story about the blind men and the elephant comes to mind here. Depending on where one stands, the thing observed reveals itself differently. Also, although the various definitions of risk appear idiosyncratic and inconsistent with each other, it is nevertheless true that there is a whole thing called 'risk', and risks, like elephants, are fascinating objects in no way diminished by the difficulty in defining them.

This book does not intend to labour over theory or terminology, so the purpose of Chapter 1 is to establish a workable understanding of the meanings of risk. After considering the definitions of risk, the chapter turns to the matter of uncertainty and concludes by identifying 'public risks' and explaining why these risks should be managed.

# What is risk?

Risk arises from what might be called the 'dynamic' characteristic of reality; a static, certain world would not contain risk. This dynamism produces change through the outcomes, outcomes that may fall within a definable possibility set (a coin toss will produce either a heads or tails outcome) or that may not be defined or anticipated in any obvious way (e.g., space exploration in the early 1960s). However, simply noting that risk exists when there is more than one possible outcome in a given situation does not seem adequate. We must know the relative likelihood of each outcome, and have some expectation of what is likely to happen the next time similar circumstances arise. If such information could be gathered, the ingredients for a 'baseline' definition of objective risk would be present.

Risk is the variation in outcomes around an expectation

Mathematicians offer a quantitative version of the definition of risk. It is called 'the coefficient of variation' and is determined by dividing standard deviation by the expected value. The coefficient of variation measures the degree of standardised dispersion relative to the 'average' or expected value. The problem with relying on the mathematician's interpretation of risk is that a risk manager may learn that a particular coefficient of variation is 2.8 (see Sidebar 1.1) and not believe that he or she has any better understanding of the risk in question. Part of the limitation of the coefficient of variation is that it is a relative value, and must be compared with other risks to increase its usefulness. However, another limitation is that this 'objective' measure does not capture much of the texture of risk. The concept of risk, it would seem, contains both quantitative (objective) and qualitative (subjective) dimensions.

'Texture', this book will argue, refers to the subjective or qualitative aspects of risk that seem to be missing from the mathematical definition given above. After all, two individuals might know objectively that some event has a 1 in 10 chance of producing a £1000

---

## Sidebar 1.1 The coefficient of variation

To demonstrate how the coefficient of variation is computed, consider Table 1.1.

**Table 1.1** Total property losses per year to a fleet of five cars

| Losses per year (£) | Probability |
| --- | --- |
| 0 | .606 |
| 1000 | .273 |
| 2000 | .100 |
| 4000 | .015 |
| 10 000 | .003 |
| 20 000 | .002 |
| 40 000 | .001 |

The average or expectation for this distribution is found by:

£0(.606) + £1000(.273) + £2000(.100) + £4000(.015) + £10 000(.003) + £20 000(.002) + £40 000(.001) = £643

The standard deviation for this distribution is found by calculating the square root of the following:

(0–£642) (.606) + (£1000–£643)(.273) + (£2000–£643)(.100) + (£4000–£643)(.015) + (£10 000–£643)(.003) + (£20 000–£643)(.002) + (£40 000–£643)(.001) = £3 199 312
The square root of which is: £1789 (the standard deviation)

Thus, the coefficient of variation = £1789/£643 = 2.8

loss, but have very different reactions to the knowledge. Subjectivity, perspective and attitude would seem to be a part of risk. Furthermore, texture would have to include not just perceptual factors, but also what might be thought of as 'fuzziness' factors. Fuzziness suggests a lack of clarity, the hidden interrelatedness of risks and the complexity of our environment.

Thus, a provisional list of the fundamental elements of risk might include:

- the number of possible outcomes that might occur and relative frequency of occurrence of each
- the quantitative value and magnitude of possible outcomes relative to some expected value
- the qualitative/perceived nature of the possible outcomes
- an ability or confidence in an ability to know or define the possible outcomes – that is, the level of uncertainty present
- attitude towards risk and uncertainty
- the externalities, interdependencies, and complicating factors associated with the risk.

Can each of these elements be woven into a clear, elegant definition? No. However, a working definition might be as follows:

> Risk is a characteristic of our world that is present when certainty is absent. Objectively, risk is the variability of outcomes around an expectation; while subjectively, risk is our attitude towards or perception of risk – which is influenced by uncertainty, personal, social, and cultural factors, and the risk's relationship to the larger environment (its context).

Although this definition is not elegant, it is useful enough and should signal that the management of risk will not aspire merely to manage probabilities and outcomes, but also to manage uncertainty and attitudes towards risk – and also, to recognise that the management of a risk may have broader social (even ethical) considerations not easily captured in a narrow, quantitative assessment of risk (see Sidebar 1.2).

## What is uncertainty?

The dictionary definition of uncertainty is 'doubt about our ability to know', and this is a useful way to think about the concept. 'Knowing', or cognition, requires data, a means of receiving the data, and the capability of processing or converting data into information.

---

## Sidebar 1.2 Fundamental elements of risk

The six elements of this book's definition of risk can be illustrated in an example. Assume a public body is contemplating hiring an individual to fill an internal auditor position. One risk presented by the hiring process is the possibility that the new hire might perpetrate a fraud. The elements of this risk are listed here.

1   Since behaviour is either fraudulent or it is not, only two possible outcomes can occur. One might be able to quantify the risk by gathering data on fraud committed by internal auditors. How often does it happen?
2   What are the ranges of magnitude of loss when fraud occurs? What are the effects of such losses on a public body?
3   The qualitative nature of those outcomes is readily imaginable, but this is not to say that fraud is simple to understand. What causes someone to commit fraud?
4   How much information can be gathered on this risk and on the interviewees – and at what cost? What is the confidence level in this information?
5   How do the public body and its managers account for personal biases and attitudes in the analysis of the risk (e.g., whether the interviewee's race factors into managers' judgement)?
6   The hiring of an individual does not present just one risk. The worker may bring intangible value to the organisation through exceptional industry, he or she may be injured at work, refusal to hire may bring a discrimination claim or the worker may discover potential losses and prevent them from occurring elsewhere.

---

Numerous factors can produce doubt: data or information may be incomplete, one may be incapable of receiving the data, or one may be able to receive the data but be unable to process or understand it.

For the purposes of this book, note that risk and uncertainty are separate concepts that are inextricably linked. The characteristics of a risk may influence the level of uncertainty; but other factors (such as attitude towards risk) can affect uncertainty as well. It is necessary to note the distinction here because the book considers the importance of managing uncertainty in Chapter 4 (see Sidebar 1.3).

---

### Sidebar 1.3 Michael L. Smith's four levels of uncertainty

Professor Michael L. Smith of the Ohio State University has developed an important conceptualisation of uncertainty. He argues that, like risk, uncertainty exists in varying degrees, and he has proposed a scheme for classifying levels of uncertainty. His 'certainty-uncertainty continuum' is shown in Table 1.2.

**Table 1.2**  Smith's certainty-uncertainty continuum

| Levels of uncertainty | Characteristics | Examples |
|---|---|---|
| None (certainty) | Outcomes can be predicted with precision | Physical laws |
| Level 1 (objective uncertainty) | Outcomes are identified and probabilities known | Games of chance |
| Level 2 (subjective uncertainty) | Outcomes are identified but probabilities unknown | Fire, investments |
| Level 3 | Outcomes not fully known and probabilities unknown | Space exploration |

---

## Other important concepts

Any good insurance textbook can provide a solid discussion of concepts and terms related to risk and uncertainty. This section focuses on just a few of these concepts and terms.

Scholars from many disciplines study how humans behave under conditions of risk and uncertainty. For instance, economists and psychologists instruct us to recognise that individuals have differing *attitudes towards risk*. Economists tend to focus on the impact of risk on the individual's quest to maximise utility (satisfaction) and hypothesise that most humans tend to be risk averse, especially as more and more financial resources become exposed to loss possibilities. Psychologists argue that economic rationality is only one factor governing attitudes towards risk, and so focus more on personality, family upbringing, personal history and other behavioural characteristics. Although the psychological research is rich and complex, patterns can be seen that are related to knowledge and understanding of a risk, and the degree to which fear or dread governs the individual perspective. By contrast, anthropologists place considerable credence in the notion that culture influences attitudes towards risk, largely by imposing 'filters' through which individuals broadly judge risks as being important or unimportant. Even medical researchers are involved actively in risk-related research and have uncovered gene-based influences in attitudes towards risk. Practical implications of these competing views are developed in Chapter 11.

Different categories of risk have been developed. While all the categories may be useful, the most commonly discussed are *pure risk* and *speculative risk*. Pure risks are those risks with two outcomes – either nothing will happen or a loss will occur. Speculative risks have three possible outcomes – nothing happens, a loss occurs, or a gain occurs.

The pure risk/speculative risk distinction is somewhat arbitrary. However, psychologists have demonstrated that individuals react differently to pure and speculative risks (basically, people tend to be less risk averse in speculative risk situations), and thus risk managers should recognise that reaction to risk will differ depending on the type of risk involved. However, in most respects risks are risks, and this book's general concern is the impact of all risk on a public body's mission.

Risk arises from *sources of risk*. A source of risk is an environment from which *hazards* or *risk factors* emerge. Hazards are characteristics of a risk source that elevate the chance for loss (or potential severity of loss), while risk factors are those characteristics that elevate the chance or magnitude of loss or gain. For example, icy roads would be a hazard arising from the physical environment source of risk. Voter unrest or uncertainty would be an example of a risk factor arising from the social or political environmental source of risk.

Hazards may produce *perils*, which are actual causes of loss; the hazardous condition of an improperly maintained heater may result in the peril of fire. In this book, the term *'opportunity'* serves as a speculative risk analogue to 'peril'. Use of 'opportunity' is open to some debate, but this book develops the concept of 'opportunities arising from risk factors'.

Finally, although our discussion is based on the notion of risk arising from sources of risk, the imagery is somewhat imprecise. Risk also requires *exposure*, which does not arise from sources of risk. An icy road cannot produce a loss to a driver who does not drive on that road. Likewise, an individual who does not invest does not face market risk. It could be argued that, like the tree falling unheard in the forest, the icy road does exist physically as a hazardous condition whether anyone experiences the icy road or not. However, in the context of organisations managing risks, it is exposure that provides the primary motivation to act.

# Risk in the public sector

If public sector managers were asked whether they think management in public bodies differs from private sector management, the
majority would – undoubtedly – answer yes. Comments about the
'absence of a bottom line', 'public accountability' and the 'separation
of power and authority' would be heard; and these would all be valid
points. However, additional differences can be noted – differences
that are important in understanding whether public sector risks
possess unique perspectives.

Drawing distinctions between the public and private sectors is not
straightforward. Broadly speaking, the distinctions are rooted in cultural and social factors (at least) and this means that 'public' is whatever a society says it is. While this idea may be a bit unsatisfying for
some readers, it does explain a wide range of inconsistencies observed
in the public life of Western democracies. Some nations believe health
and health care are public matters, others do not. Some nations
believe that government should run utilities while others do not. The
values ascribed to role of public education can vary widely as well.

The subject of 'publicness' is fascinating and intellectually challenging, but of course a full discussion here would take the book far
afield from its intended purposes. However, avoiding the topic is not
entirely appropriate either, so the following section offers a brief
treatment of the subject of publicness and – importantly – its implications for risk management in public institutions.

## *What is publicness?*

The concepts of public and private are best understood as points on
a continuum rather than as mutually exclusive states. Since this is
so, it is important to understand how things move from private to
public, and also how publicness relates to government as an institution. Two views, the political scientist's and the economist's, seem
relevant, and serve to suggest the contrasts in views and the political difficulties such differences promote.

### A political science perspective

Political scientists remind us that in the UK power to govern derives
from consent of the governed. Powers may be enumerated or implied,
but in a most fundamental sense, government exists to:

• protect individual rights
• advance politically agreed upon values and purposes
• balance interests.

This view of government's role is something of an amalgamation of two distinct philosophical traditions, republican and liberal. The republican view puts its emphasis on the citizen's responsibility to society, while the liberal view tends to look at government's obligation to assure individual freedom.

When considering government's fundamental role, it seems to be an instrument by which society imposes order on itself. Societies have basic desires to express identity, values, beliefs and aspirations. Informal social mechanisms such as religious institutions and fraternal associations, indeed even culture itself, cannot always connect to fulfil communal needs. Thus, government may serve as a vehicle for expressing communal values (and often serves to form them) when they cannot be expressed elsewhere – and value expression and clarification can create order. Likewise, in the process of forming and expressing values, democratic government serves the related purpose of balancing interests. Balancing interests is an imprecise science, but it is a critical element of the government's 'ordering' role. The preceding points can be summarised by saying that, from a political science perspective, government in the UK mediates republican and liberal impulses in the pursuit of social order. But it also should be remembered here that public endeavour is not synonymous with government endeavour. Government need not be the only occupant of the public sector.

## The economics perspective

Modern economists approach the role of government in a slightly different way. They maintain that fully functioning markets can also serve a public purpose in that markets organise the desires of individuals and organisations (in a manner of speaking), allocate scarce resources, and also – like governments – provide order to human affairs. Economists further assert that, all else being equal, markets coincide best with the political values of democracy inasmuch as competitive markets rely fundamentally on individual choice – a distinctly classic liberal argument. However, it is widely recognised that the concept of markets assumes that rules are abided by and that enforceability of interests occurs in an orderly manner. Thus, government has a clear *de minimis* role (in the eyes of economists) in serving as a referee. Beyond that, however, is a consensus that the assumptions underlying free, fully functioning competitive markets often are not met. Economists call this phenomenon 'market failure' and have developed a fairly elegant argument as to how government's role might be characterised in part as a response to market failure.

Markets also might fail because some goods or services are 'public goods'. Public good is a status conferred on goods or services that are non-appropriable, meaning that the consumption of the good/service cannot be restricted to those who pay for it. The classic example of a public good is national defence; even if an individual does not pay for it explicitly, they enjoy the benefits of expenditure for the common defence.

'Externalities' also could be a justification for government intervention. Externalities exist in goods and services when the costs and benefits cannot be captured fully in the price system. A relevant example is pollution. A polluting organisation can damage the environment without cost, in the sense that the cost of pollution can be passed on to the surrounding community, and thus is not captured in the market price. Those bearing the cost of pollution are not involved in the market transaction for the good produced and thus cannot, through the buy-sell transaction, impose that cost on the polluter.

The fact that public goods and externalities exist does not mean (to the economist, anyway) that aggressive government intervention need occur. For one thing, there can be 'government failure' as well, suggesting that a less than efficient market with no government intervention might still be preferable to a similar market with ineffective governmental intervention. As a result, public economists speak of a hierarchy of government responses to market failure – ranging from doing nothing, to providing information, to light intervention to restore the functioning of a private market, to absolute monopolistic provision by government of the good/service (this concept is derived from Catholic Canon Law and is related to the concept of subsidiarity – see 'Read more about it' later in this chapter). The idea of market failure can be connected to the political science view by suggesting that it reflects part of a more republican view of government – that is, society is more than a collection of utility-maximising individuals, and collectiveness gives rise to social obligations and responsibilities. We need also observe that economists, like political scientists, would argue that not all public matters need involve government.

What does all this suggest about the public sphere? First, the distinction between public and private is a rather fuzzy abstraction. One might be tempted to suggest that any human action is public inasmuch as it will have some effect on other humans. In such a restrictive view only a person's interior life is truly private. Culturally and politically, we have extended that view to include familial and other close relational activity. Publicness becomes a more distinct feature of human endeavour as its impact broadens to the larger community.

Second, even when a circumstance is deemed to be public in nature, we do not automatically assume that government has a natural role. Depending upon whether the economist or political science view is employed, justification for governmental involvement derives from the failure of private or market based efforts or from the need to secure and protect rights or to arbitrate interests.

## Is there such a thing as public risk?

Set aside for the moment the more general discussion of publicness, and turn now to the matter of risk and uncertainty. Since risk is pervasive, it is reasonable to wonder whether public and private risk actually exist.

Economic theory implies that efficient markets manage risks. This means that the efficient market allocates the cost of responsibility for risks attendant to the product or service. However, it might be imagined that some (or many) public risks might not be suited to 'market management'. Indeed, the risk properties of certain goods and services may be key contributors to their publicness. Once again, pollution is a good example in that the risk of collateral damage to surrounding communities is a feature (if not *the* feature) of the market that precipitates 'failure'. If this is true, it suggests an idea that is very important to this book: *since the nature of certain risks is influential in making goods and services 'public', risk management would seem to be a fundamental, rather than peripheral (or narrowly technical), function of government.*

How, specifically, does publicness affect risks and how does it influence the practice of risk management in public bodies? There seem to be two answers.

First, the exposure to risk is different. When a public body is exposed to a risk – what we call an 'organisation risk' – that risk is public by definition; the risk of a fire to a local authority controlled school is a public risk because the school building and contents are publicly owned. This sounds rather elementary, but it is an important point. Government's authority and legal justification for existence is based on powers derived from statute and the explicit relationship a government has with its citizens is not duplicated in private organisations. It is tempting to compare the citizen with the shareholder of a publicly held company, but there are many differences, both obvious and subtle. There is no market for trading shares of citizen ownership, and the nature of the citizen's financial obligation is different. The nature of legal liability differs as well. Further, peripheral matters like intergovernmental relations complicate the situation. Thus, government risk management is different from non-governmental risk management because the exposure to loss (or gain, for that matter) is politically, legally and socially unique.

Second, economists might argue that a public risk is defined similarly to a public good. A risk moves towards publicness when a private market (or individual action) is incapable of managing or distributing efficiently the burden of the risk. More precisely, a market's failure to manage a risk would be attributable to:

- a market's inability to incorporate the cost of risk into the price of the good or service due to non-appropriability, the presence of externalities or other reasons
- a market's inability to distribute the burden for risk-bearing to parties with the responsibility for and/or the capacity to bear the risk
- a sufficiently high level of uncertainty to impair the ability of a market to function.

The preceding comments structure our thinking about the characteristic differences that arise as risks become more public (from, at least, the economist's perspective). Risks move into the public domain when there is a high level of uncertainty and when the risk is either externality producing or non-appropriable, and/or when the risk cannot be distributed privately to the responsible parties with the ability to bear the risk.

A political scientist's view would differ in several key areas. Since government's functions include protecting rights, advancing politically agreed upon values and purposes, and balancing interests, the definition of public risks might be as follows:

> Public risks are characterised as those pertaining to issues or processes that arise from the assertion of matters of public interest – those matters relating principally to the protection of rights, the balancing of interests, and the assurance of fairness in the political process.

Notably here, government's role in this regard may be passive or active in that it may decide either to act or not to act in a given situation. Often, as noted later, government becomes indirectly involved in public risks through the establishment of policy (mandates) that directs others to manage risks that fall within the public domain but outside the realm of government direct action. This area of public risk is known as 'social risk management' (as distinguished from organisation risk management) and, although there are overlaps between the two, one represents the realm of policy while the other represents practice.

Thus, we come to the culmination of this line of reasoning. Somewhere in the territory where the private begins to become public, risks move to the public. Risks enter the public domain when they become characterised, to an increasing degree, by one or more of the following attributes:

1   The risk cannot be distributed, with recognition for political equity, to responsible parties capable of bearing the risk.
2   The risk produces externalities (or is imbued with externalities) that cannot be meaningfully captured in market pricing.
3   The risk is made manifest by the political process (an extreme example is the risk of revolution).
4   The risk imposes significant concerns with respect to the protection of individual rights.
5   The risk, in addition to the characteristics above, has an associated high level of uncertainty.
6   The exposure is public.

The entire preceding discussion, then, gives rise to three propositions that will be carried forward in the remainder of this book:

1   Although governments do not address all public risks directly, the risks that fall ultimately under government's purview have particularly challenging properties.
2   Public risks come in two broad forms: social risks (that affect society as a whole) and organisation risks (that affect particular public entities). Governments can have responsibilities in both areas – but other institutions can occupy space in the public sector too. This book is concerned mainly with organisation risk management.
3   Since the nature of particular risks frequently contributes to the publicness of some good, activity, service or process, the management of public risks is a fundamental role of government.

## Afterward: contracts, obligations, commitments and agreements – units of analysis

Before concluding this introductory chapter, it is useful to discuss briefly a concept that will serve an important analytical role throughout the book. Although it stands alone as an organising idea, it does relate in very significant ways to the preceding discussion of public risks and public risk management, and in an important sense is the means by which the rather abstract discussion in this chapter begins to give shape to the practice of organisation risk management. The concept is known as the 'COCA organisation'.

Earlier discussion in this chapter has proposed the idea that the management of risks is a central or general management function in governmental entities. But how is this core role of risk management adequately conveyed – especially when risk management historically has been viewed as a narrow technical or specialised function?

The answer can be found by recognizing that public bodies are collections of contracts, obligations, commitments and agreements between managers (and/or elected members) and resource holders. These contracts, obligations, commitments and agreements (COCAs) are assembled, or in any event accumulated, in the service of the overall purposes or objectives of the organisation. The concept of a resource holder is similar to that of a stakeholder, but the emphasis on possession of an asset or claim (a resource) that serves the purposes of the organisation probably is more useful in a risk management setting. For this book, the COCA concept's importance can be summarised as follows:

1   COCAs create an organisation's exposure to risk. Some risks are created literally by the COCAs, while some risks 'pass through' the COCAs.
2   Risks are fundamental characteristics of COCAs.
3   COCAs are expressly or implicitly multiparty, meaning that only rarely are entities in a position where only their interests are served.
4   Formation of COCAs is a key moment in risk management as it is the first and best opportunity to manage and distribute risk.

The COCA concept is developed in Chapter 3 as a foundation for risk assessment and in Chapter 4 as a means of risk control.

---

# APPLICATIONS

## Judging attitudes towards risk

Perhaps one of the greatest difficulties risk managers encounter is understanding their organisation's attitude towards risk. Of course, organisations like a local authority do not have an 'attitude towards risk' *per se*, but certainly the leaders and key managers do and their attitudes influence how the organisation behaves under conditions of risk and uncertainty.

Indeed, it can be argued that attitudes towards risk – or 'subjective risk' – really is the critical aspect of risk to manage. The risk manager can have very accurate and objective data on public sector risks, and still face considerable obstacles in getting managers and members to act – or even to reach a consensus on a view of those risks.

Although Chapters 2 to 11 provide numerous insights on the management of subjective risk, it is appropriate here to think about the specific objective of managing subjective risk and how a risk manager might set about doing it.

First, the objective. At several points in this book the overall purpose of risk management is discussed, and readers will see that risk management is not just about reducing or eliminating risk. Rather, risk management is governed by the overall purposes of the organisation, meaning that risk-taking may become a central element of the risk management programme. In other words, risk management involves striving for a balanced portfolio of risks that supports the organisation's overall objectives. But what about the specific issue of subjective risk?

Dispense with the idea that there is one true attitude towards a given risk or set of risks. Yes, there may be a scientifically objective description of a risk, but to say that there is an absolute value for subjective risk is nonsensical. Certainly, as later chapters argue, information management can reduce uncertainty and help managers better understand the objective characteristics of a risk – and this is a desirable outcome – but this is not the same thing as managers having an identical attitude towards that better understood risk.

The previous paragraph will not strike public sector managers and politicians as remarkable, for these comments could apply to any matter of public concern. People's attitudes about any policy – paving streets, expanding a public park, changing curricula in schools – will not be identical even if the outcomes are known with certainty. Public policy in democracies is driven by compromise and consensus building, which means that unity of purpose and perfection of outcome is largely unattainable. The same is true with the management of subjective risk within public bodies. The risk manager's role in managing subjectivity is to champion a process by which convergence or consensus may occur. Like all public sector management challenges, this means that the process is nearly as important as the outcome.

Numerous books on organisational behaviour and management can provide an insight into the challenge of consensus building, so we do not go into detail here. However, with respect to building consensus on an organisation's attitude towards risk, the following information may be useful.

Elected members and managers have very different perspectives – and certainly this includes attitudes towards risk. Chapter 2 develops the concept of 'levels of risk' within organisations, but simply note that an elected member's perspective is going to be influenced by deeply personal factors but also by the context of his or her position. Cynics might observe that the overarching objective is to get re-elected but, even if true, it requires a degree of responsiveness to the needs of the constituency being served. Thus, in an important sense, the elected member represents a means by which community attitudes towards risk are processed and converted into a policy form. The point here is that, while risk managers often lament that elected members do not have the same view of a particular risk, it actually would be more surprising if they did. Elected members' attitudes towards risk exist in a political realm mainly and only occasionally in a managerial or operational realm.

This suggests that when risk management matters are presented to the politicians of a public body either the matter needs to anticipate the political realm of the risk, or the issue of subjective risk needs to be explicitly raised and discussed.

Equally, managers within a public body have a distinctive perspective and this influences their attitude towards risk. While assuming that these individuals generally have the best interest of the electorate in mind, they face a host of pressures, incentives and disincentives that tend to focus their attention on their specific operating unit.

As an application of Chapter 1, the preceding discussion might be characterised as follows:

1   Risk managers have an obligation to engage both elected members and managers in a discussion of risk and attitudes towards risk. The objective is to create a basic awareness of attitudes towards risk, why they exist and how they differ.
2   Risk management education is a duty of every risk manager. As Chapters 10 and 11 discuss, risk is a complicated subject and effective communication is a serious challenge. However, the development of a 'culture of risk management' begins with education.
3   The process of educating managers and elected members on risk management can serve as a springboard for establishing the risk management mission, for obtaining top-level buy-in,

for setting a more participatory environment for the practice of risk management, and for creating a better appreciation for the differing attitudes towards risk and how consensus might be obtained.

---

## TOOLS YOU CAN USE

### Building a risk management library

A wealth of resources are available to help risk managers better accomplish their objectives and, specific to this chapter, educate members of their organisation. The following represent a reasonable and manageable starting point for a risk management library:

1   The Association of Local Authority Risk Managers (ALARM) is the pre-eminent association of public sector risk managers. Membership of ALARM is essential for a number of reasons but, from a library or resource perspective, ALARM offers:
   (a)   a library
   (b)   a good practice guide
   (c)   links to other risk management and public sector risk management related web sites both in the UK and internationally
   (d)   an annual conference and regionally based meetings and activities.

ALARM can be contacted at: Association of Local Authority Risk Managers, Queens Drive, Exmouth, Devon EX8 2AY; phone 01395 223399; fax 01395 223304; e-mail admin@alarm-uk.com; web site www.alarm-uk.com

Readers should note the presence of one other association of possible relevance; the Association of Insurance and Risk Managers in Commerce (AIRMIC).

2   John Adams's *Risk* (UCL Press, London, 1998) is a good introduction to the subject of attitudes towards risk, and the specific implications of subjective risk on public policy.
3   Peter Bernstein's *Against the Gods: The Remarkable Story of Risk* (John Wiley, New York, 1996) is a very readable introduction to both a history of risk and risk management, but also of modern practices.
4   C. A. Williams, Jr, Michael L. Smith, and Peter C. Young's *Risk Management and Insurance* (Irwin/McGraw-Hill, New York, 8th

edn, 1999) is co-authored by one of the authors of this book and is generally recognized as the most widely used university-level textbook on the subject of risk management.

5   Mark Dorfman's *Introduction to Insurance* (Prentice Hall, Englewood Cliffs, NJ, 1998) is a very accessible introduction to the concepts of risk and uncertainty, as well as an excellent reference on insurance and risk financing.

6   Neil Doherty's *Corporate Risk Management* (McGraw-Hill, New York, 1985), while focused on private sector bodies, offers many important insights into the larger purposes of risk management. It is fairly advanced in its treatment of the subject, and readers looking for an accessible introduction to the subject should look elsewhere.

7   The Institute of Risk Management (IRM) programme offers a professional designation that is the current 'coin of the realm' for professional risk managers in the UK. The IRM web site address is www.irmgt.co.uk

8   Miley Merkhofer's *Decision Science and Social Risk Management* (D. Reidel, Dordrecht, Holland, 1987) is a book focused on risk assessment models and their applications to broad public policy questions. Although quite technical, it is fairly accessible and provides a number of important insights into policy formulation and risk management.

9   R. M. Trimpop's *The Psychology of Risk Taking Behaviour* (Morth-Holland, Amsterdam, 1994), while fairly advanced and technical, could make useful reading for risk managers wanting to better understand attitudes towards risk and methods for measuring and understanding its relationship to objective risk.

---

## READ MORE ABOUT IT

## Private sector and public sector risk management: is there a difference?

### By Peter C. Young[1]

Are there meaningful differences between management in the public and private sectors? This question rests at the center of a long-standing debate among management scholars. Almost invariably it is a debate laden with political overtones, which in itself is instructive as public and private management are never free from political influence. As a professor who has spent time in both public administration and business administration programs, I have had several opportunities to think about both sides of the debate. On one side, we have those who argue that management is management and that differences in the public and private sectors are modest and in any event are differences in degree rather than in kind ('if only government were run like a business . . .').

For public risk managers and those concerned about public risk management, this point of view has a particular ring of familiarity. In recent years we have heard two arguments that reverberate with echoes from the 'management is management' thesis. First, many observers have expressed the belief that public risk managers could import a great number of private sector risk management practices, and that this effort would bring the public sector up to the level of private sector practices. I, myself, have made this point from time to time, albeit in limited contexts. Second, both public and private sectors have been subjected to the outsourcing phenomenon, which at its heart is based on the argument that risk management is risk management and that knowing a particular set of skills is sufficient to be successful in any organization. Again, I have been associated with parts of this argument, and our Master of Business Administration (MBA) curriculum at St Thomas (like most MBA programmes) is partly predicated on a belief in a universally applicable set of managerial skills and knowledge.

Opponents of the preceding point of view argue that the public sector is so differently configured that it constitutes a distinctly separate thing and, thus, requires substantively different knowledge and management skills. For a very long time, I simply did not buy this argument. Politics exist in private and public organizations, as do multiple stakeholders. Some large private organizations have dispersed authority, while some public institutions have fairly focused authority. Some private organizations are very process oriented and some public entities emphasize outputs. Further, increasingly, it is difficult to draw demarcation lines between public and private sectors. What do you call, for instance, an arrangement where a private transportation company is contracted to a non-profit care facility for disabled individuals, which in turn is under contract with a county government?

In recent years, however, I have begun to back off my views on public v. private management, and I now believe that while there are important commonalities and similarities, the 'public' aspect of public risk management does present some important and meaningful distinctions. Further, I have grown a little less enchanted with the 'management is management' school. With respect to the argument that the public sector needs to catch up with the private sector, I am not sure that is true in the case of risk management.

For one thing, as the following discussion will attempt to establish, there are aspects of public risk management that have no private sector analog – so there is a comparability problem. Also, when we survey the state of the art in private sector risk management, we find much less advancement than you might expect. Indeed, the garden variety public risk manager probably has a broader range of responsibilities than is the case for the average private organization risk manager. For another thing, leading management scholars like Peter Drucker and Henry Mintzberg have concluded (as have a growing number of graduate schools of business) that knowledge of the specific business you are in is as critical to success as – perhaps even more critical than – your understanding of management principles and practices. With respect to outsourcing, this view does not mean that an organization cannot contract for technical services – but it does mean that the idea of outsourcing the entire risk management function is wrong-headed.

Many readers will respond to the previous paragraph by saying, 'Of course government is different from business; business strives for profit! Do we really need a whole article to come to this conclusion?' I believe that a more subtle explanation is necessary, however, when looking at the question of publicness and risk management; and I hope, by this section's end, to have persuaded readers that the effort was worthwhile.

There are a number of ways to approach the subject of publicness. A political science-based approach would engage us in considerations of how societies formalize, institutionalize and legitimize government and how government, once constituted, interacts with society. We might try to define publicness through legal reasoning; how does the law differentiate between the public and the private? A sociological/anthropological approach would ask us to consider how societies distinguish 'the collective from the individual' and the 'private collective from the public collective'. Other avenues of investigation are possible; for instance, in the public administration literature there is fairly extensive analysis of the differences between organizational structure and processes in public and private institutions.

For a publication like *Governmental Risk Management Reports* it probably is not the best use of ink to survey academic research as wide-ranging as that mentioned above. Therefore, I would like to discuss only briefly the concept of publicness, and provide readers with a framework for thinking about intrinsic differences between the public and private sectors. Then, readers will be asked to think about whether risks can be separated into public and private categories. Finally, those discussions will serve as a basis for a general commentary of the characteristics of the public sector and of public risks that give public risk management its distinctiveness.

## The public, the private and government

The notion of publicness is a rather fuzzy one, demarcating as it does actions that are of private concern with those that have social or collective interests. Societies tend to specify the distinction somewhat broadly and resolve questions individually. In the USA we rely on national and state constitutions to set basic boundaries of the private and public (as well as government), and then look to social expressions, culture and common law to identify specific characteristics of publicness.

Because this is so, it is probably not possible to draw a clear distinction between the public and private sectors. Additionally, since virtually every human activity has consequences for individuals other than the actor, we have to recognize that publicness is a matter of degrees. But what about the distinction between 'public' and 'government'? They are not, after all, synonymous terms.

In the USA we have been particularly mindful of the distinction between things that are imbued with a public interest and those public things that merit government involvement, and it has become a topic of great interest. The following comments illustrate this point.

While many nations have pursued the belief that government has active responsibility for most, if not all, public activity, Americans have tended to adopt the view that public matters need not necessarily give rise to governmental activity. Indeed, since the 1960s, there have been several powerful trends that, cumulatively, have changed attitudes formed in the 1930s, 1940s and 1950s about the centrality of government in the public and private lives of citizens. In particular, critics have raised questions about the relationship between central or national governments and public sectors, and between government and the governed.

It would be misleading to state that anti-government sentiment has won the day, but it probably is true that the political center of gravity today is found at a point in the electorate where misgivings about government are the highest they have been in sixty years. This antipathy to active central government is traceable not just to conservative politics, but also to market-based economics (greater choice, greater mobility of capital, consumption preferences, technology) and a rising valuation of individual rights (the civil rights movement). Admittedly these forces have sometimes come to cross-purposes; the civil rights movement, after all, did require active national government involvement and advocacy. However, it is arguable that general social, political, legal and economic forces have run in the direction of 'the primacy of the individual' and, correspondingly, 'the primacy of the private'. Since the influences come from across the political spectrum and from fundamental economic dynamics, the general direction of the trends is not likely to reverse itself short of a political crisis or some other unforeseeable circumstance.

Having noted the general direction, we should not ignore completely the discomfort many Americans feel when we constantly place the individual before the group. Voices as disparate as William Bennett and Louis Farrakhan have expressed concern over the loss of community values. The Communitarian movement is striving to identify communal values and a clearer sense of publicness. In fact, if we were to judge our current state of affairs from the *New York Times* bestsellers' list, we might conclude that concerns about 'public values' are in the ascendancy.

So, what can we say here about the distinction between the public, the private and government that will move our discussion along? Well, first we must recognize that the threshold between public and private sectors is not a clear one (in and of itself a useful conclusion), and we need to think about human affairs as existing on a spectrum with most human activities exhibiting 'degrees of publicness'. Second, we must recognize that while 'government' is not necessarily popular in America, there is wide recognition that society is more than a collection of individuals; that is, we do believe that some things are imbued with publicness. Recognition of these points compels us to alter slightly the initial trajectory of this section. It seems that a critical issue for public risk managers is recognition that the public/private debate does not present us with an either/or proposition. Rather, a public risk manager will be more interested in the implications of increasing publicness and, most importantly of all, the implications of the distinction between public affairs and governmental affairs.

Let us finish this section with some thoughts on the public sector and on government. Since we are operating from a basic premise that all human activity has some degree of publicness, we need to think about how publicness relates to government. Political scientists remind us that in the USA power to govern derives from consent of the governed. Powers may be enumerated or implied, but in a most fundamental sense, government exists to:

- protect individual rights
- advance politically agreed upon values and purposes
- balance interests.

This view of government's role is something of an amalgamation of two distinct philosophical traditions: republican and liberal. The traditional republican view puts the emphasis on the citizen's responsibility to society, while the liberal view tends to look at government's obligation to assure individual freedom.

When one considers this view of government's role at its fundamental level it is apparent that government is an instrument by which society imposes order on itself. Societies have basic desires to express identity, values, beliefs and aspirations; and informal social mechanisms such as religious institutions or fraternal associations cannot always connect with communal expression. Thus, government may serve as a vehicle for expressing communal values (indeed, often serves to form them) when they cannot be expressed elsewhere, and value-expression and clarification can create order. Likewise, in the process of forming and expressing values, government serves the related purpose of balancing interests. Balancing interests is an imprecise science but a critical element of the democratic government's 'ordering' role.

To put this in the context of the text, we might summarize the preceding by saying that government in the USA mediates republican and liberal impulses in the pursuit of social order.

Modern economists approach the role of government in a slightly different way. They maintain that fully functioning markets also can serve a public purpose in that they organize the desires of individuals and organizations, allocate scarce resources, and also can provide (like government) order to human affairs. They further assert that, everything else being equal, markets best coincide with the political values of democracy inasmuch as competitive markets rely fundamentally on individual choice – a distinctly classic liberal argument. However, it is widely recognized that the assumptions underlying free, fully functioning competitive markets often do not hold (see Sidebar 1.4). Economists call this phenomenon 'market failure' and have developed a fairly elegant argument as to how government's role might be characterized as a response to the failure of markets.

How, specifically, do economists explain government's role? First, as mentioned above, they note that markets may be weakened when fundamental assumptions do not hold. Thus, if the supplier of some good is a monopolistic provider, economists would be concerned that the market may be inefficient. Thus, government might have a role in addressing the failure by, say, monitoring the monopoly.

A weakening of any one of the basic assumptions of efficient markets might prompt a governmental response, but there are other non-assumption factors that may lead to failure. Markets might fail

## Sidebar 1.4 Characteristics of pure competitive markets

A pure competitive market is efficient, meaning that economic forces operate unimpeded. There are seven assumptions or conditions that must exist for a pure competitive market:

1   The number of firms (sellers) is large.
2   Buyers and sellers are price-takers.
3   There are no barriers to entry.
4   The product is homogeneous.
5   There is costless, instantaneous entry and exit.
6   Selling firms are profit-maximizing organizations.
7   There is complete information.

Item 1 refers to the presence of a large number of competitors, none of which has any particular market advantage over the other. Item 2 means that no single party can set the price or unduly influence the determination of the price of the good. Item 3 is self-explanatory, and item 4 means that the product is undifferentiated, or identical. Item 5 means that actions to move in and out of markets are 'frictionless', while item 6 means that suppliers of the good are motivated to maximize wealth. Finally, item 7 states that all parties in a market must have equal access to all pertinent information on the product and the market.

It is plain that these assumptions are stringent, and readers might readily conclude that many markets for goods and services violate one or more of these underlying characteristics. However, violation of assumptions does not devalue the meaning of the pure competitive market idea, since purely competitive markets serve more as an analytical benchmark enabling us to understand the performance and behavior of markets.

---

because some goods or services are 'public goods'. Public good is a status assigned to goods or services that are non-appropriable. Non-appropriability refers to an inability to restrict the use of the good/service to those who pay for it. The classic example of a public good is national defence. Even if you do not pay for it, you enjoy the benefits of expenditure for the common defence. 'Externalities' might also be a justification for government. Externalities exist in goods or services where the cost and benefits cannot be captured entirely in the price. Pollution is a topic of relevance, and it illustrates the characteristics of an externality. A polluting organization can damage the environment 'costlessly' because the cost of damaging the environment will not be captured in the price (unless the cost is imposed by a party outside the market transaction, like a governmental regulator). Those bearing the cost of pollution (neighboring communities) are not involved in the market for the good produced and thus the buyers and sellers enjoy a transaction that does not incorporate the cost of pollution into the price.

The fact that public goods and externalities exist does not mean that aggressive government intervention need occur. For one thing, there can be 'government failure', suggesting that a less than efficient market with no government intervention might still be preferable to a similar market with ineffective governmental intervention. As a result, there is an implicit hierarchy of government responses to market failure – ranging from doing nothing, to providing information, to light intervention to restore the functioning of a private market, to absolute monopolistic provision by government of the good or service. We could connect the concept of market failure into the political science view by suggesting that it reflects part of a more republican view of government; that is, society is more than a collection of individuals and collectiveness gives rise to social obligations and responsibilities.

In further contrasting the economist's view of government with the political scientist's, we might generalize that economists look to matters of economic efficiency and private equity, while political scientists are more concerned with process and fairness, or what we might call social adequacy. While this statement glosses over the complexity of both points of view, it does serve a rhetorical purpose here. Government serves mixed purposes that may be in conflict with one another, and may not be entirely reconcilable. Most public administrators recognize that they manage in an environment where conflicting objectives prevail, and that the good ones realize that this feature gives rise to an important maxim of public administration: Managing in the public sector is the art of the possible informed by the science of the ideal. Squaring 'efficiency' objectives with 'social adequacy' goals is a common public administration challenge, and it illustrates plainly a previous point – balancing interests is a fundamental purpose of government.

Before we depart the subject of publicness, we must discuss briefly the concept of 'subsidiarity' and its relationship to the public sector.

If we recall that government does not act in every part of the public sector, we have a very practical question to answer: on what basis does a society conclude that a public matter requires governmental involvement? For our purposes, the general answer is to be found in the concept of 'subsidiarity'. Subsidiarity may be explained as follows: individuals possess rights and responsibilities for control of their lives, and government's role is to intervene in human affairs when individual action, choice or responsibility fail to meet a test of adequacy or appropriateness. The concept of subsidiarity does not clarify the exact points at which the private becomes public and at which point public matters become governmental matters, but it does provide us with a rough framework for analysis: in democratic societies, the individual enjoys primacy in the general determination of his or her affairs. When individuals are incapable of managing personal affairs, a 'subsidiarity hierarchy' is assumed to exist to resolve this incapability. The rank ordering of this hierarchy is:

1   The individual.
2   The family.
3   Informal/voluntary social institutions (including markets).
4   Public sectoral/social institutions.
5   State governmental/social institutions.
6   National governmental/social institutions.

Increasingly, we must toss in a item 7, international institutions (such as the United Nations), which may be the only entities capable of addressing certain complex, multinational problems. In any event, we see in this rank ordering that government is, in principle, a social institution of last resort. It is also worth noting that within the governmental sector, the level of government most proximate to the problem/issue is presumed to be best positioned to respond.

Plainly, this rank ordering has a strong American flavor, and we should not let it go unremarked that cultural influences on democracy can produce different orderings (think how Japanese citizens might react to this hierarchy). Even in roughly similar cultures, with roughly similar forms of government, different ordering preferences can emerge. For instance, the UK and the USA have similar political and legal traditions, but one has a national government structure while the other operates under a federal system. Although attitudes are changing in the UK, it is evident that the subsidiary hierarchy mentioned above does not integrate as easily with such a system.

Additionally, subsidiarity principally arises from a liberal economic frame of reference and this seems to contradict the previous assertion that publicness in the USA involves a balancing of liberal and republican instincts. The clarification I would make here is that while subsidiarity appears inconsistent with social responsibility, it is not, and we can still allow for a more republican view to emerge through the process of defining relationships in the hierarchy. For instance, we could look to individuals and families as having certain obligations to society rather than merely having rights to remain separate from society.

## Is there such a thing as a 'public risk'?

Set aside for the moment the more general discussion of publicness, and turn your attention to the matter of risk and uncertainty. Since we have known that risk is pervasive, we might assume that some risks also might become 'public' when certain conditions hold. How would we organize our thinking about this?

We might begin in a manner similar to our discussion of publicness by noting that risks also exist on a continuum, and we would further observe that when the impact of a risk goes beyond the individual, we begin to see 'public' properties emerge. These risks would fall in two broad categories: social risks and organizational risks. Social risks would be those risks that affect society in part or as a whole. Viral epidemics, foreign invasion and natural disasters are examples of this type of public risk. Organizational risks are the risks that befall the public institutions themselves. Wrongful termination liability lawsuits, fires in public facilities, and pension funding and other financial risks are examples. Of course, there is some overlap in these two categories; changing legal liability standards might present both social and organizational risks.

Economic theory implies that efficient markets manage risks; the efficient market allocates the cost of and responsibility for risks attendant to the product or service. However, while not yet articulating the reasons, we readily might imagine that public risks may not be suited to 'market management', and further we might speculate that the risk properties of certain goods are key contributors to their publicness. Pollution, once again, is a good illustration in that the risk of collateral damage to surrounding communities is a feature of the market that precipitates failure. If this is in fact true, it suggests that risk management is a fundamental, rather than peripheral, function of government. We will revisit this point shortly.

Earlier this section argued that the concepts of private and public are best considered as points on a continuum, and likewise we might consider that there is not absolute distinction between public and private risks. So, rather than asking what the difference is between public and private risks, it is probably more appropriate to ask: What are the properties of risks that introduce publicness? There seem to be two answers.

First, the exposure is different. When a public institution is exposed to a risk – what we called organizational risks – that risk is public by definition; the risk of a fire to a public school is a 'public risk' because the exposure is public. This sounds obvious; however, we must appreciate the fact that this statement suggests an important point. Government's authority is based on constitutionally derived powers, and the explicit relationship a government has with its citizens is not duplicated in the private sector. One is tempted to compare the citizen with the stockholder of a publicly held corporation but there are many differences, both obvious and subtle. Citizen 'ownership' of that burned school building is by definition distant from stockholder ownership; there is no market for trading shares of 'citizen ownership' and the financial obligation is different.

Also, the government's taxing authority presents a risk-spreading financing vehicle not seen in the private sector. Additionally, intergovernmental relations complicate, but in many ways enhance, the risk-bearing capabilities of the public sector, and statutory liability limits will have an impact as well.

We might contrast this illustration with a situation where a publicly held firm suffers a similar fire. Although employees, creditors and customers will be a concern for the firm's risk manager, the impact on the stockholders is fairly plain, and certainly measurable.

The second answer to the question can be found by revisiting the earlier economic and political discussions of publicness. Economists might argue that a public risk is defined similarly to a public good. So, a risk moves towards publicness when a private market is incapable of either managing it or distributing 'efficiently' the burden of the risk. More precisely, a market's 'failure' to manage a risk would be attributable to:

1   The market inability to incorporate the cost of risk into the price due to non-appropriability, or to the presence of externalities, or other reasons.
2   The market's inability to distribute the burden for risk-bearing to parties with the responsibility for or the capacity to bear the risk.
3   A sufficiently high level of uncertainty as to affect the ability of the market to function.

Regarding point 3, it does not follow that high uncertainty alone precipitates government intervention. However, the presence of high levels of uncertainty may be an accompanying condition of publicness when other factors are present. This third point suggests a fundamental tenet of public economics, which is that, in a market-based democracy, government has a basic role in assuring access to information since 'complete information' is a foundation principle of market economics.

The preceding paragraphs give us some structure to thinking about the characteristic differences between public and private risks from an economist's perspective. Risks move into the public domain when there is a high level of uncertainty and when the risk is either externality producing or non-appropriate and/or when the risk cannot be distributed to responsible parties with the ability to bear the risk.

My version of the political scientist's take on this would yield a somewhat different answer. Since government's functions include protecting rights, advancing politically agreed upon values and purposes, and balancing interests, the explanation for public risks might appear as follows: public risks are characterized as those pertaining to issues or processes that arise from the assertion of matters of public interests, those matters principally relating to the protection of rights, the balancing of interests and the assurance of 'fairness' in the political process.

Thus, we come to the culmination of this line of reasoning. Somewhere in the territory where the 'private' begins to become the 'public', we see risks move to the public. While it is not possible to draw a distinct line, we can say that risks enter the public domain when they become characterized, to an increasing degree, by one or more of the following attributes:

1   The risk cannot be distributed, with recognition for political equity to responsible parties capable of bearing the risk.
2   The risk produces externalities (or is imbued with externalities) that cannot be meaningfully captured in market pricing.
3   The risk is made manifest by the political process (an extreme example is the risk of revolution).
4   The risk imposes significant concerns with respect to the protection of individual rights.
5   The risk, in addition to the characteristics above, has an associated high level of uncertainty.
6   The exposure is public.

We must remind ourselves once more that, like public goods, the fact that a risk is a public risk does not automatically presume active government involvement except in cases where the exposure is a governmental entity. A public risk only requires public 'consideration' of a governmental risk management response. And, our subsidiarity rule influences the decision for government to become involved.

## Sidebar 1.5 Are hurricanes a public risk?

It is useful to test a sweeping assertion like the description of public risks given in this section. A very topical example is the exposure to losses arising from natural disasters. The formation of a catastrophic loss pool in Florida suggests that the state has decided that hurricanes are public risks. Why?

The six characteristics mentioned in the text are all met to varying degrees in the case of hurricanes – from the need to maintain public order, to the inability of citizens to bear equally their common exposure, to the problem of maintaining public infrastructure in the wake of a disaster. Knowing the risk is 'public' does not tell us how it should be managed, however. That decision requires a critical analysis of the risk and the exposures (and the risk-bearing capacity of exposures). Subsidiarity is an important idea here, not just in support of economic and political values, but also because the financing of risk involves tradeoffs between private equity and social adequacy. Financing risk based solely on individual ability to pay provides incentive for those who can pay to do so, but it does fail to address the public issues (e.g., externality costs) that arise from those who cannot bear the cost. Conversely, tipping the balance towards social adequacy can create huge moral hazard problems.

Historically, this balance point between adequacy and equity has been hard to find in the case of hurricanes. For instance, the National Flood Insurance Program provides taxpayer-subsidized insurance for commercial and individual property owners in high-risk areas. Arguably, the presence of this subsidy (a social adequacy mechanism) has provided incentive for the construction of commercial and residential property in areas that would not be built upon if the risk were borne privately. For the public risk manager, the question is whether the public benefits derived from enhancing the exposure to catastrophic loss (subsidizing the building of private and commercial properties along the Florida coastline) are greater than the costs. Also, are the derived benefits being enjoyed by those who are financing those benefits, or is there an agreed-upon political purpose that offsets the privacy inequity of subsidization?

# The public risk management distinction

The discussion thus far may strike readers as academically inter-esting, perhaps, but of uncertain relevance to the practicing risk manager. The risk manager rarely has the time or inclination to think about risks in broad conceptual categories, and the effort to detail the characteristics of public risks may not seem to pass the 'materiality' test for most risk managers. However, I do believe the effort to draw distinctions is important.

To explain this belief, consider the following proposition, which summarizes the discussion thus far. Public sector risk management differs from its private sector counterpart because:

1   Governmental entities, as social institutions, present an expo-sure to risk that is substantively different from a private entity.
2   The characteristics of risks that produce publicness present a set of risk management issues not fully present in the private sector, including:
    (a)   inability of government to avoid responsibility for risks within its purview
    (b)   frequent absence of markets as a risk management tool
    (c)   complexity of relationships between risks
    (d)   the interaction of risks with governmental purposes
    (e)   the breadth of the government's exposure to risk.

Publicness does present public risk managers with a set of distinct challenges. If we accept the concept of subsidiarity, which rests on the principle of 'primacy of the individual and the private' (but which also may incorporate social responsibility considerations), then we are subscribing to a belief that individual behavior – exhibited alone or in the context of a private market – generally precedes government action. This means that government involvement in public affairs arises when private behavior (and markets) is somehow unable to deliver the good or service efficiently, if at all, or to manage a risk. Although we know there are degrees of govern-ment intervention, the main point here is that risks, goods and services that meet the test of government intervention have done so because of characteristics which are not 'market manageable'. Consequently, under the subsidiarity regimen, risks with strong public attributes (and thus the public risk manager's challenge) are substantively different from 'private' risks. They exhibit character-istics of high complexity and high uncertainty (often), they are market-failure inducing and their effects on the public are diffuse. The effects of these risks, often by definition, call into question matters of fairness and social adequacy, and thus may be impervious to tests of economic efficiency.

So, as was suggested in the previous section, one distinction between private and public risk management is that the risks are substantially different. It is true that numerous risks overlap, and it is also true that with the erosion of the distinction between the public and private sectors this overlap will expand. However, we must be reminded that even if the risks that public and private risk managers face become more alike over time, another important distinction remains. The nature of government and its authority and responsibility is different. Whereas government might privatize garbage collection, or the National Aeronautics and Space Administration (NASA), or prisons, government's responsibility and authority for those activity areas remains. To put it even more plainly, government has very limited ability to avoid public risks that fall within its purview. So, publicness makes the risks different, and it makes exposure different too.

I think the preceding discussion suggests some other relevant lessons for the practicing risk manager. The first of these is implicit in the preceding discussion. To begin, the typical risk manager has responsibilities for a set or risks that can be characterized generally as falling within the 'organizational risk' domain – property loss exposures, legal liability-based risks, workers' compensation exposures, and so on. While all these areas are important, we need to be reminded that public organizations may have responsibility for organizational and social risks, and that traditional risk management skims the surface and fails to attack risk comprehensively. Thus, the earlier introduction of the concepts of social and organizational risks provides us with a broader frame of reference for thinking about the responsibility of risk management – a frame of reference that goes well beyond the perimeter of present risk management practices.

Second, by raising the possibility that the management of social risks is part of public risk management, we extend the accumulated knowledge of the risk management field into the public policy arena, where – I believe – it has been woefully absent. For example, the systematic and critical analysis that risk managers apply to complex property and liability risks would be a breath of fresh air in the debate over public investment in professional sports facilities. This approach, based on economic and finance principles and integrated with actuarial analysis and judgement informed by an understanding of contingencies, is a policy model with considerable relevance to many current problems and issues. It is sad to say that today's risk managers are rarely involved in public policy planning and execution, and I would hope that this text might begin a discussion on how public risk managers work their way past present barriers.

Third, this more comprehensive interpretation of risk management forces us to face a critical question: what is the purpose of risk management? Let us reflect on the question for a moment.

Risk imposes potential costs. A car accident inflicts economic and physical harm, a liability suit against a city reduces funds available for meeting public needs. Risk exacts costs other than losses, however. The mere presence of risk can cause fear, worry and misallocation of resources. Thus, we might make the general claim that we are motivated to practise risk management by the cost risk imposes on us – costs that largely serve no productive purpose other than to provide disincentives to undertake loss-producing activities.

Conversely, many risks can yield benefits. No doubt, risk certainly makes life more interesting. It also can produce a reward incentive and 'reward' itself. An investment can produce wealth; the construction of a public marina can produce income for a municipality and can also contribute to the ambient quality of life in that community. There are risks that we do not wish to eliminate or reduce, but may wish to actively pursue. As a result, we could say that the motivation to practice risk management is not to reduce or eliminate risk, at least not necessarily. The purpose of risk management is to develop a risk profile that best suits an organization's (or society's) goals and purposes. Some risk is worth taking, and the cost of eliminating or reducing other risks is prohibitively high. Thus, the traditional view that risk management is all about reducing or eliminating risk is one dimensional and too limiting for organizations today.

But a question (at least one!) still remains. Stating that the purpose of risk management is to manage risks in accordance with overall organizational or societal objectives is a little vague. What specifically, readers may well ask, is the risk manager supposed to accomplish? What is the core objective of risk management?

My answer would be, in the furtherance of organizational objectives the fundamental purpose of risk management is to ascertain the organization's attitude towards risk and to reduce the long-term cost of risk while maximizing the probability that long-term benefits will be achieved.

Herein we encounter a final important distinction between public risk managers and private risk managers (at least with private risk managers in publicly held corporation). In publicly held firms, the preceding objective statement can be translated into a decision rule that subjects all risk management decisions to a 'value-maximizing' test. For instance, does buying insurance increase firm value or not? Unfortunately, for reasons discussed earlier, public activity often cannot rely on this type of market-based reasoning. In fact, although economic thinking supports the central contentions of this text, it is difficult to reduce public sector decision-making to quantitative formulations, or to even organize qualitative analysis around a central decision rule.

## Conclusion

I tend to look at this section as an 'opening argument' in a debate, and fully expect that readers might have very different feelings about the nature of public risk management. I would encourage such readers to contact me as I think some 'give and take' would be helpful in further developing these ideas. In anticipation of reader responses, let me summarize the central argument one final time.

This section has asserted that the public and the private are social constructs that are ends of a spectrum – that is, all human activities have some degree of publicness and privateness. Therefore, it probably is misleading to characterize public sector management and private sector management as discrete alternatives. Rather, each arises from a general structure of skills, practice and knowledge that we might refer to as 'management'. The characteristic difference that emerges as we move away from the 'private' is a thing we have chosen to call 'publicness'. In discussing publicness, the text has made two basic assertions. First, as organizations become increasingly 'public' they represent an exposure to risk that has properties not found in mainly private organizations (the nature of ownership, legal rights/remedies, objectives and purposes) and, as a result, they establish an environment for risk managers that is qualitatively different from the environment in which private organization risk managers operate. So, public organizational risks differ from private organizational risks because the exposure (government) is different.

Second, as we move from the private to the public the nature of risks begins to change. Truly public risks exhibit characteristic differences (they induce market failure, they have political dimensions, and so on). Thus, social risks (and a number of public organizational risks) exhibit different characteristics from those that are found to be private in nature.

When we combine these two points, it is arguable that you have a type of risk management that is 'risk management' but which is so substantively different in the particulars that it challenges our ability to compare public and private practices.

One final word. This section's central argument is not meant to suggest that a public risk manager cannot adopt, say, a return to work program developed by a private organization. Obviously, at a day-to-day operational level, some aspects of management 'are management' whether public or private. The section does contend, however, that publicness does intrude substantially on the public risk manager's job and does create a distinctiveness that must be recognized and appreciated.

## Note

1    Reprinted with the permission of Tillinghast-Towers Perrin, from *Governmental Risk Management Reports*, September 1996.

# Public sector risk management: an introduction

## EXECUTIVE SUMMARY

In the public sector in the UK traditional risk management practices have been observed since the 1980s. These practices have tended to focus on the management of insurable risks (fires, thefts, liability claims), plus responsibility for the buying of insurance and, occasionally, for occupational safety and health.

Over the last decade, predominantly in the private sector, there has been a visible trend towards the expansion of general risk management duties into the areas of financial risks, political risks, operational risks and strategic planning. This trend is leading to a transformation in the practice of risk management, moving it away from a narrow technical function to a broad and integrated management of all organisation risks. This book develops a model for understanding the co-ordinated management of public sector risks, a model called organisation risk management (ORM).

Notably, the ORM concept views risk management as an organisation-wide effort, with managers throughout the organisation dealing with the range of risks within their purview, but doing so in a way that is aligned with the public body's goals and objectives. This concept differs from a narrower department-oriented approach, and offers readers a sound reference point for thinking about the risks within their areas of concern.

## PRINCIPLES AND CONCEPTS

This chapter sets a general framework for understanding risk management in public organisations, based on the idea that organisation risk management involves the management of all risk, and that its objectives are mission driven.

To develop the concept of ORM, Chapter 2 has two tasks: to describe historical and current risk management practices and trends, and to explain how current developments support the idea of organisation-wide risk management. The second task will culminate with the creation of a framework for understanding the ORM idea.

## The history of public risk management

It certainly is true that public bodies have practised risk management, in the general sense of the term, for thousands of years. Ancient cities, by building walls to keep out invaders, were practising an elementary (but sound) form of risk management. Indeed, as Chapter 1 indicates, risk management is a fundamental purpose of government – government is, to a considerable degree, risk management.

Still, readers should distinguish between risk management as a general purpose of government and the functional nature of the practice of risk management. In that somewhat narrower sense, public sector risk management is a relatively recent phenomenon. Certainly, its foundations do not extend back much before the 1980s in the UK.

Broadly speaking, risk management – whether in the public or private sector – is a post-Second World War development. The massive effort in conducting the war proved to be a significant influence on management and management science theory and practice. Strategic management, operations research, operations management and risk management can all trace roots to the war, and their growth as fields of study and practice in the 1950s and 1960s reflect the application of those wartime experiences to business and government practices.

Research on the general history of risk management has shown that the term 'risk management', applied in the modern sense, began to appear in the mid-1950s. The 1950s and early 1960s still represent the high-tide era of scholarly research on the subject of risk management, although practitioner interest and research has proliferated since that time.

The development of risk management in the public sector lagged behind the private sector. Certainly, readers may assume that public bodies tend to adopt innovations more slowly than the private sector; and this assumption is not entirely incorrect – but it is a bit misleading. The lag in adoption more likely was due to the particular characteristics of the insurance market formed to serve local authorities in the UK.

A mutual insurance company, that is, one owned by its policy-holders rather than shareholders, was founded in 1903 by a group of local authorities in response to what was a hardening insurance market where coverage was limited and perceived to be expensive. By the mid-1970s Municipal Mutual was providing the whole or part of the insurance programme for over 90 per cent of the local authorities in the UK. This market dominance continued until the late 1980s.

Municipal Mutual sold its insurance programmes directly to its client base without using customary distribution channels such as brokers and consultants. It was able to offer all the covers a local authority was perceived to need and it provided cover from the ground up. While this was all good news from the narrow perspec-tive of insurance buying, the mutual's position as the preferred provider of services to the public sector and as a predominantly ground-up insurer had the unfortunate side effect not only of dimin-ishing the role of the insurance buyer within the local authority, but also of reducing the incentive to improve risk profiles that a degree of risk retention encourages.

However, the 1980s saw the emergence of a number of external factors that were to change the face of public sector insurance in the UK. Local authorities were put under financial constraints by central government with the result that the resources to maintain the quality and level of services expected by the community were not as readily available. The public grew more litigious. The reduc-tion in the quality of services provided and the unpopularity of local government following the introduction of the Community Charge (also known as the Poll Tax) resulted in a significant increase in the number of claims made against local authorities. As a ground-up insurer, Municipal Mutual bore the full brunt of the increase in claims frequency.

By September 1992 the combination of these external and internal factors – the aggressive diversification strategy of the 1980s with its consequent loss of focus, the mutual's inability to access external capital and its investment strategy – meant that Municipal Mutual could not continue to write new or renew existing business. Local authorities had to look elsewhere for their insurance protection.

Certainly, the demise of Municipal Mutual (see Chapter 9 for a fuller discussion) was a significant catalyst for the development of risk management in the public sector. It allowed brokers and consultants to act as advisers to local authorities and introduce new ideas and programme structures. A number of new insurance carriers entered the market and the availability of choice enhanced the status of the insurance buyer. All the new entrant carriers required the authorities to retain some degree of risk, as indeed had Municipal Mutual in its last few months of trading. This prompted the need to understand, manage and control risk and uncertainty within the authorities, and spawned the creation of the risk management function.

It would be wrong, however, to assert that no risk management was practised in any local authority in the UK prior to the demise of Municipal Mutual. Certainly in the 1980s a number of individuals were introducing risk management initiatives into their authorities and some authorities were investigating the wider insurance market and practising some form of risk retention. The Association of Local Authority Risk Managers (ALARM) can trace its origins to the late 1980s. But it is true to say that the exponential growth in the number of risk managers in local authorities and the evident practice of risk management in the vast majority of local authorities can be traced back to the autumn of 1992 when the local authority mutual ceased trading. ALARM, formally founded in 1992, now has over 1200 members.

Municipal Mutual shared many of the characteristics of public sector risk financing pools which can be found in the USA, Canada, the Netherlands, Japan and Australia, to name but a few territories. That Municipal Mutual ultimately failed does not *per se* predict the ultimate demise of the global intergovernmental pooling movement. Indeed, Chapter 9 argues that there are significant lessons that pools can learn from the Municipal Mutual saga that can enhance the prospects of their long-term viability.

## What do risk managers do?

Previously, insurance-buying was identified as a historic function of risk management, and undoubtedly the management of insurance and insurable risks is the core activity of the average risk manager.

Responsibilities for buying insurance tend to push a risk manager's duties into a number of related areas, what might be called 'insurable risk management'. For example, responsibility for employers' liability insurance almost inevitably compels the risk manager to address workplace safety and health matters, integration issues with employee benefits, training, equipment maintenance, and so on. Similar extensions occur when risk managers deal with property and liability insurance.

Summarising typical risk manager responsibilities is subject to the ordinary caveats that one would cite in any attempt to generalise a fairly diverse occupation. That said, the average scope of duties likely would include:

- insurance buying
- insurance risk management
- occupational safety and health matters
- claims administration and handling
- loss information management
- training and risk management education
- compliance with regulatory and legal requirements
- catastrophe planning
- security
- risk assessment and loss control.

If any current trends are in evidence, they would be the gradual addition of human resources related responsibilities and the slower addition of financial risk management (interest rate risk, currency exchange risk, etc.) into the risk management portfolio. However, the importance of these trends is more abstract than real – at least at the current time. Well over 90 per cent of all public sector risk managers are limited to the activities listed. But, it still probably is true that forces are afoot that will lead to a broader definition of risk management. This observation is explained in the following section, and this explanation will serve to introduce an important organising framework for understanding both the practices and the possibilities of risk management in public bodies.

## Organisation risk management

In the private sector, there are significant changes occurring in the practice of risk management; changes which, taken as a whole, are tending to redefine risk management as the management of all organisation risks on an integrated basis. While the number of organisations practising this 'holistic' form of risk management is limited, most observers predict that this new definition eventually will prevail. Why?

The explanation varies a bit from industry to industry, but in general the trend seems to be driven by the following factors:

1   The restructuring of organisations has tended to broaden the responsibilities of all managers.
2   Increasing competition has forced organisations to scrutinise cost structures, leading to insights into the reduction of the cost of risk.

3    Just-in-time processes, total quality improvement practices, and other modern developments all stress the need to control risk and to do so in an integrated fashion.

4    Consolidation in financial services has resulted in an increasing integration of insurance, banking and other financial services – which in turn has led to broader thinking about risk financing.

5    The absence of co-ordinated risk management practices (or, occasionally, the demonstrated effectiveness of the same) has been a feature of many sensational and highly publicised stories, disasters and events (e.g., the collapse of the Bank of Credit and Commerce International [BCCI], Year 2000 preparedness, the 1987 and 1990 storms).

As a consequence, there has been a move towards a more organisation-wide approach to risk management. For instance, recent years have seen the emergence of the chief risk officer (CRO) concept, the mandate that risk management is an important ingredient of corporate governance, and heightened evidence of 'boardroom risk management'.

Anticipating the destination of this emerging trend is difficult, but the general structure of an organisation-wide risk management scheme can be easily framed, and that is the objective of the balance of this section.

## The organisation risk management model

Organisation risk management is a general management function that seeks to assess and address the causes and effects of uncertainty and risk on an organisation. In principle, the purpose of ORM is to enable an entity to progress towards its goals in the most direct, economical and effective path.

To appreciate the relationship between risk management and other functional aspects of management within a public body, it is useful to think about the central purposes of management. One construction of the management function would describe management as entailing strategic management, operations management and risk management components. The strategic management component consists of activities that involve the determination of an organisation's (or functional unit's) mission, goals and objectives and, of course, the creation of strategy and the management of progress towards strategy fulfilment. The operations management component consists of those actions and decisions that enable the organisation or functional unit to 'do what it does'. The risk management component consists of those decisions and actions that facilitate the most direct achievement of organisation objectives via its operations (see Exhibit 2.1).

Readers must realize that this model applies to the organisation as a whole, but is equally applicable to each position within that organisation. In other words, risk management is central to the overall management of a public body, but it occupies a segment of the specific responsibilities of all managers and employees. As an example, the director of highways within an authority would have strategic responsibilities with respect to budget setting, and the identification of specific goals and objectives. Additionally, the manager would have operational responsibilities, ranging from work force management, task supervision, allocation of department resources, and general reporting activities. But equally, that manager would have responsibilities that entail an assessment and appreciation of relevant risks and the application of risk management measures to control those risks. This would be as true of employees as managers. One could easily imagine that a road repair worker could identify actions and decisions made each day that would be characterised as 'risk management'.

The strategic, operational, and risk management activities are not mutually exclusive. Indeed, overlap (see Exhibit 2.1) is an important element of the ORM idea as it demonstrates the centrality of risk management. Risk management, in this conceptualisation, is not a peripheral technical function but rather a core management

**Exhibit 2.1**   Strategy, operations and risk management model

function – something each employee does within the scope of his or her duties, but also something the organisation does to itself.

The ORM idea ties in neatly with the discussion of public risks in Chapter 1. Conceptually, risk management is a central reason for the existence of public bodies, and the ORM concept simply explains why and how risk management relates to the other functional areas of management.

## The elements of organisation risk management

The practice of risk management varies from organisation to organisation, but the ORM idea incorporates five distinct elements into its structure:

1    Mission identification.
2    Risk and uncertainty assessment.
3    Risk control.
4    Risk financing.
5    Programme administration.

Throughout this book, the distinctions between these elements will be subject to a degree of overlay. Some tools and techniques will be shown to be both 'control' and 'financing', for instance. Thus, readers should appreciate that there always is a certain level of arbitrariness in labelling management practices. Nevertheless, for introductory purposes, these element categories allow newcomers to the risk management field to better understand the overall purpose and practice of risk management.

### Mission identification

A risk manager has a responsibility to assure that risk management goals and objectives (indeed, the 'mission' of the risk management function) align with the overall purposes of the organisation. In this sense, ORM is described as mission driven, which means that the practice of risk management is measured by the degree to which it supports the central purposes of the organisation. These central purposes serve as the yardsticks against which success or failure is measured, but they also provide the basis for the philosophy that supports risk management activities.

### Risk and uncertainty assessment

Risk and uncertainty assessment involves three overlapping activities:

- risk and uncertainty identification
- risk analysis
- risk measurement.

Identification involves the systematic process of discovering an organisation's risks and exposures to risk. Identification is a continuous process.

Analysis involves the examination of risks in an effort to determine how hazardous conditions lead to actual losses. Increasingly, analysis also involves the study of risks with upside potential – that is, situations where risk factors can give rise to opportunities.

Measurement entails the assessment of the impact of risk on an organisation. This invariably will be undertaken in different ways. For example, measurement might be highly quantitative or quite subjective. Measurement also might focus on the impact of risk on specific objects or on the organisation as a whole.

## Risk control

Risk control involves those activities that focus on avoiding, preventing, reducing, transferring and neutralising risks and uncertainties. Risk control can range from simple measures like wearing hard hats to complex measures like catastrophe management plans.

## Risk financing

Risk financing activities enable an organisation to reimburse losses that occur and to fund programmes to reduce uncertainty and risk, or to enhance positive outcomes. The financing of losses can include measures like the purchase of insurance, the establishment of a letter of credit or total retention. A less obvious risk financing measure would be the use of earmarked taxes to fund a highway safety and maintenance programme.

## Programme administration

The administration of a risk management programme involves a range of technical and general management activities, from the buying of insurance, to claims administration, to the development of a hedging arrangement, to safety training and the institution of loss control programmes. Risk management requires technical competence but, equally, a risk manager must have solid general management capabilities.

## Organisation risk management within the public body

The ORM idea leads to an organisational scheme that differs from traditional risk management practices. Most traditional risk managers are located within a government's finance or purchasing department (or, somewhat less frequently, in the legal and audit areas). If a separate risk management department exists (or if a distinct risk management unit exists within a finance department), the risk management unit typically consists of one to three individuals. A moderately sized unit would probably have a risk manager, a secretary and, perhaps, an insurance manager. Larger public bodies might have as many as a dozen employees, but this large number commonly would be indicative of the presence of in-house claims management personnel.

Contrasted with the traditional approach, the ORM idea suggests that the risk manager is proximate to the executive function. Overall direction should be provided by the executive level, particularly because the scope of ORM is organisation-wide. Additionally, the ORM idea is not particularly conducive to a 'risk management department' model per se. Rather, many or most risk management activities would be practised throughout the organisation, so the ORM risk manager would serve more as a link co-ordinating and organising risk management efforts. Risk management responsibilities would be written into every employee's job description, and the risk manager would co-ordinate these responsibilities and facilitate implementation. Under this idea, the risk manager is idealised as the chief risk officer, connoting the elevated position within the organisation and also the broadened scope of responsibilities. This model function is further developed in Chapter 10.

The fact that the ORM model is rarely, if ever, seen in the public sector today does not diminish its importance. Like all good models, it serves as a frame of reference for current practices and promotes critical examination to explain and justify the differences. To be sure, many differences from the ideal are warranted and desirable. But, conversely, examination of these inconsistencies may reveal that the 'old way' of doing things is no longer the best way.

---

# APPLICATIONS

## The levels of organisation risk management

Chapter 1's applications section refers to differences in perspective between elected members and managers. Chapter 2's applications section develops and formalises this observation.

The central premise of ORM is that a public body seeks to establish both a philosophy and a culture of risk management. Risk is so pervasive and complex that it is difficult to imagine that a single department can manage the wide-ranging needs of a local authority. Thus, the objective is to establish an environment of goals and expectations that each manager and employee can use to frame their specific risk management duties. From this perspective, ORM is not holistic in the sense of being a highly integrated and centrally administered system. Rather, ORM establishes a context and allows the particulars of risk management to develop according to the specific issues involved in a particular situation.

While ORM approaches the actual management of risk in this loose-jointed fashion, there do seem to be four strata of risk management within a typical local government: the political stratum, the strategic stratum, the tactical or managerial stratum and the operational or functional stratum.

## The political stratum

Risk management in a public body has a distinct political dimension. This is the governance dimension of local government, entailing the relationship of elected members to the citizens, the overall purposes of government and the legal dimensions of institutional existence. Primarily, but not exclusively, this is the domain of the elected member.

## The strategic stratum

Sometimes overlapping with the political stratum, this is the policy-setting, mission/goal/objective formulation of local government. Generally, this level can be characterised as being represented by the chief executive and the senior management team.

## The tactical/managerial stratum

This level of risk management within local government represents – essentially – a mid-level manager perspective. It is focused on risks related to budget execution, programme management, tactical decision-making and intermediate-range decisions.

## The operational/functional stratum

This can sometimes overlap with the tactical/managerial stratum, but is focused on risks related to day-to-day operations, short-term planning and execution, and functional performance.

An example is a local government's consideration of a new leisure centre. The politics of this initiative tend to be broad and are focused on issues of community prestige, economic impact, jobs and image. The political risks generally arise from the process by which elected leaders manage the decision-making at this level. The strategic stratum involves the capital budgeting planning, the tying of long-range planning to political purposes and processes, and the integration of this initiative into other government activities – and, of course, the risks associated with that level of management. The tactical or managerial dimension entails the risks associated the execution of the initiative – meeting medium-term objectives, managing resources, supervising human resources, and being held accountable for meeting overall objectives. The operational or functional level of risks would be associated with day-to-day matters like worker safety, audit procedures, procurement of insurance and contract negotiations with subcontractors or finance partners.

The principal insight for risk managers is that risk means different things at different levels of the organisation, and the process of educating/training/communicating with colleagues will be influenced by the vantage point they occupy. For instance, elected members commonly will not render judgements on whether construction site workers need to wear lumbar support belts. Effective risk management communication requires an anticipation of what the audience does and does not need to know and the most appropriate form in which to deliver the information.

## TOOLS YOU CAN USE

## A sample risk management policy statement

The council will apply to the risk of accidental and fortuitous loss a risk management process that includes a systematic and regular identification of loss exposures, the analysis of these loss exposures, the application of sound risk control procedures, and the financing of risk consistent with the council's financial resources.

The council is to be protected against accidental loss or losses that in the aggregate during any financial period would significantly affect the budget or the ability of the council to continue to fulfil its responsibilities to taxpayers and the public. Loss prevention and contract activities are of paramount importance to the council.

## Risk management purposes

1  Objectives
   (a) The council with respect to the management of all risks
       of accidental loss shall have as its objectives:
       (i)   the protection of the council against the financial
             consequences of accidental losses which are cata-
             strophic in nature
       (ii)  the minimisation of the total long-term cost to the
             council of all activities related to the identification,
             prevention, and control of accidental losses and their
             consequences
       (iii) the creation of a system of internal procedures
             providing a periodic assessment of fluctuating expo-
             sure to loss, loss-bearing capacity, and available
             financial resources, including insurance
       (iv)  the establishment to the extent possible of an expo-
             sure-free work and service environment in which
             the council employees as well as the public can enjoy
             safety and security in the course of their daily
             pursuits.
2  Risk management functions
   (a) The risk manager shall have authority for:
       (i)   identification and measurement of risks of accidental
             loss
       (ii)  selection of appropriate risk management techniques
             for resolving exposure problems – risk assumption,
             risk reduction, risk transfer, other systems, as appro-
             priate, including the purchase of insurance
       (iii) development and maintenance of a risk information
             system in co-ordination with existing systems for the
             timely and accurate recording of losses, claims,
             premiums and other risk-related costs and informa-
             tion
       (iv)  allocation of insurance premiums, uninsured losses
             and other risk costs and information
       (v)   risk management consultation with the council, its
             agencies, departments and commissions
       (vi)  benchmarking the council's performance relative to
             risk management against agreed performance indica-
             tors.
3  Risk retention
   (a) With regard to risk of accidental loss, it shall be the
       council's policy to self-insure all losses:

(i) which occur with predictable frequency, and

(ii) which will not have a significant impact on the council's financial position, and

(iii) will be in compliance with the laws of the UK, in so far as they can be held to apply.

(b) The intention of the council as a general guideline is to self-insure aggressively and to maintain high standards of claims handling and risk management capabilities. Exceptions to these guidelines should be allowed:

(i) whenever certain necessary services can be obtained only through the purchase of insurance

(ii) when the council is obligated by contract or law to purchase insurance and no alternate method is available

(iii) when deductibles, noninsurance, and self-insurance do not result in long-term economies.

4 Purchase of insurance

(a) The procurement of all property/casualty insurance in the council will be co-ordinated through the division of risk management.

(b) Insurance shall be purchased from any source determined to be in the best interest of the council and in accordance with European Union Procurement procedures.

(c) Whenever possible, the remuneration of agents and brokers providing services to the council shall be made on a fee basis.

---

# READ MORE ABOUT IT

## Local authority risk management: state of the profession[1]

### *Introduction*

Risk management is an issue of increasing concern for local authorities. Governmental entities are encountering forces of profound change; advancing technology, blurring of private/public distinctions, constraints on financial resources, internationalisation, devolutionary pressures. Arguably, this uncertain environment has begun to highlight the impact of risk on organisations and underscore the value of managing that risk actively and aggressively.

Although lessons are being learned, the late 1990s clearly is a period of transition in that the quality of risk management practices observed in local authorities seems to be highly variable – from nonexistent in some authorities to extremely sophisticated in others; and the nature of those practices appears to be quite different even when comparing sophisticated programmes with other sophisticated programmes. For instance, the risk management function may be located in many different places within the organisational structure, the scope of responsibilities may be quite different, and the actual tools and strategies employed can range far and wide.

Despite the high level of variability and uncertainty, indeed perhaps because of it, the Association of Local Authority Risk Managers (ALARM) has supported this first 'State of the Profession' study as an initial step towards understanding the world of public authority risk management in the UK. Given the lack of information on risk management and the level of change occurring in public authorities, the study's specific objectives are investigative and descriptive, rather than analytical – meaning it intends to describe (as well as is possible) the current state of practices and to explore and define the gaps in the knowledge of those practices. The study does not intend to critique and evaluate the effectiveness of policies and practices, and in fact was not designed to elicit that type of information. However, this report will produce several suggestions for future research that do spell out evaluative concerns and questions.

The results of this study are taken from a survey instrument that was mailed to 500 local authorities (all London and metropolitan boroughs; all English, Scottish and Welsh unitaries; all county and district councils; and a sample of police and fire authorities) on 10 May 1997. Each survey instrument contained a questionnaire to be completed by the individual responsible for general risk management activities within that authority. A separate question-naire was enclosed for the supervisor of each of those individuals.

The intention of the risk manager's questionnaire was to obtain descriptive information on the risk management practices within each local authority as well as information on the attitudes and opinions of those directly responsible for risk management. The supervisors' questionnaire sought to elicit attitudes and opinions from those to whom risk managers report.

The response was very positive. One hundred and sixty-one local authority risk managers returned completed usable questionnaires, representing a 32 per cent response rate. This compares favourably with the 35 per cent response rate achieved by the Public Risk Management Association's (PRIMA) 1992 study of risk management practices in the USA (the Public Risk Management Association's State of the Profession survey, 1992). Indeed, the UK response is particularly significant since the PRIMA study was mailed to association members only, while the ALARM survey was sent to every local authority in the UK. Perhaps even more encouragingly, 135 supervisor questionnaires were returned (27 per cent response). Although there will be some difficulty in ascribing statistical significance to particular individual responses, the response rate suggests that – taken as a whole – the results provide a fairly meaningful window on the state of the public sector risk management profession in 1997.

## Survey of local authority risk managers

### Part 1: Respondent profiles

One hundred and sixty-one local authorities (out of a survey population of 500) provided usable responses for this survey. The breakdown by organisation is shown in Table 2.1.

The response rates for each authority type were generally representative of the local authority population. Only in the case of district councils and Scottish unitaries did response rates differ significantly from actual proportionality. In the general population, district councils represent 62 per cent of all local authorities, but they accounted for only 53 per cent of the survey respondents. Conversely, Scottish unitaries account for only 6 per cent of the local authority population, but made up 12 per cent of the responses. Given the nature of this study, these anomalies do not hamper the meaning of the results, and in the case of the Scottish unitaries, add credibility to findings regarding unitaries. Because unitary response rates generally were high, however, several of the findings recorded below include recognition of the possible effects arising from over-representation.

**Table 2.1** Types of local authorities and respondents

| Authority type | % of respondents | Number |
|---|---|---|
| District councils/borough councils | 53.0 | 85 |
| Scottish unitary | 12.0 | 19 |
| County council | 9.0 | 15 |
| Metropolitan borough | 7.0 | 11 |
| English unitary | 7.0 | 11 |
| London borough | 5.0 | 8 |
| Welsh unitary | 4.0 | 6 |
| Fire authority | 1.0 | 2 |
| Police authority | 1.0 | 2 |
| Other | 1.0 | 2 |

Respondents were next asked to identify the job title that fits (or best fits) their current position. The responses are shown in Table 2.2.

**Table 2.2**   Respondents' job titles

| Position title | % of respondents | Number |
|---|---|---|
| Insurance officer/manager | 26.0 | 42 |
| Insurance and risk manager | 16.0 | 26 |
| Risk and insurance manager | 14.0 | 23 |
| Risk officer/manager | 8.0 | 13 |
| Health and safety officer | 1.0 | 2 |
| Other | 35.0 | 55 |

The most dominant response was 'Other', but the specifically cited position titles were distributed across a fairly wide range. The leading responses in this category were some type of head or assistant accountancy position (principal accountant, senior accounting assistant, for instance, which represented nearly one-third of the 'Other' responses); and head or assistant finance officer (exchequer services manager, finance support manager, treasury manager, assistant treasurer, senior finance assistant, for instance, which represented just over one-third of the 'Other' responses). The remaining reported titles were distributed among legal services, central administration, and audit.

Reporting relationships were explored, with the following results:

* 37 per cent indicated that they reported to the director of finance (supervisors' titles varied somewhat).
* 12 per cent indicated that they reported to an assistant finance officer.
* 12 per cent said that they reported to the director of accountancy (supervisors' titles varied somewhat).
* 2 per cent reported that their supervisor was an assistant accountancy director.
* 12 per cent indicated that they reported to the chief executive or a deputy chief.
* 22 per cent reported that they were supervised by other managers, ranging from legal managers, to audit managers, to other line management positions.

Respondents were asked to comment on their time in the field of risk and insurance management (Table 2.3).

Finally in Part 1, respondents were asked about their professional preparation, training and education experience (Table 2.4).

**Table 2.3** Respondents' years in risk management

| Number of years in field | % of respondents | Number |
| --- | --- | --- |
| 0 to 1 | 13.0 | 21 |
| 1 to 2 | 16.0 | 26 |
| 2 to 5 | 26.0 | 42 |
| 5 to 10 | 26.0 | 42 |
| 10 + | 19.0 | 30 |

**Table 2.4** Respondents' educational qualifications

| Professional qualifications | % of respondents | Number |
| --- | --- | --- |
| University degree | 20.0 | 32 |
| ACII | 15.0 | 24 |
| FCII | 5.0 | 8 |
| AIRM | 5.0 | 8 |
| FIRM | 2.0 | 3 |
| IOSH | 1.0 | 2 |
| Other | 52.0 | 84 |
| None | 22.0 | 35 |

*Notes*: Respondents may have reported more than one qualification.
ACII – Associate of the Chartered Insurance Institute
FCII – Fellow of the Chartered Insurance Institute
AIRM – Associate of the Institute of Risk Management
FIRM – Fellow of the Institute of Risk Management
IOSH – Institute of Occupational Safety and Health

Of those who responded 'Other', the dominant qualifications were:

- CIPFA – Chartered Institute of Public Finance and Accountancy (22 per cent reported qualifications through this organisation)
- FMAAT/MAAT/AAT – Fellow/Member of the Association of Accounting Technicians/ Association of Accounting Technicians (45 per cent reported these qualifications)
- Other accounting designations (20 per cent of the 'Other' respondents).

Less than 1 per cent of the respondents indicated having obtained an MBA, a law degree or any other advanced degree.

## Part 2: Structure of risk management

An effort was made to determine the size and structure of risk management programmes/departments/sections. Nearly all the respondents provided basic information on the number of full- and part-time employees dedicated to risk and insurance management work. The responses ranged from 0.5 to 13 employees, with the average being 2.79 full-time equivalent employees. Four responding authorities dramatically skewed the range, and if they are removed from the computation, the average drops to 2.42. This suggests that the 'typical' risk management department likely consists of an individual responsible for risk management, an assistant responsible for (perhaps) insurance-buying and a part-time clerical support person.

There is a notable difference in average size when respondents are separated into categories based on authority-type. For instance, if district councils are considered alone, the average drops to 2.08 full-time equivalents. London and metropolitan boroughs, counties and the unitary authorities average 3.62 full-time equivalents. Authority size would appear to be the relevant differentiating factor, although an examination of specific responses indicates that the number of department staff also seems to be positively related to the presence of an in-house claims management function – at least with respect to the risk management departments reporting five or more employees.

## Cost of risk

The cost of risk is a widely recognised measure of the impact of risk on an organisation. It reflects both the direct cost of losses an organisation sustains in a given period and the indirect costs arising from the risks (intangible costs, misallocation of resources, costs of risk-reducing measures). Respondents were asked to address the cost of risk. Specifically, they were given a worksheet that asked them to produce a cost of risk estimate based upon the following formula:

Cost of risk =   risk management department payroll +
                 health and safety/loss control expenditures +
                 insurance premiums + uninsured losses +
                 risk management service vendor fees

Given the general size differentials between district and non-district local authorities, responses were segmented into three categories:

- district councils
- county councils
- London and metropolitan boroughs and unitaries.

The smaller single-purpose authorities (police and fire) were insufficient in number to separate for the purposes of the cost of risk computation (Table 2.5).

**Table 2.5**  Reported cost of risk

| Cost of risk range | % of total Counties | Metropolitan/ London/unitary | District |
|---|---|---|---|
| £0 to £250 000 | 0.0 | 2.0 | 26.0 |
| £250 001 to £500 000 | 0.0 | 2.0 | 29.0 |
| £500 001 to £750 000 | 0.0 | 7.0 | 13.0 |
| £750 001 to £1 million | 9.0 | 14.0 | 8.0 |
| £1 000 001 to £1.5 million | 0.0 | 26.0 | 8.0 |
| £1 500 001 to £2 million | 9.0 | 12.0 | 4.0 |
| £2 000 001 to £2.5 million | 9.0 | 5.0 | 1.0 |
| £2 500 001 to £5 million | 36.0 | 16.0 | 6.0 |
| £5 000 001 + | 36.0 | 14.0 | 5.0 |

*Note*: Columns may not add to 100 per cent due to 'Don't know' responses.

The findings here seem to offer a general picture. Counties and other non-district councils report a higher cost of risk than district councils – which makes intuitive sense given the relative sizes of these types of local authorities. Based upon responses, county councils reported an average cost of risk of £3.6 million, while London and metropolitan boroughs and unitary authorities reported a figure of £2.125 million. The district councils reported an average cost of risk of £900 000.

However, the specific numbers must be viewed with great suspicion. The cost of risk is a concept open to many interpretations. Even when a common definition is used (as in the case of the survey), the components of the cost of risk may be difficult or impossible to obtain. Further, a certain degree of subjectivity factors into an individual's estimate. Thus, while the cited figures accurately reflect the responses, it is clear that the development of cost of risk data cannot be based upon a self-reporting regimen. Data must be developed consistently across all organisations.

## Part 3: Programme administration and scope of responsibilities

Respondents were asked to report on the duties for which they were responsible and the administrative tools they employed in the practice of risk management (Table 2.6).

Only in two categories were differences significant between district and non-district authorities. First, 67 per cent of the non-district authorities reported having a risk management goal and objective statement, while only 51 per cent of district authorities supplied the

**Table 2.6**   Administrative tools employed

| Tool | % of total Used currently | Not used | Planning to use |
|------|-----|-----|-----|
| Training programmes | 88.0 | 5.0 | 6.0 |
| Cost allocation system | 57.0 | 25.0 | 14.0 |
| Risk management goal and objective statement | 56.0 | 19.0 | 23.0 |
| Newsletters/other forms of communication | 50.0 | 23.0 | 23.0 |
| Risk management information system | 49.0 | 26.0 | 18.0 |
| Risk management audit process | 33.0 | 43.0 | 21.0 |
| Risk management manual | 16.0 | 42.0 | 39.0 |

Note: Rows do not add to 100 per cent due to responses of 'Don't know'

same response. Second, 65 per cent of the non-district authorities reported having a risk management information system (RMIS) in place, while only 45 per cent of the district authorities indicated they had adopted an RMIS.

In terms of the activities for which they were responsible, respondents were asked to indicate whether they were involved in a list of general risk management activities, and if so, were they solely or jointly responsible for execution and management (Table 2.7).

**Table 2.7**   Risk management responsibilities

| Activity | % of total Sole responsibility | Joint responsibility |
|----------|-----|-----|
| Insurance-buying | 95.0 | 2.0 |
| Risk management cost allocation | 73.0 | 4.0 |
| Loss information management | 72.0 | 10.0 |
| Other risk financing | 65.0 | 13.0 |
| Claims handling | 57.0 | 26.0 |
| Training/risk management education | 47.0 | 35.0 |
| Loss control | 40.0 | 36.0 |
| Risk identification | 34.0 | 59.0 |
| Financial risk management | 22.0 | 3.0 |
| Catastrophe planning | 17.0 | 47.0 |
| Public relations | 6.0 | 21.0 |
| Health and safety | 4.0 | 31.0 |

Finally, respondents were asked about their reliance on third party providers and vendors of particular risk management activities. Sixty-eight per cent indicated that they used outside claims handling/ management services, either through their insurer or through a separate claims service provider. Fifty-two per cent said they had used general consultation services, while another 33 per cent said that specific risk management consultation services had been used. Loss control services had been procured by 28 per cent of respondents and 22 per cent had contracted for outside actuarial services. Another 10 per cent reported that they viewed 'broking' as a contracted service and included insurance brokers in their list of contracted service providers.

There were no significant differences in the responses of district authorities when compared to non-district authorities.

## Part 4: Risk financing

Local authorities were asked to provide basic information on their insurance/risk financing programmes across four lines: property, motor third party, motor comprehensive and liability. Key findings are as follows.

### Property

Respondents reported an aggregate total sum insured of just over £74 billion, with individual entities reporting insured property values between £25 million and £4 billion. Through straight extrapolation, it is possible to suggest that local authorities in the UK have up to £353 billion in property under cover in 1997.

Information was sought on the deductible or excess levels used in property programmes. Those respondents providing deductible/excess levels reported an overall average of just under £10 000. District council averages were roughly half that overall average, while counties, London and metropolitan boroughs, and the unitary authorities reported an average about 50 per cent higher than the overall average.

Stop-loss levels were reported ranging between £50 000 and £5 million with 50 per cent of stop-loss levels under £250 000. Stop-loss levels for non-district councils averaged nearly twice the overall figure, while the district council reported an average 25 per cent below the overall average.

### Motor

Motor programmes showed deductible/excess levels ranging between £250 and £25 000 whereas stop-loss programmes (much less

numerous than deductible programmes) ranged between £20 000 and
£1 million. A number of reporting errors and incomplete data limited
the value of further analysis.

## Liability

Liability (employer's liability and public liability) limits of indemnity varied widely between district and non-district authorities, as
might be expected. Non-district authorities reported limits ranging
from £10 million to £100 million, with an average value of just over
£23 million. District authorities reported limits ranging from £5
million to £25 million, with an average value of just over £15 million.

Deductible or excess levels differed between authority type. For
non-district authorities, the average deductible level was just below
£100 000 – ranging between £500 and £500 000. For the district
authorities, the average excess level was computed at just under
£7500, ranging between £250 and £100 000.

Finally, levels of stop loss were computed. Non-district authorities reported stop loss levels ranging between £100 000 and £6
million, with an average of just over £1.2 million. For district authorities the corresponding numbers could not be produced given the
number of respondents (only nine of the district authorities provided
any stop-loss information and three of these responses were deemed
to be errors).

## Future financing direction

Respondents were next asked to indicate in which financing direction they expected to head over the next three years (Table 2.8).

Responses were sorted by authority type, but no significant differences were found between district and non-district authorities.

When asked to indicate why they were likely to move one way or
the other, respondents overwhelmingly indicated that self-insurance
provided a better means of promoting risk management within their
authority and in capturing the attention of fellow managers. A large

**Table 2.8** Risk financing trends – next three years

| Programme | % of total Increasing self-insurance | Decreasing self-insurance | No change |
|---|---|---|---|
| Property | 51.0 | 0.0 | 47.0 |
| Motor third party | 19.0 | 0.0 | 64.0 |
| Motor comprehensive | 34.0 | 1.0 | 62.0 |
| Liability | 48.0 | 1.0 | 50.0 |

*Note*: Rows do not add to 100 per cent due to 'Don't know' responses.

number of respondents also thought that self-insurance would materially reduce the cost of risk to their local authority.

Since insurance continues to play a key role in risk-financing, respondents were asked to comment on the factors that influence their insurance purchase decisions (Table 2.9).

**Table 2.9** Factors influencing risk financing decisions

| Decision factor | % of total Very important | Important | Somewhat important | Unimportant |
|---|---|---|---|---|
| Premium competitiveness | 81.0 | 19.0 | 0.0 | 0.0 |
| Financial stability of risk carrier | 73.0 | 26.0 | 1.0 | 0.0 |
| Willingness to share loss information | 51.0 | 40.0 | 7.0 | 2.0 |
| Commitment to risk management | 46.0 | 43.0 | 10.0 | 1.0 |
| Knowledge of public sector | 38.0 | 57.0 | 4.0 | 1.0 |
| Flexibility in underwriting approach | 34.0 | 55.0 | 10.0 | 1.0 |
| Local representation | 11.0 | 29.0 | 36.0 | 24.0 |
| Other | 7.0 | 8.0 | 0.0 | 0.0 |

*Note*: 'Other' responses focused on flexibility in claims services and policies.

## Part 5: Trends, issues and challenges

Respondents were asked to comment on the key issues they thought would impact local authorities in general and their authority in particular, and the risk management issues of note in their local authority. First, information on their perception of professional development needs was sought (Table 2.10).

**Table 2.10** Overall local authority challenges over next three years (percentage)

| | |
|---|---|
| Financial limitations/constraints on local authorities | 43.0 |
| Compulsory competitive tendering | 36.0 |
| National government policy changes | 13.0 |
| Litigation/liability issues | 12.0 |
| Maintaining service quality | 11.0 |
| Devolution/reorganisation (including unitary) | 9.0 |

*Note*: A wide range of responses fell in the 0 to 3 per cent range, the principal responses being worker stress, European Union (EU) directives, performance benchmarking and litigiousness.

**Table 2.11**  Issues facing public risk managers generally (percentage)

| | |
|---|---|
| Risk management training and awareness-raising | 21.0 |
| Finding resources for risk management projects | 16.0 |
| Marketing risk management to managers | 13.0 |
| Compulsory competitive tendering | 13.0 |
| Limited overall financial resources for authority | 11.0 |
| Litigiousness/liability issues | 9.0 |
| Quality of risk management services | 8.0 |

*Note*: There were many responses that fell in the 0 to 3 per cent range, the principal among those being worker stress, exploring alternative risk financing strategies, environmental management, and general health and safety.

**Table 2.12**  Issues of concern for your risk management programme (percentage)

| | |
|---|---|
| Funding for RM activities | 29.0 |
| Compulsory competitive tendering | 23.0 |
| Risk management training/awareness raising/marketing risk management | 20.0 |
| Reorganisation (including unitary) | 18.0 |

*Note*: There were many responses that fall in the 0 to 3 per cent range, notable among them were the influence of the EU directives and national government legislation, liability concerns, service quality and cost of risk reduction.

## Professional development needs and concerns

Overall, respondents reported an overwhelming need to find both technical and managerial training opportunities. A dominant theme in the comments was frustration over a lack of time to commit to education and personal development, difficulty in finding and accessing appropriate opportunities, and a general sense that, even if found, the actual number of opportunities for professional development were limited.

## *Survey of supervisors of local authority risk managers*

Questionnaires were sent to individuals in local authorities who were defined to be the supervisor of the risk and insurance manager within that authority. Information was sought that would gauge supervisor attitudes about risk management practices and issues within that local authority.

## Part 1: General descriptive information

Respondents were asked to identify the type of organisation that best describes their local authority (Table 2.13).

When asked to identify their job titles, respondents indicated as shown in Table 2.14.

As a point of comparison, the risk manager respondents reported that 37 per cent reported to the head of finance and 12 reported to an assistant finance officer. Twelve per cent reported to the head of accounting while another 2 per cent reported to assistant or deputy accounting positions. Twelve per cent of the respondents indicated that the executive or general management managers were their supervisors, and another 12 per cent reported having reporting relationships with legal managers, audit managers and other line management positions.

Respondents indicated that 18 per cent had been in their position for less than one year; 21 per cent had been in their field for one to two years; 17 per cent for two to five years; 27 per cent for five to ten years; and 15 per cent had been in their field for over ten years.

**Table 2.13** Responding supervisors, by organisation type

| Type of authority | % of respondents | Number |
| --- | --- | --- |
| District council/borough council | 56.0 | 76 |
| Scottish unitary | 11.0 | 15 |
| County council | 8.0 | 11 |
| English unitary | 8.0 | 11 |
| Metropolitan borough | 7.0 | 10 |
| London borough | 4.0 | 5 |
| Welsh unitary | 4.0 | 5 |
| Police authority | 1.0 | 1 |
| Other (Northern Ireland) | 1.0 | 1 |

**Table 2.14** Responding supervisors' job titles

| Position title | % of respondents |
| --- | --- |
| Head of finance/treasury (various titles) | 29.0 |
| Deputy finance/treasury (various titles) | 25.0 |
| Head of accounting (various titles) | 20.0 |
| Deputy accounting (various titles) | 5.0 |
| General management | 9.0 |
| Legal | 3.0 |
| Other | 9.0 |

## Part 2: Perception of the risk management function

Supervisors of risk managers were asked to comment on the overall importance of risk management in the attainment of their local authority's overall goals and objectives (Table 2.15).

Respondents were then asked to comment on the effectiveness of the risk management programme within their local authority (Table 2.16).

## Part 3: Trends, issues and challenges

Respondents were asked to comment on issues and challenges related to local authorities generally, their local authority generally and risk management issues facing their local authority (Tables 2.17, 2.18 and 2.19).

Finally, supervisors were offered an opportunity to comment on any aspect of risk management they wished to address. Just over half provided additional comments. These comments can be summarised as follows:

> Risk management is of increasing importance to local authorities, especially given broad sources of uncertainty affecting these entities today: financial restrictions, a new national government, demands for increasing quality of services, reorganisation of local authorities,

**Table 2.15**  Supervisors' view on importance of risk management

| Authority type | Percentage of respondents | | | |
| | *Very important* | *Important* | *Somewhat important* | *Unimportant* |
| --- | --- | --- | --- | --- |
| District councils | 27.0 | 52.0 | 17.0 | 2.0 |
| Non-district authorities | 35.0 | 57.0 | 5.0 | 3.0 |
| County councils | 50.0 | 40.0 | 10.0 | 0.0 |

*Note*: Rows do not add to 100 per cent due to 'Don't know' responses.

**Table 2.16**  Supervisors' view on effectiveness of risk management in their entity

| Authority type | Percentage of respondents | | | |
| | *Very effective* | *Effective* | *Somewhat effective* | *Ineffective* |
| --- | --- | --- | --- | --- |
| District councils | 5.0 | 42.0 | 39.0 | 8.0 |
| Non-district authorities | 3.0 | 30.0 | 51.0 | 5.0 |
| County councils | 0.0 | 89.0 | 11.0 | 0.0 |

*Note*: Rows do not add to 100 per cent due to 'Don't know' responses.

**Table 2.17** Supervisors' views of key public sector issues

| Overall issues facing local authorities | % |
|---|---|
| Financial limitations and challenges | 61.0 |
| Compulsory competitive tendering | 44.0 |
| New policies from national government | 25.0 |
| Maintaining quality of services | 21.0 |
| Reorganisation/devolution (including unitary issues) | 20.0 |
| Community relations | 14.0 |
| Computer-related issues | 5.0 |
| Other | 24.0 |

*Note*: There were a wide range of responses in the 0 to 3 per cent range, the key among them being growth demands, devolution, computer security, community relations/governance and managing public/private partnerships.

**Table 2.18** Supervisors' views of their entities', key issues

| General issues facing your local authority | % |
|---|---|
| Financing limitations and challenges | 53.0 |
| Compulsory competitive tendering | 43.0 |
| Maintaining quality of services | 29.0 |
| Reorganisation/devolution/unitary | 26.0 |
| Policies of new national government | 8.0 |
| Information technology challenges and issues | 7.0 |
| Other | 47.0 |

*Note*: 'Other' comments ranged from 0 to 3 per cent, the principal responses among them being community governance, housing issues, employee morale and crime.

**Table 2.19** Supervisors' views of their entities' key risk management issues

| Principal risk management challenges within your authority | % |
|---|---|
| Risk management education/raising awareness | 24.0 |
| Developing a risk management strategy | 15.0 |
| Reducing insurance/loss costs | 14.0 |
| Funding for risk management programmes | 14.0 |
| Risks arising from unitary/reorganisation | 10.0 |
| Security issues | 8.0 |
| Developing upper-level support | 7.0 |
| Other | 84.0 |

*Note*: There were a wide range of comments provided that registered in the 0 to 3 per cent range, among the principal responses were catastrophe planning, developing a holistic approach to risk management, liability concerns and computer concerns.

demoralisation of the workforce. However, it is difficult to get upper management's attention with respect to risk management, and this presents a specific challenge to public authority risk managers. Risk managers have important issues within their brief, but these issues are not fully appreciated by upper management. Training, educating and consciousness-raising are key issues for local authority risk managers.

Less emphatically, supervisors indicate that measuring risk management success is both difficult and essential.

## Summary comments

This survey has accomplished its primary purpose by providing a baseline picture of local authority risk management practices in 1997. The picture that has emerged may be summarised as follows.

Risk management is widely practised in the UK and can be described generally as a management function concerned principally with insurance-buying and the management of insurable risks. Because insurable risks intermingle with other general organisational risks, local authority risk managers report a diversifying brief, with many having involvement in planning, public relations, financial risk management, internal audit and health and safety. Nevertheless, 'insurable risk' management remains at the heart of local authority risk management practices.

Commonly, risk management is seen to be a financial function as illustrated by the fact that the majority of risk managers report to either a finance or accounting officer. If a dedicated department or section exists (and it often does), it tends to consist of two or three individuals who may have other financial or accounting responsibilities. The size of risk management department is a function of size and authority type. In general, district councils have smaller departments, whereas county councils, London and metropolitan boroughs, and the newer unitary authorities report larger departments. The largest departments tend to have in-house claims administration responsibilities, which seems to be as much a factor in department size as is the size of the authority itself.

Risk managers (and it should be noted here that various titles are used) report a wide range of backgrounds and professional development pathways, and it is apparent that there is not a standard preparatory route available for those pursuing a career in public sector risk management. Interestingly, the single most commonly seen background area is accountancy, which was a specialisation reported by around one-third of the respondents.

The study sought to develop an understanding of risk-financing practices, and a wide range of information was provided by respondents. In general, it can be observed that conventional insurance plays a dominant role in most respondents' financing programmes. Additionally, retention levels (deductibles, excess and stop-loss levels) appear to be low relative to the size of insured values. Nearly half of the respondents, however, indicated that they were moving in a direction of greater retention over the next three years. Significantly, both small and large authorities reported the same intention to expand retention practices. Elsewhere in the survey, respondents indicated that retention was important in motivating the authority to practise risk management and in communicating the risk management message. Additionally, risk managers suggested that retention offered the prospect of lower costs over time.

While the survey highlighted the growing desire among risk managers to increase retention levels, citing increased control and quality and advancing the risk management ethos as key reasons, price competitiveness and financial solidity far outstripped considerations such as risk management expertise, knowledge of the public sector and service quality, in the factors determining insurance provider selection. Insurance-buying decisions are driven mainly by price, primarily as a result of the need to meet with *Official Journal of the European Community* (*OJEC*) tendering requirements, but as the lowering of costs was also cited as a factor in the retention decision, it may be the fundamental objective of risk-financing is seen as the reduction of the explicit cost of risk.

The survey sought to better understand the cost of risk, and provided respondents with a means of self-reporting their authority's cost of risk. The results, while indicating a broad distinction between district councils and other local authorities, must be viewed with great suspicion. The degree of subjectivity evident in the reported answers suggests strongly that a self-reporting scheme is not the appropriate method for gathering such information.

As was suggested in the previous paragraph, differences were noted between district councils and all other authorities with respect to the cost of risk, but this was an across the board finding. In almost every respect (save the intention to increase retention practices), district councils reported significant differences in risk management practices from all other entities. Their 'risk managers' were likely to have non-risk management duties, the risk management departments/sections were smaller, they retained less risk, their insured values and limits of coverage were lower, and the breadth of the risk manager's duties tended to be narrower. On the face of it, this should not be surprising given the size of district councils relative to county councils, London and metropolitan boroughs, and the unitary authorities.

Both risk managers and their supervisors were asked about their concerns and views related to local authority risk management. There was a broad consensus as to the key issues. Risk managers and supervisors both indicated that selling and developing a risk management culture and training, and educating managers, was the top internal challenge. Compulsory competitive tendering, shrinking financial resources, changes in national government policies, devolution and reorganisation were all cited as critical 'external' concerns.

Interestingly, issues such as increased litigiousness, deteriorating infrastructure, crime and worsening public safety were only reported as important by a very few respondents. These topics frequently are cited as major problems for local governments, but the survey results provided scant evidence that this was the case.

While risk managers and supervisors seemed to be in agreement on many issues, one set of findings suggested an area of possible concern for risk managers. Supervisors were asked to comment on the relative value they place on risk management within their organisation. Overwhelmingly they responded that risk management was 'very important' or 'important'. However, when later asked to assess the quality of risk management practices within their local authority, over half indicated that they were only 'somewhat satisfied' or 'unsatisfied'. Levels of satisfaction did not vary significantly across organisation types, except in county councils where supervisors reported a significantly higher level of satisfaction than was reported elsewhere. Allowing for the fact that the structure of the survey may have allowed supervisors to easily ascribe a high value to risk management while reporting a lower level of satisfaction with their own authority's efforts, there is still an internal consistency among responses that suggests that the difference in attitudes is real.

## Suggestions for further research

There are nearly as many questions as answers arising from this study, and there appears to be a great number of subjects warranting further investigation. The key suggestions are:

1   Risk managers, as a group, exhibit a significant connection into the accounting field. Does, and if so how does, the accounting perspective influence public authorities' risk management strategies?

2   The cost of risk is an issue worthy of further investigation. While this study found rather basic information on the cost of

risk, a focused study of the subject is likely to gather more meaningful information. The subject is worth studying as it has broad implications for the future success of the risk management function.

3    By inference, professional development and training seems to be an issue of some importance for risk managers. General responses regarding developmental needs point in this direction but, equally, the existing educational backgrounds of risk managers suggests that there are not significant preparatory programmes for those interested in careers in the field of risk management. This, however, raises an important question; 'what constitutes appropriate educational preparation for a risk manager?' Such a question is important in its own right, but is more broadly meaningful as it addresses the question of risk management's identity. What is risk management and what is the distinguishing knowledge and skill set of the risk manager? These are critical questions for an emerging profession.

4    It appears that the relationship between risk managers and their supervisors is a subject warranting further investigation. There is some evidence to suggest that supervisors view the risk management function in their organisations as less than effective, both supervisors and risk managers believe that convincing upper management of the importance of risk management is difficult but important, risk managers do not believe that there is strong upper level support for risk management and supervisors have a somewhat different attitude with respect to what are important risk management issues for their organisation.

5    Apropos 4, the differences in supervisors' views of risk management relative to those of the risk managers may be due to their different vantage points within the organisation, but the differences may also suggest that risk management means different things at various levels within public authorities. The issue of differing levels or meanings of risk management within an organisation presents important concerns for effective risk management and should be a topic for further exploration.

6    Levels of risk retention appear to be relatively low. This is particularly true of district councils, but even among non-district authorities, deductible and stop-loss levels are not large. The study was not designed to determine risk-bearing capacity for local authorities, so the question of financing efficiency (that is, the cost-effective balance of transfer versus retention) is a subject meriting further study.

7    Respondents' comments reflect a general concern with possible changes arising from the 1 May 1997 general elections. A large number of comments centred on possible changes in compulsory competitive tendering, continuation of devolutionary trends, adjustments to central government financing patterns for local authorities, new regulations and statutory changes arising from Labour-Party inspired regulation, as well as significant national government changes in policies towards schools, public transport, housing, policing and welfare reform. This suggests a possible research topic – the expressed or implied risk management philosophy of the new national government.

## Note

1    Reprinted from report prepared by Peter C. Young and Am Re Managers International Ltd for the Association of Local Authority Risk Managers, 1997.

# Risk assessment

## EXECUTIVE SUMMARY

The ORM concept challenges managers to develop a means of identifying and managing all risks encountered by their public body. The
ambition of this goal puts considerable pressure on those managers
to develop a systematic process for identifying, measuring, and
analysing risks.

Risk assessment is the systematic and ongoing process by which
a public body's risks are identified, analysed and measured. A foundation concept that governs risk assessment is the insight that public
bodies are, in effect, collections of contracts, obligations, commitments and agreements between the body and resource holders. Those
arrangements serve as means by which the public body becomes
exposed to risk. Those risks, in turn, arise from the physical, social,
political, economic, legal, operational and cognitive environments.

Part of risk assessment involves an analysis of the public body's
exposures to risk. Broadly speaking, there are five general exposure
areas: physical assets, financial assets, human assets, legal liabilities
and moral/ethical responsibilities. An effective assessment process
will produce not only a clear understanding of the risks themselves,
but also a sophisticated understanding of the organisation's specific
exposures to those risks.

## PRINCIPLES AND CONCEPTS

Risk assessment is the fundamental activity of risk management,
meaning that risk management tools, techniques and strategies cannot
be applied until an organisation identifies and understands its risks.

Assessment involves three distinct but closely related elements: risk identification, risk analysis and risk measurement. The purpose of this chapter is to enable readers to develop an appreciation for the governing concepts and practices of systematic, organisation-wide assessment. To that end, the chapter begins with the development of an assessment framework that is based on the organisation risk management concept. This is followed by a discussion of identification methodologies. The balance of the chapter is devoted to a discussion of risk analysis basics and applications, and to a presentation of risk measurement principles. Both qualitative and quantitative dimensions of measurement are presented and analysed.

## The risk assessment framework

The ORM concept, coupled with the notion of the COCA organisation, imposes a stiff challenge for the practising risk manager. In principle, the ORM view asserts that risk management is the management of all organisation risks, while the COCA organisation idea establishes that risks arise from all the contracts, obligations, commitments and agreements that jointly form the basis for an organisation's existence.

A moment's reflection on the implications of the previous paragraph will reveal the daunting challenge of identifying, analysing and measuring every single risk in an organisation's risk portfolio (and doing so in a systematic, timely and ongoing basis at that). The chapter establishes the framework for comprehensive risk assessment, but does so with an important caveat: It will be impossible to assess all risks because organisations are highly complex and exist in a dynamic environment. Thus, although the ambition of risk assessment is lofty, the effort to assess must be leavened with a healthy dose of humility and scepticism.

### *Risk assessment begins with contracts, obligations, commitments and agreements*

The concept of the COCA organisation is a basic assumption of risk assessment, and consequently its premises are restated here.

An organisation like a local authority is the result of many years of conscious and rational, spontaneous and opportunistic, and required or unavoidable arrangements entered into between the locality's managers or elected leaders and resource holders. These arrangements mainly serve the declared purposes of the organisation, but sometimes impose purposes on that local government (e.g., a central government mandate). These arrangements can be described as contracts, obligations, commitments or agreements.

1    Contracts are legally enforceable arrangements that meet the ordinary tests of offer and acceptance, consideration, legality of purpose and legal capacity.
2    Obligations refer to legally binding arrangements that are required of an organisation and, typically, are not the fruit of party/counterpart offer and acceptance.
3    Commitments also may appear to fulfil the test of an agreement, but the concept of a commitment is intended to convey self-imposed duties. The duty of present generations to future generations is cited in current debates about social security and this is a good illustration of a commitment. Certainly, moral and ethical values represent commitments. The principal governing characteristic of commitments is that only one party need be involved in the formation and implementation of a commitment.
4    Agreements often may enjoy legal enforceability – like contracts and obligations – but the term is intended to connote less formal arrangements between parties that may fall somewhat outside a legal sphere. Politically motivated agreements between communities to lobby for some particular purpose illustrate this non-legal dimension of agreements.

Taken as a whole, the COCAs that constitute a public body are referred to as that body's risk field, and this is intended to reflect the fact that an organisation becomes exposed to risk through the COCAs (see Exhibit 3.1). The risks that arise from the risk field collectively are defined as the organisation's risk profile. Both of these terms are fully explained in the discussion of the risk assessment process, but a few final words are necessary here regarding COCAs.

   The COCAs either create risks for the organisation or they serve as a portal for risk. For example, an employment contract will specify certain contractual matters that are unique to that contract – salary, job duties, measures of performance, and so on. In that sense, the contract is creating expectations, duties and rights that have enforceability. Absent the contract and the organisation would not encounter the risks. But, that employment contract might also allow external risks to pass through to the organisation. For example, the Disabilities Discrimination Act exists independently of individual employment contracts, but by entering into an employment contract, the organisation becomes exposed to risks associated with providing reasonable accommodation for employees.

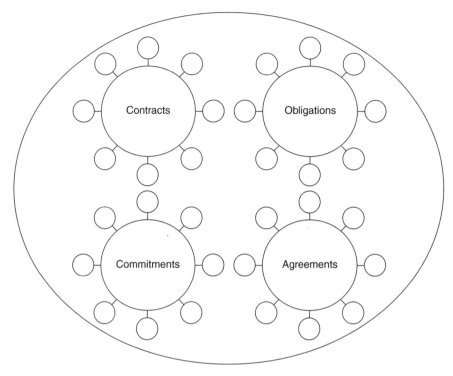

**Exhibit 3.1**  The risk field

The COCAs can further be characterised by the possible risk-distributing characteristics of the arrangement. A commitment to some moral value does not permit risk distribution to occur, as it is a single-party, self-imposed duty. However, a multiparty contract with vendors may create numerous opportunities for distribution. In general, distribution and transfer of risk would seem to be a function of some, if not all, of the following:

* the number of parties to the arrangement
* the relative negotiating strength or leverage of the parties
* the legal or moral enforceability of the arrangement
* the risk-bearing capacity of the parties
* the relationship of a particular arrangement with other COCAs
* the influence of external interests (i.e., external to the specific arrangement).

Finally, COCAs have a history, and while the process of risk assessment tends to focus its efforts on describing what exists and how it might be managed, there always is value in understanding why the arrangement exists in the first place. One of the challenging complications of the ORM view of risk management is that it forces the matter of 'interdependencies' (and history) into the forefront of analysis. In later chapters, the book discusses statistical methods for measuring risks and making decisions, but almost invariably these methods assume independence of exposure – that is, it is assumed that a collection of risks (motor vehicles, for instance) are independently exposed to risk. If the relationships or interdependencies between these exposures are too strong, statistical analysis diminishes in its power to predict and measure.

The irony of this limitation of statistical analysis is that it tends to force risk managers to view interdependency as a nuisance to be assumed away or controlled for in analysis, whereas the ORM view plainly states that interdependencies are the point (or at least a key point) in understanding organisation risk management. The COCAs are entered into, more or less, intentionally and they are expected to serve a common mission or set of purposes for which the organisation exists. It would, in this light, be absurd not to wonder about the interrelatedness of risks and COCAs, so when analysis of the risks within COCAs occurs, it must be plainly understood that each contract, obligation, commitment and agreement is expected to have an impact on other COCAs.

## Environmental sources of risk

The COCAs are the risk field, but additional concepts must be introduced to help in the assessment process. For example, while the risk field is the point of contact between an organisation and a risky world, it would be useful to develop a basis for categorising the various sources of risk. This book relies on a model that incorporates seven environmental sources of risk (see Exhibit 3.2):

1   Physical environment – geological and climatic risks arise from the physical environment.
2   Social environment – citizens' changing tastes and preferences, morals/values, and demographic factors can all give rise to risks.
3   Political environment – political institutions and decisions create responsibilities, interests, and expectations that produce risks.
4   Legal environment – the formalised legal system establishes rights and duties that create risk for organisations.
5   Economic environment – while often influenced by the political, social and legal environments, the global economic system has a degree of independence that warrants separate analysis.

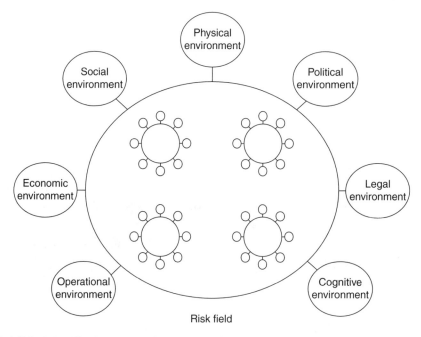

Risk field

**Exhibit 3.2**   Environmental sources of risk

6   Operational environment – the manner in which an organisa-
    tion goes about its work gives rise to a wide range of risks,
    most of which are influenced by the other environments.
7   Cognitive environment – the environment of the mind; a
    manager's knowledge may be influenced by absence of infor-
    mation, attitude towards risk, misinformation or, even, mental
    limitations, and this gives rise to both risk and uncertainty.

There certainly is overlap among these environments, but each is
sufficiently distinct and the separation enhances analysis. In general
terms, risk assessment involves a scan of each environment with
the purpose of being able to describe the environment and being
able to identify risks that arise from each of these environments.

## Hazards and risk factors/perils and opportunities

The specific purpose of environmental scanning is to identify
characteristics that give rise to risk. In the nomenclature of risk
management this means that assessment is concerned principally
with discovering hazards (which produce perils) and risk factors
(which produce opportunities).

Hazards are conditions of an environment that enhance either the likelihood of loss or the potential severity of losses. Ice on a road enhances the likelihood of an accident, and at least indirectly can influence the extent of the damage should an accident occur. Sometimes, an entire environment is deemed hazardous – such would be the case with the social/political environments in Kosovo – but, more commonly, hazards are nodes within an environment that can be detected through careful investigation.

Perils are actual causes of loss, so assessment ultimately is concerned with understanding how hazardous conditions produce losses. After all, most cars driving on icy roads do not crash. Thus, recognising that hazards exist only partly explains the nature of a risk.

Risk factors are a speculative risk analogue to hazards. Certain features of, say, the economic environment are favourable to gain (as well as loss); exchange rate differentials can be profited from with timely investing. These risk factors produce opportunities that offer upside outcome potential. For example, a finance officer might use an arbitrage situation (misalignment in exchange rates, for instance) to speculate on rate movements – an opportunity that might produce returns greater than otherwise would be available.

The identification of hazards and risk factors involves a process known as environmental mapping (see Exhibit 3.3).

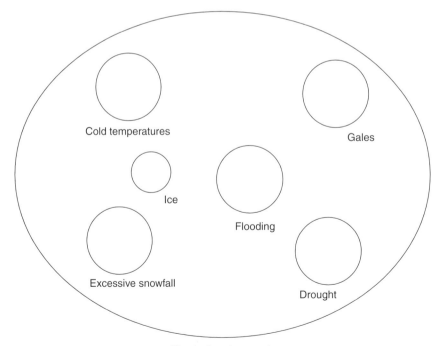

**Exhibit 3.3**  Environmental mapping

## Exposures to risk

Earlier, we explained that COCAs are the risk field where the risk portfolio arises. These risks might be characterised as the product of the environmental sources of risk; as a practical matter, the COCAs are directly responsible for production of the risk or serve as a conduit.

Looked at from another direction, the COCAs bring the 'exposure' to the risks. In other words, an organisation has elements that become exposed to risk through the creation of the COCA. It is not fruitful to spend too much time making terminology distinctions here, however, because commonly the creation of a contract in many senses spontaneously generates exposure. For example, financial assets of a local authority become exposed to a number of risks the instant a vendor agreement is signed.

While COCAs create exposure in a general sense (the public body is exposed to loss), there is an analytical value in categorising types of exposures (see Exhibit 3.4). These exposure types – and there are five – are discussed in Chapters 5 and 6.

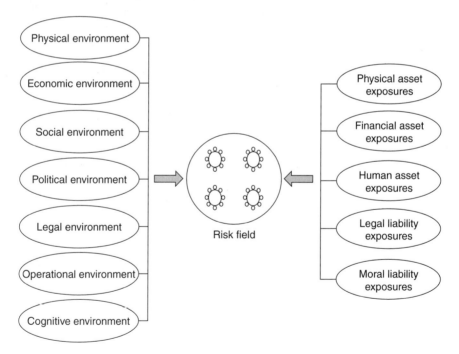

**Exhibit 3.4**   Types of exposures

1   Physical asset exposures – motor vehicles, buildings, bridges, docks, roads, revenue and expense flows.

2    Financial asset exposures – money, investment instruments, debt obligations, derivatives, insurance.
3    Human asset exposures – employees, managers, elected members, key stakeholders.
4    Legal liability exposures – public and employer's liability claims, public officials liability claims.
5    Moral liability exposures – ethical and value-based commitments and obligations.

Since the focus of this book is ORM, it is practically true that risks mean nothing without exposure. An icy road in the Highlands of Scotland certainly is a hazardous condition, but if no one drives on the road there is no exposure. In the context of ORM, exposure is the trigger and while, as human beings, managers might be concerned about certain hazards where no exposure exists, a discussion of such circumstances does little to advance the purposes of this book.

# Risk identification tools and techniques

Ideally, a risk manager would like to develop a process for identifying risks that ensured comprehensiveness and allowed for some degree of confidence that identification was systematically and consistently undertaken. One approach is described below, but readers should note that a wide variety of methods might be adopted and, in fact, the unique attributes of an organisation will be most influential in the approach that ultimately is created.

## *A comment on risk checklists*

A straightforward way to initiate an identification effort is to acquire a risk checklist and use it as a road map for evaluating a public body's risks. Certainly, risk checklists abound; virtually all insurance agencies, brokerages, insurance companies, accounting firms and management consultancy firms have them, as do many professional associations.

The benefits of having a checklist are fairly self-evident. However, there are problems with using them. First, virtually all checklists available are derived from insurance industry sources and thus tend to limit assessment to insurable risks. Second, by design, such checklists are standardised methods, meaning they may not be suited to any particular organisation. Third, the presence of an existing checklist permits an organisation to miss an important opportunity, which is the chance to think broadly and critically about its own exposure to risk.

The balance of this discussion assumes that some type of organising idea is present – whether a customised or standardised checklist – to govern the identification process. However, further discussion of that organising idea will not occur. Curious readers are directed to the sample checklist provided in this chapter's 'Tools You Can Use' section.

## Sources of information

Conventionally, risk assessment processes rely on the following sources of information.

### Environmental scans

Critical to the risk assessment process is the initial effort to characterise and understand the environmental sources of risk. The sources of information for evaluating the physical, social, economic, political, legal, operational and cognitive environments will be varied. However, the environmental scanning process should at least produce answers to such questions as:

• What is the general nature of the environment?
• In broad terms, what is the public body's exposure to this environment?
• What are the specific hazards or risk factors in the environment?
• How does the public body see itself being exposed to hazards and risk factors?

Ordinarily, a risk assessment document will include a short narrative discussion of each environment. The purpose of the scan is more descriptive than analytical; the information sources discussed later will aid in analysis.

### Financial documentation

Budget documents, fund statements and other financial documents provide a very good starting point for analysis. In principle, financial analysis can yield at least:

• the overall financial position of the public body
• general representations of resource flows

- broad identification of physical and financial assets (exposures to risk)
- material events and activities that may affect future budgets
- the overall organisational structure of the public body
- some reflection of goals and objectives of the departments and units within the public body
- general descriptive information on the political unit/community the organisation serves.

## Legal documentation

Relevant legal documentation is difficult to summarise as it will differ significantly from body to body. However, certainly a review of existing contracts would be central to the analysis. Additionally, review of relevant statutes, regulatory rules and laws pertinent to the public body is critical. Commonly, a risk manager relies heavily on the body's legal counsel to conduct a significant portion of the analysis.

## On-site inspections

There is no substitute for actually seeing an organisation's exposures to risk. A formal risk assessment process would include comprehensive site visits, and such inspections probably should be a regular feature of the ongoing risk management process.

## Interviews

Employees and managers are the best sources of information on risks pertinent to their scope of authority and activity. Talking to all levels of employees is important because relying on managers only can result in an 'official version' of things that may not be accurate.

The benefit of interviews also is strategic. By involving employees in the identification process, the risk manager signals the importance he or she places on employee input, and this participatory approach helps the risk manager to obtain institutional buy-in when the risk management programme is rolled out.

## Statistical analysis

Certain important areas of risk management are amenable to statistical analysis – fire losses, worker injuries, motor vehicle risks and general liability claims, to name the most obvious. Further, process or operations analysis can be important in analysing work processes, material flows, and other operational sources of risk.

Data may be internally available, but often the organisation's insurance companies can produce data that can provide important understanding of particular risks.

## Benchmarking/best practices

Partly in response to the challenge of demonstrating best value the Association of Local Authority Risk Managers (ALARM) is spearheading work in the UK to develop benchmarks relative to public sector risk management. Benchmarking involves the development of standards or measures of practice for a wide-ranging set of risk management practices – third party claims administration and other vendor costs, loss control cost/benefit performance, risk manager compensation.

Best practices differ from benchmarking measurement in that benchmarking is concerned with showing average or customary practices, whereas best practices is an effort to find standards of excellence and to emulate them. Less work has been done in this area, but for many public bodies, a best practices approach may be more meaningful. For the practising risk manager, this could mean investigating entities similar to one's own and selecting the top-performing bodies within that grouping for intensive analysis.

Benchmarking and best practices are identification techniques, to be sure, but they also are risk measurement tools and can aid in the selection of risk control measures.

## Consultancy services

There are numerous sources of professional advice and service that can be useful in risk assessment. Notably, insurance agencies and brokerages have highly competent consultants who can provide valuable assistance; and often this is considered part of the overall servicing of the insurance that is purchased.

Several risk management consultants specialise in public risk management clients and can provide a wide range of services. More specialised consultants also exist – actuaries, claims management, safety and security, engineering, legal, and so on – and they may have a particular value with challenging risk assessment projects.

## Citizen forums

Feedback or input from the public can be an invaluable means of identifying risks and – importantly – identifying attitudes and public perceptions of risk.

# Risk analysis

Previously, the discussion of risk assessment introduced the role of hazard and risk factor analysis in the overall risk assessment undertaking, but little was said specifically about analysis processes.

The roots of risk analysis can be found in operations management and safety engineering principles and practices. Further, specialisations have evolved over time bringing specific technical processes to bear on environmental risks, construction risks, workplace safety risks and road safety, among others. For the purposes of this book, it is sufficient for readers to know that this specialised expertise exists. The remainder of this section is devoted to a conceptualisation of risk analysis that can be employed flexibly in a variety of settings.

## The risk chain

Losses (or gains, for that matter) may be reduced to a set of interlocking elements, thereby allowing for close analysis and examination (see Exhibit 3.5). These elements collectively are known as the risk chain; the 'links' of which are:

1   The environment link – the general conditions in which loss or gain events occur.
2   The hazard/risk factor link – within environments, certain conditions elevate the chance of loss or gain or the potential magnitude of loss or gain.
3   The exposure link – the nature and condition of the organisation's exposure, whether asset or liability.
4   The peril/opportunity link – the process through which the interaction of hazard/risk factor and exposure produces loss or gain.
5   The outcome link – the direct and measurable impact of the hazard/risk factor on the exposure.
6   The consequence link – the longer term effect of the loss or gain on the organisation.

There are numerous schools of thought regarding the appropriate perspective or organising idea in conducting a risk analysis. Some

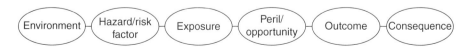

**Exhibit 3.5** The risk chain

view analysis as a mainly scientific process, whereby events are mapped and modelled with the hope of developing a highly detailed picture of risks. Often, this view is accompanied by a somewhat 'engineering'-based perspective that focuses on the mechanics of accidents.

Others view analysis as largely a matter of behavioural psychology. In other words, accidents and events are characterised by the human dimension (fault, carelessness, malicious motives, improper training).

In general, either or both views may be appropriate at any given time, and the main point here would be for a risk manager to be open to a range of possible interpretations.

As a practical matter, the following comments can be made regarding use of the risk chain concept in risk analysis:

1    The environment link is best understood in the context of the broader environmental scan mentioned previously. The evaluation of specific risks or events should be placed in a wider ranging view of the overall convergence of environments on an organisation. Thus, if one is examining the environmental link of a problematic series of accidents in city parks, the physical environment may explain a great deal of the problem – but it is possible that the political, social and economic environments (e.g., a history of insufficient spending on park maintenance) provide a deeper appreciation of the ultimate sources of the problem.

2    The hazard/risk factor link relates to the nodes that exist within a given environment that increase probabilities or potential magnitudes. Carrying forward the example of accidents in council owned parks, the environmental link would compel us to consider all council owned parks as an environment, while the hazard/risk factor link would force us to identify potential and real accident sites (e.g., playground equipment, swift flowing streams, improperly lighted areas).

3    The exposure link isolates the actual loss exposures. Obviously, in the case of park accidents, visitors and other park users would be the principal exposure units – although it can easily be imagined that pets, property, motor vehicles, political support, legal liability, and moral and ethical values also could be exposures. Beyond simply identifying the exposures, consideration of this link would entail describing the nature and scope of the exposure (children v. adults? many or a few? night v. daytime? and so on).

4   The peril/opportunity link ordinarily will be the focus of much attention and analysis as it is the link that moves a risk from 'potential' to 'actuality'. For example, not everyone who uses playground equipment is injured. What are the elements of a hazardous situation that actually produce the losses that occur? Analysis often reveals that perils are not singular elements but are the product of a convergence of elements (improper design and carelessness, for instance). Quantitative assessment of frequency and magnitude (how often accidents occur, and what their impact is when they do occur) logically will be associated with this link.

5   The outcome link is associated with the immediate and, mainly, direct effects of an event or accident. A child falls off a piece of playground equipment, and the risk manager needs to understand specifically what occurs – bruises, broken limbs, concussions. Additionally, the outcome link forces an examination of immediate or initial accident response efforts. Were playground supervisors adequately trained to respond quickly? Did response efforts worsen the situation?

6   The consequence link may not be relevant in some circumstances, but it exists as a reminder that the effects of an accident may be long term and indirect. For example, a spate of accidents may lower park use for an extended period of time, or the situation may have broad political consequences.

One is tempted to frame risk analysis as a highly statistical process, which it may be. However, the preceding discussion suggests that intuitive and qualitative approaches may be wholly appropriate for certain situations.

Readers should make note here of one critical caveat regarding risk analysis. There is a strong and obvious motivation to focus on an analysis of past losses. Losses tend to be known and remembered, and naturally data exist to explain what happened, how much it cost, and even who was to blame. However, from a risk management standpoint, a mapping of only past accidents could be misleading. There may be dozens and dozens of incidents that occur in the parks that do not result in losses, but which may be important to know. For example, a dangerous intersection may have numerous near misses but no actual accidents. Focusing on accidents and ignoring near misses in a risk analysis may give risk managers a comfort level they do not deserve, distract the risk manager from looming or real problem areas and influence the distribution of risk management resources.

# Risk measurement

Ultimately, the purpose of risk assessment is not just to identify and understand risks but also to rank them in some way. The ranking of risks is important because it will influence the allocation of risk management resources. Specifically, risk measurement requires the risk manager to develop yardsticks for measuring the importance of risks to the organisation, and to apply these yardsticks to identified risks.

The distinction between direct and indirect costs is important to the discussion of risk measurement. Direct costs are a direct consequence of a peril acting on an asset. If a fire damages the roof of a town hall, for example, the direct loss is the cost to repair and replace the damage to the roof. An indirect cost is related to the damage caused directly by the peril, but the financial consequences are not a direct consequence of the action of the peril on the asset. For example, the inability of an authority to use its town hall during roof repairs might force the authority to incur expenses in renting a temporary facility. Indirect costs often are hidden, although their consequences may be greater than those of direct losses.

## *Hidden costs/benefits of losses and gains*

Considerable research has been undertaken to evaluate the relationship of indirect costs to direct costs in loss-producing situations. Much less evident is work examining the direct/indirect gain relationship. This section briefly addresses the latter before turning to a fuller discussion of the former.

The ORM idea has begun to force risk managers to think more completely about the overall impact of risk, meaning that attention is starting to be paid to upside potential. Naturally, positive outcomes would have direct and indirect characteristics. For instance, economic development efforts may produce direct benefits in that a new business might choose to relocate to a community, thereby producing tax revenue benefits for the locality. However, the tax revenue benefit likely will be dwarfed (if the development effort is successful) by the numerous indirect benefits – diversification of the job base, jobs, spillover effects on other businesses and effects on future development efforts. Although economic development experts have long been cognizant of direct and indirect benefits, the role of risk management in ascertaining the impact of risk on economic development has only recently come to the fore.

With respect to direct and indirect costs, a number of studies have been undertaken to better understand the impact of losses on organisations. A well-known set of industrial accident studies, for instance, seemed to suggest that the ratio of 8:1 (i.e., £8 of indirect losses for every £1 of direct losses) was a common phenomenon. While this ratio is widely disputed as anything other than an abstract rule of thumb, it does suggest an important risk measurement point – the 'total cost of risk' is greater than the 'direct cost of loss'.

'Cost of risk' has special meaning in risk management, historically serving as one particular way of measuring the impact of risk on an organisation. However, the fundamental definition of the cost of risk is not fully agreed upon by practitioners. Most working measures of the cost of risk include the costs of losses (insurance premiums, uninsured losses and administrative costs – claims management services, for instance) and certainly these are obvious candidates for inclusion. However, the costs of uncertainty are not so obvious or easy to measure. The salary of a risk manager certainly is a knowable cost of uncertainty, but the misallocation and inefficiencies of resource deployment due to uncertainty are not so easily seen. Fear and worry among managers, employees and other stakeholders also take a toll, but measurement of those costs is problematic.

The point here is that risk exacts direct and indirect, quantifiable and unquantifiable, costs on the organisation and risk managers must be alert to the fact that the overall impact of risk extends far beyond the visible effects. But, striving to incorporate a more comprehensive measurement is critical to managerial success, because the case for investment in risk management (made to upper managers) becomes more persuasive when the full effect of risk is known and appreciated.

## Dimensions of exposure to risk

Information is needed concerning at least two dimensions of each exposure. In the case of pure risks these are the frequency of the number of losses likely to occur and the potential severity of those losses that do occur. In the case of speculative risks, these are the frequency of both positive and negative outcomes, and the range of magnitude of possible outcomes. For each of these two dimensions, it would be desirable to know at least the value in an average budget period and the possible variation in the values from one budget period to the next.

These data can be directly useful in determining the best methods for handling an exposure to risk. For example, multiplying expected loss frequency and average loss severity provides an estimate of the expected value of losses. This estimate can be compared with the amount an insurer charges for insurance protection, and estimates of possible variation allow the risk manager to estimate the likelihood that losses will exceed the cost of insurance.

In Chapter 11, statistical/financial information is used in the context of making decisions about risk management strategies and techniques. Concepts necessary to appreciating these approaches are best discussed at that time, so the purpose of the remaining discussion here is to help readers gain an intuitive understanding of the concepts that support more sophisticated measurement approaches. Further, the ideas here serve a useful function when statistical data are limited or nonexistent, a fairly common circumstance in real risk management situations.

Measurable dimensions of risk are shown in Exhibit 3.6, which provides a conceptual structure to the risk measurement challenge. For example, Cell I represents risks that are low frequency/low severity; these risks only infrequently result in loss, and when loss occurs, it is relatively unimportant. Cell III represents risks that are low frequency/high severity; losses occur infrequently but each loss is costly. Cell VII represents risks that are high frequency/low severity; losses occur with great frequency but each loss is relatively inexpensive. Cell IX represents risks that are high frequency/high severity; losses occur with great frequency and are costly each time they occur. From a practical utility standpoint, this matrix is limited in its usefulness because high, medium and low are relative terms, and the model is a single-period model, meaning it does not easily capture the fact that losses may recur over an extended period. However, as an introductory idea, Exhibit 3.6 helps readers through a basic distribution of risks into nine broad measurement classifications.

The measurement matrix in Exhibit 3.6 helps frame an intuitive overall measurement of an organisation's risk profile. A risk manager is able to group risks into broad categories that can serve as a first-round effort to separate the important from the unimportant, the

|  |  | **Magnitude** | | |
|---|---|---|---|---|
|  |  | Low | Medium | High |
|  | Low | I | II | III |
| **Frequency** | Medium | IV | V | VI |
|  | High | VII | VIII | IX |

**Exhibit 3.6**  The measurement matrix

problematic from the manageable. For example, the risks falling into the upper left-hand quadrant of the matrix (roughly, cells I, II and IV) appear to be harmless in the sense that they produce events occasionally and those events are of minor consequence. This is the realm of risk toleration, meaning little or nothing may need to be done other than to monitor those risks that could change frequency and magnitude characteristics over time.

Contrast the previous cells with those found in the lower right-hand quadrant (roughly, Cells VI, VIII and IX) where the likelihood of events is high and the impact of events is dramatic. Public bodies rarely encounter such risks in the assessment process, largely because the frequency and magnitude characteristics could not have escaped the attention of even the most distracted of managers. Organisations that encounter these risks do not last long or, conversely, if it is a huge upside risk, that windfall benefit will only last for a limited period of time. Still, local authorities look for such fertile opportunity-producing circumstances and sometimes they succeed (exploiting a favourable geographic resource, such as an excellent climate or beautiful scenery).

The remaining cells represent the 'messy middle' – those risks that produce events frequently, but at low magnitudes (roughly, the lower left-hand quadrant), and those that rarely produce events, but when those events occur, they are dramatic (the upper right-hand quadrant). Anticipating the discussion in Chapter 4, it could be said that the former risks are risks to be controlled while the latter, echoing discussion in Chapters 7 and 8, are risks to be financed and transferred.

## A brief comment on frequency and magnitude measurement terminology

One method for estimating event frequency is to consider the probability that a given method of exposure to a single risk will result in an event during a year. For example, a risk manager may estimate the probability that a single-storey building will be damaged by fire or the probability that a police authority will be sued for failing to provide an adequate law enforcement service. One traditional, non-numerical approach to estimating probabilities uses four measurement values, which are:

1   *Almost nil*, meaning, in the opinion of the risk manager, the event will not happen.
2   *Slight*, meaning that, though possible, the event has not happened to the present time and is unlikely to occur in the future.

3    *Moderate*, meaning that it has happened once in a while and
     can be expected to occur some time in the future.
4    *Definite*, meaning that it has happened regularly and can be
     expected to occur regularly in the future.

Most exposures to risk are more complex than single-peril/opportu-
nity or single-exposure estimates would imply. For example, a given
building can be damaged from windstorm, earthquake, or flood as
well as from fire. The value of financial assets can be influenced
by foreign exchange rates, inflation, monetary policy, and interest
rates. In addition, a single-peril/opportunity may influence multiple
assets. The accuracy of event-frequency estimates can depend on
whether the relationships between perils/opportunities and objects
exposed to risk are considered. These considerations return us to
the issue of the amount of information the risk manager has on the
nature of the risk. Most risk management decisions are made on
the basis of what the risk manager considers a reasonable subset
of full information. Almost any decision can be improved by additional information allowing more precise estimates of possible
outcomes and their likelihood. The risk manager's judgement is
needed to integrate all available information and use it to develop
estimates.

Two measures commonly used in reference to event magnitude are
the *maximum possible outcome* and the *maximum probable outcome*.
For the moment, consider occurrences causing only one type of loss
or gain. The maximum possible outcome is the largest outcome that
possibly could occur. The maximum probable outcome is the largest
outcome that the risk manager believes is likely to occur.

The maximum probable outcome, which is the most commonly
used magnitude measure, depends on the nature of the peril/oppor-
tunity causing the outcome as well as the person or object exposed
to that outcome; usually the maximum possible outcome is not
affected by the peril/opportunity being considered. For example, a
local authority leasing office space from a commercial property
manager faces the possibility of fire and theft losses to its office
equipment. The maximum probable outcome (loss) to the tenant
authority may be the full value of this equipment in the event of a
fire, but may be limited to the value of the items that have high
value relative to weight and size in the case of theft. In contrast,
the maximum possible outcome (loss) is the full value of all the
equipment, regardless of which peril is considered.

Finally, the concept of *maximum probable yearly aggregate outcome*
is used to apply to a single-peril/opportunity (or exposure) or multiple
perils/opportunities (exposures). This concept reflects the largest total

amount that an exposure unit or group of exposure units is likely to suffer or enjoy during, say, a budget period. Like the maximum probable outcome, this amount depends on the probability level selected by the risk manager, but unlike the maximum probable outcome, this measure does not refer just to magnitude of a single occurrence. Instead, it depends on the number of occurrences as well as their magnitude.

A representation of the complete ORM risk assessment process is given in Exhibit 3.7.

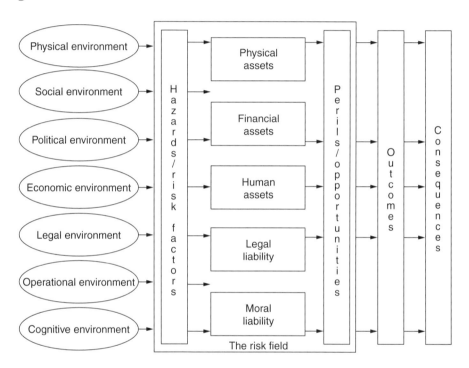

**Exhibit 3.7**   Risk assessment model

# APPLICATIONS

## The cost of absenteeism

The Confederation of British Industry (CBI) published its latest survey into the cost and causes of workplace absenteeism in July 1999, entitled *Focus on Absence: 1999 Absence and Labour Turnover Survey*,[1] providing an update on the level of absenteeism within both the public and private sectors in the UK. Of the 537 respondents to the survey some 22 per cent (approximately 118) came from the public sector. The public sector definition encompassed National Health Service trusts as well as local government.

On average, across all sectors – both private and public – 8.5 days per employee were lost because of sickness absence, compared with 8.4 days in 1997. Based on a working year of 228 days, this represented an absence rate of 3.7 per cent. Absence, so far as the survey was concerned, was defined as any absence other than resulting from holiday and public holiday entitlement. If the results were extrapolated across the total UK workforce then over 200 million workdays would be lost per annum.

When levels of sickness absence are split between manual and non-manual employees the results are as shown in Table 3.1.

Clearly the level of absenteeism among manual workers remains higher than that among non-manual employees, although, specifically in 1998, that level of manual absenteeism fell while the rate of non-manual absenteeism rose.

The survey also reported on absenteeism by size of organisation. The results were as shown in Table 3.2.

With most local authorities in the UK having a workforce in excess of 500 it is not surprising that the level of absenteeism within the public sector is higher than that within the private sector (Table 3.3).

Absenteeism rates were compared between organisations that recognised and did not recognise trade unions. Although the absenteeism rate was higher where trade unions were recognised (8.6 days compared with 6.1 days) this may be as much a function of the fact

**Table 3.1**  Sickness levels

| Employees | Days lost, 1998 | Days lost, 1997 | % of working time, 1998 | % of working time, 1997 |
|---|---|---|---|---|
| Manual | 9.4 | 10.8 | 4.1 | 4.7 |
| Non-manual | 7.6 | 6.8 | 3.3 | 3.0 |
| Total | 8.5 | 8.4 | 3.7 | 3.7 |

**Table 3.2**  Absenteeism by organisation size

| Number of employees | Days lost | % of working time |
|---|---|---|
| < 50 | 4.8 | 2.1 |
| 50 to 199 | 5.9 | 2.6 |
| 200 to 499 | 7.5 | 3.3 |
| 500 to 4999 | 8.9 | 3.9 |
| 5000+ | 9.2 | 4.0 |
| Average | 8.5 | 3.7 |

**Table 3.3** Absenteeism by industry segment

| Sector | Days lost | % of working time |
|---|---|---|
| Public | 9.2 | 4.0 |
| Transport and communication | 8.2 | 3.6 |
| Other services | 8.2 | 3.6 |
| Manufacturing | 8.0 | 3.5 |
| Retailing | 7.5 | 3.4 |
| Distribution, hotels and restaurants | 7.1 | 3.1 |
| Energy and water | 6.8 | 3.0 |
| Other | 5.4 | 2.4 |
| Banking, financing and insurance | 5.0 | 2.2 |
| Construction | 5.0 | 2.2 |
| Average rate | 8.5 | 3.7 |

that absenteeism rates are higher in organisations with larger work-forces.

Of the 537 survey respondents, some 70 per cent provided an estimate of the costs to the organisation of the absences. The average cost per employee was £426 (Table 3.4) and if this were extrapolated across the whole workforce in the UK the overall cost of absenteeism would be £10.2 billion.

One hundred and seventeen of the survey respondents estimated the indirect cost of absence arising from such factors as reduced customer satisfaction and poorer quality of products and services to be a further £666 per employee. Given that this represents responses from just under 22 per cent of the total number of survey respondents, the results should be treated with some caution.

Respondents were then asked to rank on a scale of 1 to 5 in order of importance causes of absence, split between manual and non-manual employees. The findings are shown in Table 3.5.

**Table 3.4** Absentee costs by selected industry segments

| | Direct costs, 1998 (£ million) | Number of employees | Median cost for 1998 (£) | Median cost for 1997 (£) | Median cost for 1996 (£) |
|---|---|---|---|---|---|
| Public | 147.5 | 286 855 | 535 | 503 | 553 |
| Private | 227.2 | 381 534 | 465 | 438 | 351 |
| Manufacturing | 92.7 | 152 534 | 500 | 500 | 325 |
| Services | 126.0 | 229 294 | 343 | 401 | n/a |
| Other/non-specified | 6.9 | 12 128 | 343 | 779 | n/a |
| Total/average | 381.7 | 704 420 | 426 | 478 | 415 |

**Table 3.5**  Cause of absence, by labour type

| Cause of absence | Manual employees, average rank | Non-manual employees, average rank |
| --- | --- | --- |
| Minor illness | 3.72 | 3.30 (1) |
| Serious illness | 2.35 | 2.15 (3) |
| Home/family responsibilities | 2.16 | 2.09 (4) |
| Personal problems | 2.15 | 1.93 (5) |
| Absence seen as entitlement | 2.12 | 1.68 (6) |
| Lack of commitment | 2.06 | 1.59 (9) |
| Work-related accidents | 1.95 | 1.25 (13) |
| Poor workplace morale | 1.93 | 1.68 (7) |
| Workplace stress | 1.91 | 2.17 (2) |
| Unauthorised holiday | 1.87 | 1.46 (10) |
| Impact of long hours | 1.66 | 1.64 (8) |
| Drink or drugs | 1.49 | 1.30 (12) |
| Leisure accidents | 1.55 | 1.40 (11) |

The high placing of workplace stress among causes of absence for non-manual employees shows that employers are beginning to recognise its importance. However, the high ranking of external factors such as personal problems and home and family responsibilities indicate that employee stress is contributed to by a combination of work and home pressures rather than work pressures alone. Interestingly, workplace accidents, which are the focus of much health and safety, risk control and occupational health and safety work, feature relatively low down in the cause of absenteeism (seventh in respect of manual workers and thirteenth in respect of non-manual).

Respondents were asked to comment on whom within their organisation monitored absenteeism, and absence rates were calculated according to who took responsibility for managing absence. The results shown in Table 3.6 reveal that absenteeism is lower the more senior the manager is who reviews absenteeism.

**Table 3.6**  Who monitors absenteeism?

| Occupation | Percentage | Average number days lost per employee |
| --- | --- | --- |
| Senior managers | 11.4 | 5.1 |
| Human resource managers | 5.4 | 5.5 |
| Line managers | 71.1 | 8.5 |
| Other | 2.6 | 11.0 |
| No response | 9.5 | n/a |
| Total | 100.0 | 8.5 |

Respondents were asked to indicate what policies they adopted to reduce unnecessary absence and to rank on a scale of 1 to 5 the effectiveness of those policies (Table 3.7).

Return-to-work interviews were regarded as having the most impact on absence for both manual and non-manual employees.

The need for absence management, or to put a positive spin on it, attendance maximisation, within the public sector is receiving considerable central government attention. Public bodies now are required to report on their steps to control absenteeism. Central government's estimates are that if they can reduce absenteeism within the public sector by 30 per cent by 2003, then they will save the taxpayers some £1 billion.

The CBI survey suggests some pointers for future success centring on high-level management involvement. Clearly, the control of absenteeism requires a proper centralised absence recording system – not just restricted to workplace accidents. Together with this greater flow of information there should be some proactive action on the part of management such as the utilisation of occupational health services and automatic follow-up procedures in the event of prolonged absence coupled with the threat of disciplinary procedures for persistent absentees. The successful management of workplace absenteeism demands a centralised and co-ordinated organisation-wide approach.

**Table 3.7** Absence management policies by level of effectiveness

| Policy/practices | Number who operate policy | Impact on absence, leverage rank |
|---|---|---|
| Disciplinary procedures | 348 | 3.42 (3) |
| Formal notification procedures | 341 | 3.34 (4) |
| Provision of absence statistics to line managers | 308 | 3.10 (5) |
| Return-to-work interviews | 289 | 3.58 (1) |
| Pre-recruitment medicals | 278 | 2.82 (6) |
| Workplace counselling | 229 | 2.71 (8) |
| Occupational health services | 257 | 3.50 (2) |
| Steps to avoid recruitment of poor attendees | 229 | 2.92 (7) |
| Waiting days before occupational sick pay is payable | 205 | 2.62 (9) |
| Absence record as a redundancy determinant | 204 | 2.42 (10) |
| Attendance bonuses | 147 | 2.24 (11) |
| Private medical insurance | 144 | 1.94 (12) |

# TOOLS YOU CAN USE

## A 'starter' risk checklist

As Chapter 3 shows, a full-blown risk assessment can be quite complicated and detailed. For the typical local authority, just getting started
is challenge enough. This section provides readers with a straightforward risk identification checklist that can be used as a stand-alone
document or as the foundation for a more detailed risk assessment.
Readers should note that this checklist draws from a conventional
checklist developed by Tillinghast-Towers Perrin, a risk management and actuarial consultancy.

| Exposures | Do we have the exposure? | Economic value | Additional information |
|---|---|---|---|
| *Physical assets* | | | |
| *Real assets* | | | |
| Administrative Buildings | | | |
| Amusement park | | | |
| Athletics facilities | | | |
| Auditoria | | | |
| Beaches | | | |
| Bridges | | | |
| Camps | | | |
| Car parks | | | |
| Cemeteries/crematoria | | | |
| Communications masts | | | |
| Depots | | | |
| Fire stations | | | |
| Motorways, streets, roads | | | |
| Incinerators | | | |
| Libraries | | | |
| Marinas, harbours | | | |
| Museums | | | |
| Parks and playgrounds | | | |
| Premises leased from third parties | | | |
| Premises leased to third parties | | | |
| Refuse dumps | | | |
| Schools | | | |
| Sewerage systems | | | |
| Stadiums | | | |
| Street lighting and furniture | | | |
| Swimming pools and sports and leisure centres | | | |
| Theatres, concert halls and places of entertainment | | | |
| Tunnels | | | |
| Underground pipelines | | | |
| Unoccupied land | | | |

| Exposures | Do we have the exposure? | Economic value | Additional information |
|---|---|---|---|

*Personal assets*
Books
Computer Equipment
Equipment and machinery
Fine arts and civic regalia
Furniture and fixtures
Livestock
Security Protection/detection devices
Signage
Vehicles
Watercraft and boats
*Human assets*
Foster parents, respite carers etc.
Full-time and part-time employees
Labour masters, self-employed persons and subcontractors
Members
Trainees and work experience
Volunteers
*Financial assets*
Assessment records
Borrowings
Cash/cheques/securities and other financial instruments
Contracts
Council tax
Data processing media
Fees for service provision
Fines and penalties
Grants
Hire charges
Leases
Licences and permits
National non-domestic rates
Other valuable records
*Intangible assets*
Air
Critical expertise – accounting
Critical expertise – architectural
Critical expertise – consultancy
Critical expertise – data processing
Critical expertise – data processing
Critical expertise – electronic fund transfer
Critical expertise – engineering
Critical expertise – insurance
Critical expertise – legal
Critical expertise – medical services
Critical expertise – public relations
Critical expertise – public relations
Critical expertise – risk management
Critical resources – communications

| Exposures | Do we have the exposure? | Economic value | Additional information |
|---|---|---|---|
| Critical resources – protection | | | |
| Critical resources – transportation | | | |
| Critical resources – utilities | | | |
| Economic environment | | | |
| Energy | | | |
| Legal environment | | | |
| Natural environment | | | |
| Political environment | | | |
| Raw materials | | | |
| Social environment | | | |
| Water | | | |

## READ MORE ABOUT IT

## Organisation risk management in UK police authorities: an integrated management approach

*Peter C. Young. and Martin Fone[2]*

### About the authors

Peter C. Young is the E. W. Blanch Senior Chair in Insurance at the University of St Thomas Graduate School of Business (Minneapolis, Minnesota). Dr Young has written, spoken, and consulted extensively on the subject of public sector risk management.

Martin Fone is a Vice-President of Am Re Managers International and is responsible for that organisation's business activities in the public and non-profit sectors outside the USA. Based in London, Mr Fone has over nineteen years business experience in the UK and abroad.

### Abstract

Risk management is evolving into a broader, more general, management role in organisations. This emerging form, called organisation risk management, seeks to manage all organisation risks in an integrated, comprehensive and strategic manner. The public sector has been somewhat slow to adopt both this view and practice, but changing political, social and economic pressures are forcing public authorities to provide better services with increasingly limited resources; and these pressures, in turn, are heightening the awareness of the value in managing the cost of risk.

This article introduces and develops the organisation risk management concept, and provides a specific application that is a critical issue for the modern police authority – employment risk. In discussing this employment risk, the text offers both a method for analysing risks generally and a set of risk management principles that apply to the actual management of all organisational risks.

## Introduction

The creation of autonomous, or nearly autonomous, police authorities in the UK has given rise to numerous challenges, some of them related to the actual policing function and some to the management of that function. Perhaps the overarching challenge is the management of fixed and immutable budgets; budgets that are expected to support and sustain high-quality services in a social environment that is changeable, complex and increasingly costly to police. By necessity, the administrator's attention becomes trained on activities that will control or eliminate waste while maximising the effectiveness of limited funds.

Consideration of inefficient or ineffective use of resources inevitably leads to the cost of risk. Risks mainly impose dead-weight costs on authorities, meaning the money expended on losses serves no productive purpose from the organisation's perspective. For a police authority, the cost of risk manifests itself in pension fund financing concerns, in wrongful arrest claims, in motor vehicle accidents, in injuries to or sickness suffered by officers, and in other ways. The accumulated burden of these costs can be enormous, and a growing awareness of the burden has begun to heighten police administrators' appreciation of the need to manage costs.

Over the past few years, the public sector in the UK has demonstrated an increasing interest in the concept of risk management. This has been prompted, in part, by the imposition of high deductibles by insurers following the collapse of Municipal Mutual (Young and Fone, 1996). In the past, ground-up insurance tended to mute the cost of risk for local authorities, so the introduction of deductibles has served to reveal plainly the cause-and-effect relationship between risk and consequences. Not surprisingly, this increasing use of deductibles has promoted the development of sophisticated strategies for the management of insurable risks. However, other trends in local authorities (compulsory competitive tendering and downsizing, for instance) have begun to raise the more general question of whether it is sufficient to manage only insurable risks. The thesis of this text is that concentration on the management of insurable risks will only partially meet the overall challenge to control and

eliminate waste and dead-weight costs. In order to attack the fundamental costs of risk, police authorities need to broaden the focus of
risk management efforts to include the management of all organisation risks. To illustrate this argument, the text looks at perhaps
the most critical risk for police authorities – employment risk.

## Organisation risk management

A key purpose of risk management in local authorities is to assure
that funds are available when investments need to be made (Froot,
Scharfstein and Stein, 1994). Since public entities have limited
options in terms of securing funds, and since many options impose
high frictional costs (costs of borrowing, political costs of raising taxes
or asking the funding authority for an extraordinary appropriation),
it generally is presumed that existing, allocated funds budgeted to
an authority represent the least costly £s available to that authority.

Historically, risk managers have been expected to focus their attention on fortuitous, hazard-based risks – often called 'insurable' risks.
Thus, in pursuing the objective of assuring available funds for investment, the traditional risk manager would either (1) work to prevent
an unexpected drain on resources from arising, or (2) secure insurance in the hope that policy proceeds would serve to restore a budget
to pre-loss status (Young and Smith, 1995).

More recently, and due to numerous factors, risk management has
broadened its orientation to include the management of all risks. The
phrase 'all risks' is, of course, something of a rhetorical device since
it is absurd to presume that all risks can be identified and controlled.
Nevertheless, the phrase does convey the sense of developments
within the risk management discipline, which have been towards
a more integrated and comprehensive (some would say 'holistic')
approach to risk management (Williams, Smith and Young, 1995).

The logic behind the trend towards integrated risk management
is compelling, both from a conceptual and a practical perspective.
Conceptually, risk is not additive, nor is it precisely separable. This
means it is difficult for an organisation to pluck out one risk from
the array of risks it encounters, insure and manage it, and presume
that this can be done while oblivious to the effects of other factors
on that risk or, indeed, the effects of that 'managed' risk on other
risks. There are interdependencies in an organisation's risk portfolio, and these connections between risks require attention if an
organisation is to ever exert meaningful influence on its risks. On
a practical level, the current trends for downsizing, flattening
management structures and outsourcing suggests that there is a

general imperative to broaden the scope of individual managers, and to promote more effective, integrated management.

The value of this integrated approach is evident when applied to a problem plaguing nearly all police authorities in the UK. Absence of officers through sickness and injury impacts significantly on the authority's ability to deliver frontline services. Additional costs are incurred in overtime payments, loss of morale, inadequate maintenance of equipment, short cuts in safety measures, diminishment of public support, and so on.

The economic impact of such problems does not conform to the 'insurable risk' frame of reference. It is interwoven into all aspects of the authority and fundamentally influences the administrator's ability to manage the authority.

The promise of integrated risk management must be leavened with a recognition of the day-to-day difficulties of implementing such an approach. If one is advocating the co-ordinated management of all risks, then one had better clearly recognise that this 'organisational risk manager' will have to be a person of extraordinary knowledge and ability. We well might wonder whether such a person exists.

The work that has been done on the idea of integrated risk management, known as organisation risk management (ORM), offers a way around this practical problem. Organisation risk management is a general management function involving the assessment, control and financing of risk (Williams, Smith and Young, 1995). The phrase 'general management function' means that risk management is part of every employee's job. Individual employees are in the best position to manage the risks within their general purview, and the ORM concept promotes the view that risk management is not something that a risk management department does to its organisation but rather it is something every part of the organisation is doing to support the furtherance of the organisation's goals and objectives. In theory, an organisation does not need a risk manager per se, because risk management is an integrated piece of the operating environment. However, practically speaking, risk management does require certain technical knowledge and expertise and most importantly it needs overall co-ordination and facilitation. Thus, the ORM view notes that the co-ordinator/facilitator will need a central and elevated vantage point with sufficient authority to make risk management work. As a general convention, this person is referred to as the chief risk officer, because this title reflects both the organisational level and the scope of responsibility such an individual will have.

## Organisations, risks, and organisation risk management

But what about all the risks the CRO is responsible for managing?

The ORM view of risk management rests upon an important idea about organisations. This idea is known as the 'contractarian' view of organisations. The contractarian view states that organisations are collections of agreements between resource holders and managers (Williams, Smith and Young, 1995). These agreements can be explicit, such as the employment contract where a worker holds his or her capacity to work and the manager negotiates an agreement to compensate that worker in return for the use of that capacity. Some agreements, many in fact, are less explicit. For local governments an example might be the obligation a present government has to future generations. This particular example is important but always problematic because the claim on resources that future generations possess is difficult to ascertain. Further, future generations are unable to negotiate on their own behalf. Nevertheless, while extreme, this example does underscore the fact that many of these contracts have important peculiarities, limitations or distinctions that pose management problems for the organisation.

In risk management, these agreements collectively are known as an organisation's exposure field inasmuch as they are where an organisation encounters risk (see Sidebar 3.1). Some organisational risks arise from the agreements themselves; for example, the terms of an agreement may create an obligation that an organisation may or may not be able to fulfil. More commonly, however, agreements serve as a conduit for risks, as when an agreement between a police authority and a lending institution exposes the authority to certain financial risks (Williams, Smith and Young, 1998).

Logically, particular agreements will be more important than others for organisations. In the public sector, certain general characteristics tend to influence the shape of the risk profile (Young, 1996). Most public organisations deliver services, thus service delivery is a core management issue. Some services are technology dependent (processing of licences), but many public services are human resource dependent. Unquestionably, public safety falls into this category.

For organisations whose purpose is the provision of public safety, the employment agreement is a central (perhaps, the central) source of risk. In the case of police authorities, such a statement cannot be surprising. The act of offering employment to an individual gives rise to an array of risks – from employers liability claims, to wrongful arrest claims, to improper conduct investigations – that must be counted as among the most important management challenges

## Sidebar 3.1 The risk assessment schematic

An organisation's exposure field is that collection of agreements that presents it with the risks that constitute the organisation's risk profile. The nature of an organisation's exposure to risk is dictated by the terms of the contract or agreement, the organisation's 'interest' in the contract or agreement, and enforceability.

In general terms, the typical organisation has interest in certain assets that are the tangible exposure to risk. They can be categorized as:

- physical assets (building, motor vehicles, computers)
- financial assets (stocks, bonds, derivatives)
- human assets (employees, managers, vendors, partners).

Conventionally, risk managers often refer to legal liability as a fourth exposure area because while the law delineates rights – which in turn influence the value of physical, financial, and human assets – it also imposes duties and obligations with respect to the assets of others. Thus, an organisation's duties represent another exposure to risk.

Risks arise from seven sources of risk:

1   The physical environment.
2   The social environment.
3   The political environment.
4   The legal environment.
5   The economic environment.
6   The operational environment.
7   The cognitive environment.

The first five generally are self-explanatory. The physical environment refers to geographic, climatological sources of risk. The social environment refers to social and cultural factors that give rise to risk. The operational environment refers to the source of risk that arises within the organisation; its production processes, corporate policies, its information systems. The cognitive environment refers to the 'environment of the mind'. Humans are fallible and risk can arise from our inability to know or understand objective reality.

The environmental sources of risk may be hazardous in their entirety (a nation in a state of revolution might be deemed to have a political environment that is a hazard), but mainly it is thought that hazards are special conditions/circumstances of an environment that elevate the probability or magnitude of loss. Within hazardous conditions may be found perils, which are causes of loss. It is the interaction of perils and exposures that is a key concern to risk managers.

It would be remiss, however, to fail mentioning 'upside' risk. The physical environment may produce perils, as when a subarctic climate (the hazard) gives rise to icy roads (the peril) that exposes an organisation's fleet of motor vehicles (the exposure) to loss. However, the physical environment may contribute positively to an organisation. Certainly the potential for favourable weather in Florida, presents Disney World with significant opportunity for gain. When risk managers speak of managing such risks, the terms 'hazard' and 'peril' are inappropriate. In such cases, it is common to refer to risk factors as conditions of an environment that give rise to gain (rather than loss), and opportunities (causes of gain) arising from those risk factors. Risk assessment consists of those efforts an organisation undertakes to systematically and comprehensively identify, analyse and measure risk in the framework of this schematic.

facing modern police authorities. However, we quickly must remind ourselves that the employment relationship also presents 'upside' potential, in that an employee who is well trained, motivated and effective will enhance the organisation's performance (and, critically, those same attributes help minimise the 'downside' – a clear example of the risk interdependencies mentioned previously).

## The employment agreement

The employment agreement is not synonymous with an employment contract. The contract for employment is part of the employment agreement, but the agreement really is a collection of agreements and contracts that attach to the relationship between employer and employee. It includes implied 'moral agreements' that most humans assume exist in any interaction. It also includes agreements that attach to the employment contract, but which are independent of it – in the USA, workers' compensation laws are an example; in the UK, employers liability laws have a similar relationship.

For purposes of introduction, the employment agreement might be decomposed as follows:

1   The direct employment contract.
2   Statutory rules and laws pertaining to employment.

3    Civil law generally.
4    Criminal law generally.
5    Moral and ethical considerations generally.

Each of these five elements of the employment agreement can be construed as an implied or express contract between the employee and the organisation's managers. And, importantly for this text, each of these contracts gives rise to risks that the organisation must manage.

Fundamentally, the core risk of the employment agreement is the risk associated with the fulfilment of the direct employment contract. Managers face the possibility that a hired worker will be unable to produce labour in accordance with the contract. Conversely, the employee faces the risk that the employer can not fulfil its obligation to pay for labour rendered.

Emanating from that core risk are others, of only slightly less importance. Employers Liability laws, and other laws – arising from both common and statutory law – impose certain rights and obligations on the employer and the employee.

Civil law pertaining to agency relationships also is important. An employee enjoys certain rights and bears certain duties of agency, meaning the law understands an employee, acting within the scope of the employment agreement, to be representing the employer. To the extent that actions fall outside the law, that employee's actions are the responsibility of the employer. The same issues arise under criminal law, though the context clearly is different.

Beyond secondary risks, other risks arise and merit consideration. Moral, ethical and religious convictions can impose duties and rights on the employment agreement. These tend to be less obvious and definable in Western cultures, but are very present in the Middle East and in Asia. They present risk management challenges for organisations because these rights and obligations may have a degree of enforceability.

The principal insight gained by the contractarian approach is that agreements are the means through which organisations face risk – but as importantly, the agreements can be the means by which those risks are managed. One key implication of this insight is that the setting of terms of the agreement is the fundamental risk control technique.

## The management of employment agreement risk

Given the preceding discussion, the management of employment-related risks becomes framed in a way that would not arise from traditional 'insurable' risk management. In fact, the ORM concept gives voice to several principles that are not obvious in a more traditional assessment of employment risks.

## Risk management begins with the employment agreement

Several agreements and contracts attach to the employer–employee relationship. The manager's role is to enter into agreements that best serve the purposes of the organisation. Thus, contract/agreement negotiation is the primary risk management tool.

The manager's ability to obtain the most favourable agreement will depend in part on his or her ability to ascertain the risks that arise from the employment agreement, and to determine the best way contractually to distribute and manage those risks. Of course, the employment agreement is not unilateral, and the employees and their representatives will be seeking to advance their own interests. Consequently, the multilateral nature of the agreement means that the goal of contract formation is to 'optimise', rather than 'maximise', benefit to the authority.

For the practice of risk management, the key value of the contractarian approach is that risks explicitly are viewed as arising from multiparty agreements – agreements that presumably are entered into because the parties see benefit. In this context, management of agreement-based risks also must be approached as a multiparty arrangement.

Interestingly, in the USA there is an important historical illustration of this idea; workers' compensation. Prior to the adoption of workers' compensations laws (essentially a no-fault system where employees waive their right to sue an employer for work-related injuries and deaths in exchange for a guarantee of certain medical and lost income benefits), the USA operated under employer liability rules not too dissimilar from modern employers' law in the UK. The precipitating events that led to workers' compensation arose from a slow recognition by unions and employers that the employment agreement was a contract of mutual benefit and that the costs of workplace safety had consequences for both employer and employee. Thus, the management of workplace injuries was perceived to be a risk management issue of common interest (Williams, Turnbull and Cheit, 1982).

Of course, workers' compensation in reality falls far short of the neat social compromise mentioned above. Nevertheless, the greatest social insurance scholar of his time, Edwin E. Witte, concluded that though workers' compensation was far from perfect, it represented the kind of rough, democratic solution that allowed all parties to gain at the minimum of cost. Indeed, his view came to be known as the 'least social cost' theory of workers' compensation (National Commission on State Workman's Compensation Laws, 1973).

Engineering a workers' compensation system in the UK probably is not realistic (although the Pearson Commission pioneered the concept of a no-fault compensation system in the 1970s), but recognition that risk management cooperation between parties to an agreement can benefit all parties is realistic and is a strategy that arises from the contractarian approach.

## Understand the interdependencies of risk

Organisation risk management explicitly assumes that since agreements are interrelated, risks arising from these agreements also are interdependent. Interdependency is a characteristic of risk often overlooked by managers but, practically speaking, it is quite important. A fire at a police facility puts pressure on other facilities that must bear an additional load after that fire. Increasing frequency of workplace injury influences worker productivity. A decision to buy insurance may conflict with an organisation's general financing policy on non-insurable risks. It is tempting to view this issue as purely statistical in nature, suggesting correlations and covariations, but in fact the issue of interdependency is broadly subjective and intuitive for most risk managers. 'How do we describe the relationships that exist between agreements and how do those relationships influence the risks intrinsic to those agreements?'

## Organisation risk management relies on incentives

Arrangements can be made to manage risk, but it is useful to be mindful of incentives that exist in these arrangements. Sometimes these incentives are deliberate, but often they occur as a consequence of unintended events. For example, a worker who is injured has some choices as to how compensation and care may be received. An employer's liability claim is one method, but sick leave is another, and the health benefit plan is another. The fact that the various sickness and injury programmes only rarely are co-ordinated means that incentives may arise to select certain services over others. In the USA, this phenomenon – known as 'claims migration' – is well studied. For instance, because workers' compensation conventionally is a ground-up financing scheme (whereas group health plans tend to involve employee paid deductibles, co-payments and other expenses) non-workers' compensation claims tend to migrate into the more generous system.

Only through an integrated approach to risk management can incentives be co-ordinated and unintended effects minimised.

## The strategic goal is to control risk, not finance it

It sometimes appears that risk management is a sequence of steps; first, an organisation assesses its risks, then it attempts to control them, then it seeks to finance that which cannot be controlled. In practice this rarely happens since assessment, control and financing may – and often do – occur simultaneously. However, as a general principle, the concept of risk control does precede risk financing. Due to principles of insurance pricing, indeed of pricing for any financing mechanism, it is almost always less expensive to prevent a loss from occurring than to pay for the loss itself.

Today there is a good deal of discussion about strategic risk financing programmes that develop complex, multiyear instruments for financing insured or self-insured risks. But from the organisation's perspective this misses a key point. What is strategic is the desire to control risk. Risk control requires long-term constancy of purpose and effort and senior management commitment. Risk financing, while it should serve long-term purposes, need not be strategic in its precise form. Simply because the providers of risk-financing mechanisms (insurance companies, brokers, banks) operate in a competitive environment, it is entirely plausible for an organisation to utilise different mechanisms by which to finance its risks over time without ever deviating from the strategic goal of trying to control its risks and exposures. This is not to argue that risk-financing measures should not serve the strategic risk management objectives, but rather that the financing mechanisms in themselves are not strategic.

## Finance risk for budget stability

Insurance has been such a staple of most risk management programmes that its purpose and its value often are overlooked. For smaller local authorities with a limited ability to predict future loss experience, the role of insurance is to reduce uncertainty and help stabilise the cost of risk. For large authorities that can estimate future loss experience with some accuracy, stabilisation is the principal benefit.

Identifying budget stabilisation as the purpose of risk financing clarifies the role of insurance. Insurance adds value to a risk-financing arrangement if (1) it can predict losses better than can the local authority (thus providing an uncertainty-reducing benefit), and/or (2) it has the economic capacity to stabilise the insured's budget. Of course, the price must be right too.

The case for insurance weakens when the local authority has ability to predict its losses and when it has economic capacity rivalling the insurance company, and this is because the insurance company's margin (the premium less loss costs) becomes more a dead-weight cost. Still, if insurance is unattractive, the local authority will be concerned with budget stabilisation, and this may mean consideration of alternatives to insurance: self-insurance, finite risk insurance, banking arrangements, risk retention groups, and the like.

Risk financing arrangements for public sector organisations are quite competitive with respect to price at the moment, and it is tempting to look at the decision to insure or self-insure a risk as being driven by price alone. The preceding discussion does not ignore price, but does argue that the main motivation for risk-financing is cost stabilisation, which means that local authorities must seek some balance in their criteria for developing a risk financing scheme.

## Organisation risk management integrates its solutions

The employment agreement generates a cluster of risks that are interdependent. The article has argued that integrated risk management responds to that circumstance. To clearly understand this point, consider the following. An integrated management approach to employment risk management would have to include a co-ordinated plan involving:

1   Contract negotiation.
2   Employee screening, hiring, promotion, retention and termination policies and practices.
3   Security measures.
4   Fidelity and surety bonding.
5   Training and professional development.
6   Liability insurance.
7   Occupational safety and health measures.
8   Compensation/incentive design and administration (including employee benefits).
9   Union–management relations.
10  General public relations management.
11  Integration of human asset risk management into any contingency planning.

12    Strategic workforce planning.
13    Management of discrimination/harassment issues.
14    Litigation management policy.
15    Human asset investment strategy.

Other general management activities (audit and compliance, for instance) might be argued for and added, but the purpose of the listing here is illustrative. All of these activities relate to the organisation's efforts to manage risks arising from the employment agreement. Explicit recognition of the need to co-ordinate these efforts often is not obvious to organisation managers.

## Summary

The discussion of employment risk in this text is generalisable to all risks within an organisation. Agreements entered into with providers of raw materials can give rise to the same risk management issues. For other organisations, the agreement between that organisation and its creditors can be managed following similar approaches. The point here is that once risk management is defined in general terms, the strategy of managing particular risks will conform to the ideas discussed above.

Police authorities, like most public entities, encounter many problematic risks. The administrator's ability to address these risks in a systematic and integrated way will provide a key difference between public organisations that succeed and those that fail.

## Citations

Froot, K. A., Scharfstein, D. S. and Stein, J. C. (1994). A framework for risk management. *Harvard Business Review*, November–December, 46–57.

National Commission on State Workmen's Compensation Laws (1973). *Report of the National Commission on State Workmen's Compensation Laws*. United States Government Printing Office.

Williams, C. A. Jr, Smith, M. L. and Young, P. C. (1995). *Risk Management and Insurance*. 7th edn. McGraw-Hill.

Williams, C. A. Jr, Smith, M. L. and Young, P. C. (1998). *Risk Management and Insurance*. 8th edn. McGraw-Hill/Irwin.

Williams, C. A. Jr, Turnbull, J. G. and Cheit, E. F. (1982). *Economic and Social Security*. 5th edn, John Wiley.

Young, P. C. (1996). Public sector and private sector risk management: is there a difference? *Governmental Risk Management Reports*, September, 1–10.

Young, P. C. and Fone, M. (1996). The future of pooling. *Public Risk*, October.

Young, P. C. and Smith, M. L. (1995). Why do public entities manage risk? *Governmental Risk Management Reports*, June–July, 1–12.

## Notes

1   *Focus on Absence: 1999 Absence and Labour Turnover Survey* – available price £25.00 (non-members) or £15.00 (members) from the Confederation of British Industry, Centre Point, 103 New Oxford Street, London WC1A 1DU; e-mail enquiry.desk@cbi.org.uk

2   Reprinted with permission from *The International Journal of Police Science and Management*, **1** (1), November 1997.

# Risk control

## EXECUTIVE SUMMARY

Risk managers spend a considerable amount of time assessing risks, but once a general picture has emerged, the question of managing and controlling those risks comes to the fore. In general, the risk manager's tool kit includes two broad sets of techniques and practices: risk control tools and risk-financing tools. In this chapter, risk control is introduced and discussed.

Risk control includes all tools, techniques and strategies for avoiding risk, preventing losses, reducing risk or minimising losses, reducing uncertainty, neutralising risk and transferring risks to third parties.

In the context of risk control, risk avoidance is the fundamental tool since it commonly is the least expensive. Unfortunately, in the public sector avoidance is a highly restricted option. Therefore, most energy expended by risk managers tends to be directed towards the prevention of losses, the minimisation of the impact of losses that do occur and the transference of risks to other parties, including measures to neutralise or hedge certain risks.

The subject of risk control cannot be fully discussed without an appreciation for the phenomenon of mandated risk control. Many laws and regulations exist that compel public sector bodies to practise risk control whether they wish to or not (for example, health and safety legislation, employment-related regulations, environmental legislation).

# PRINCIPLES AND CONCEPTS

Risk control can be defined to include any measures taken by an organisation to prevent, eliminate or reduce losses, enhance the probabilities of gains, minimise the severity of losses that do occur or maximise gains. Additionally, measures taken to reduce uncertainty can be added to the definition.

The breadth of the definition and the scope of practices that fall under the definition present a challenge for the practitioner. In some respects, almost anything a manager does might relate directly or indirectly to this definition of risk control. But such inclusiveness does little to deepen the reader's appreciation of the specific characteristics that constitute a risk control measure. The purpose of this chapter is to work within this broad definition to provide a tight discussion of core risk control measures, a discussion that will enable readers to understand the specific contribution of risk control to overall management efforts.

To this end, Chapter 4 addresses the following questions:

- What are the practical working characteristics of risk control?
- Can we generalise risk control measures into categories of action?
- What is the evidence of risk control effectiveness?
- What is 'mandated' risk control, and how does it influence an organisation's motivation to control risk?

The final bullet point item will be particularly important when discussed in the context of risk management in public bodies. A high percentage of activities that might reasonably be categorised as risk control are undertaken either due to regulatory requirement or administrative rule. Employment rights legislation, health and safety regulations, and central government grant requirements, for example, all illustrate the influence of central government and, indeed, the EU on the practice of risk control in public sector organisations (as well as private sector organisations). The discussion in this chapter highlights the political dimension of this issue as well as the actual and practical implications for managers.

## What is risk control?

Risk is pervasive and its effects are both obvious and subtle. In developing the concept of ORM, this book introduces the idea of public bodies as 'collections of contracts, obligations, commitments, and agreements'. A body's exposure to risk either arises from those relationships or risks 'pass through' those relationships. So, for instance, an authority's contract with a trade union gives rise to commitments and obligations that create specific contractual risks for the local authority. However, that contract also serves as the means through which the authority's employment obligations manifest themselves.

A reminder of this book's view of public organisations is useful in this chapter, because any discussion of measures to manage/control risk must begin with an appreciation of how an organisation becomes exposed to risk. Any effort to build a comprehensive programme of risk control must first consider that the portfolio of risks a public body possesses is built over time – sometimes purposefully, sometimes not – and that the risk portfolio in some sense represents an assemblage of risks that connect to larger interrelated purposes. In other words, all organisational risks have interdependencies. More will be stated on this later in the chapter.

The preceding paragraph might suggest to some readers that an organisation is free to pick and choose the risks it is willing to be exposed to, and to a certain extent this is true. However, a developing theme in this book is the belief that public sector risk management is distinguished from private sector risk management to a large degree by the fact that risk avoidance is a highly restricted option in the public sector. A business, by contrast, might choose to avoid many risks by simply not allowing exposure to occur.

Public bodies can avoid some risks, but a distinguishing difference is the fact that risk management is a central purpose of government. By definition, many of a body's duties are risk management duties, and many of its risks are problematic. Indeed, as Chapter 1 shows, responsibility for certain risks falls to public bodies precisely because those risks exhibit characteristics that restrict the possibility for private management. And further, the relationship of a public institution and the public is different from that of a private institution and the public, and there is a much more obvious sense that the public places greater expectation on public bodies to commit to risk management measures. We might even extend that public expectation and note that the public even pressures public bodies to assure that private business is performing risk management – at least with respect to issues that affect the public at large.

So, what is risk control? Risk control is any strategy, programme, tool or technique that seeks to avoid, prevent, reduce or eliminate risk and uncertainty. This book's view of risk control also includes those measures undertaken to increase a risk's upside potential, whether through actions to increase the probability of favourable outcomes or the magnitude of those favourable outcomes.

A discussion of the second part of this definition, 'upside risk control', could quickly descend to hair-splitting over the meaning of specific words. For instance, when it is said that risk control involves measures to increase the probability of favourable outcomes, the question might arise – is this accomplished by reducing the downside possibilities, or by fundamentally affecting the upside in such a way that it is more likely to occur? Readers should rest assured that while this question is interesting enough in the abstract, it is of minor concern in this book. More often than not, risk control measures will deal with the management of downside potential, but in doing so the upside potential (where it exists) is directly enhanced. Perhaps an obvious example would be a programme to reduce back injuries among refuse collectors, which, if successful, could have a direct and powerful influence on productivity.

## Risk control tools

This book's discussion of risk control techniques and characteristics divides the subject of risk control into the following areas:

- risk avoidance
- risk transfer and distribution
- risk/uncertainty reduction
- loss prevention
- loss reduction
- risk neutralisation.

### *Risk avoidance*

It might be possible to construct a hierarchy of risk control strategies, tools and techniques using a cost basis. Almost invariably, the technique of risk avoidance would serve as the foundation. Risk avoidance involves those tools and techniques that enable the organisation to avoid completely exposure to the risk in question. While this technique seems simple enough, it is worth analysing the specific elements of avoidance, as analysis will prevent confusion when additional risk control techniques are introduced.

To begin, in its most basic form, an avoidance decision means that the risk in question simply does not exist. The risks, for instance, that might be created by entering into a contract with a vendor do not exist if the contract is not signed. This view of avoidance creates some problems, however, because it requires that an avoided risk simply does not exist for anyone (in the previous sentence, the vendor cannot contract with anyone else). For example, destruction of nuclear weapons can help a nation avoid the risk of nuclear explosion, and the risk does not fall on anyone else.

This is a rather rigorous definition, because a single public body often has little ability to eradicate a risk fully and completely through avoidance. Moving a proposed power plant from an earthquake sensitive region is 'avoidance' in the conversational sense of the word, but strict application of the definition would require the risk of earthquake to physically disappear.

As Chapter 3 indicates, this book is about management of risks in public bodies, so motivation to act is centred on 'exposure to risk'. Therefore, risk avoidance is accomplished by assuring that the organisation is unequivocally unexposed to the risk and, whenever possible, the risk does not exist in any physical sense.

Relaxation of the definition can create some confusion later in this chapter. For instance, when the discussion turns to 'risk transfer', readers might reasonably wonder whether an authority transferring an exposure to risk to a general contractor is avoidance. Perhaps the confusion is moderated slightly by observing that the risk still exists for the contractor to the organisation, who may bear the risk but who can exert some direct influence on the organisation.

Risk avoidance is the foundation risk control measure, to a large extent because it is close to costless – at least usually. Choosing to not expose an organisation does not typically consume many resources (economic, human or otherwise). However, avoidance is not always costless. Avoiding a risk also means avoidance of any benefits (upside).

Additionally, avoidance of a particular risk may actually make other risks more problematic. For example, consider a small community that has two bridges crossing a river running through the centre of town. The authority closes one bridge due to structural problems, but the re-routed traffic over the remaining bridge increases the traffic volume to such a level that the second bridge collapses a few months later. Avoidance of one risk changed the fundamental nature of a related risk.

Finally, avoidance may not be possible, and this could occur for at least three reasons. The law may mandate responsibility for the risk. Indeed, this is such a fundamental issue in risk management that it is discussed later in the chapter. Second, the risk may be so fundamental to the purposes of the organisation that avoidance is not conceivable. An authority could avoid a number of risks by not having a social services or education department, but the provision of such services is a fundamental reason for the existence of such public bodies. Third, the risk may not be avoidable in any real and physical sense. The city of San Francisco, for example, might very much wish to avoid the risk of earthquake, but it cannot.

## Risk transfer and distribution

Previously, readers were introduced to the concept and application of the COCA organisation idea. The COCAs also support a second risk control tool – risk transfer and distribution.

The principal, if not only, means by which an organisation becomes exposed to risk is through the contracts, obligations, commitments and agreements into which it enters. In Chapter 3, this idea serves as the basis for the entire risk assessment framework, showing how a risk manager might begin to develop a more comprehensive understanding of the body's exposure to risk. That chapter's discussion also alludes to the fact that entering into these COCAs affords the best opportunity to 'manage' the risks that attach to the COCAs, and the following discussion elaborates on this notion.

The term 'risk transfer' is a little misleading and takes on at least two distinct forms in risk management. It is misleading because while the actual risk itself may be transferred from one party to another, more commonly it is only responsibility (financial or otherwise) for the risk that is subject to transfer. The term also is confusing because of practical usage. Risk transfer is most widely used – almost interchangeably – with 'insurance', and it is true that insurance is an important risk transfer (i.e., risk responsibility transfer) contract. But the term also applies in a number of other transfer mechanisms. However, while the following paragraphs focus on non-insurance transfers, readers should note that the distinction is arbitrary – contractual transfers of risk differ in degree rather than in kind.

The burden of risk is both economic and psychological (and, some would say, 'moral'). Therefore, the purpose of risk distribution is to transfer one or more of these burdens to another party. An organisation's ability to do so is influenced by a number of factors – parties willing to accept the risk, negotiating leverage, and so on (see Chapter 3) – so it must be stated that many risks might not be transferable or distributable. Discussion here focuses on circumstances where the possibility of transfer exists.

Previously, the chapter noted that most transfers entail a transfer of responsibility for risk rather than transfer of the risk itself, but certainly tangible risk transfers do occur. For example, a sale/leaseback arrangement for storage facilities could be characterised as a tangible transfer because the risk of, say, fire to the facilities transfers from seller to buyer. Contrast this with the purchase of fire insurance, where the original owner remains exposed directly to the risk of fire.

The sale/leaseback strategy does suggest the outright difficulty of absolute (i.e., both tangible and responsibility) risk transfers. If an authority sells its storage facilities to a private property management firm, but then leases back the facilities, the risk has not been transferred. The authority has simply exchanged one form of exposure for another. This is not necessarily a bad thing, but the illusion of absolute transfer can create dangerous misunderstandings. Equally, risk distribution (i.e., where more than two parties are involved) may actually contribute to the confusion regarding the ultimate responsibility for a risk.

The importance of appreciating the distinction between an absolute transfer of the risk, a transfer of responsibility and a transfer of the tangible exposure cannot be underestimated in the current local government climate. Increasing efforts to privatise public services, to partner with non-profit and private organisations, and to instil private behaviour on public and quasi-public institutions elevates the issues that underlie a motivation to transfer or distribute risk. Quite simply, when an authority contracts out refuse collection to a private provider, another party enters into the risk management equation. That private vendor may supply the workers, the refuse-hauling equipment, and the administrative apparatus necessary to perform the task, so in a sense the tangible risks of harm have been transferred. But the responsibility has not been transferred. The authority still possesses a responsibility for refuse collection in both a political and legal sense. If the private service provider declares bankruptcy, many outstanding liabilities and obligations will in all likelihood revert to the authority.

A risk manager, upon reading the previous paragraph, would correctly note that responsibility for a risk can also be transferred in such a situation by requiring vendors and suppliers to demonstrate financial ability to accept risk. For instance (and this is explained in Chapter 10), an authority can insist that a contracting service provider supplies certificates of insurance to assure that risks such as employment-related injuries and motor vehicle accidents are covered and unlikely to revert to the authority.

However, while tangible risk and the responsibility for risk can be transferred, two issues arise that become critical for the authority. One is the cost of monitoring and the other is the cost of a loss of direct control. First, the monitoring cost can be appreciated by realizing that a certificate of insurance states nothing more than that insurance was in force when the certificate was issued. It is possible for the service provider to discontinue insurance cover immediately after being awarded the contract. Ongoing assurance that financial responsibility will not revert to the authority is labour intensive, and when all such arrangements that a public body might enter into are considered it could occupy the time of one clerical worker. Second, even if financial responsibility can be transferred and insured, there is the related problem of general or moral responsibility. An authority can be held responsible in more than a financial sense. Inappropriate or even illegal actions by the service provider reflect badly on the authority, and can contribute to an erosion of political support. If, for instance, it is discovered that private refuse collection workers are using their occupations as a means of committing thefts as they complete their rounds, the burden would most directly fall on the provider and the employees, but certainly the authority would be affected.

This scenario shows the 'loss of control' issue that bedevils privatisation and partnering initiatives. A public body will retain a general responsibility for public services, no matter how sophisticated the risk transference. And, that transference typically means a loss of control over the day-to-day activities that influence or give rise to the risks. It may still be in the best interest to both government and citizens that a service is provided privately, but the loss of direct control is not costless. Just as monitoring costs must be factored into the decision to 'outsource', so must the costs associated with loss of control.

## Risk/uncertainty reduction

In Chapter 1 the nature of the relationship between risk and uncertainty is explained. Risk is, in a sense, a state of nature whereas uncertainty is more a state of mind; and yet, the two concepts are intertwined. This relationship is important to remember, because it serves as the basis for asserting the centrality of risk/uncertainty reduction as a risk control tool.

Uncertainty can be the result of many factors and, indeed, it may not be possible at any particular time to understand which factors are in play. A person may be genetically predisposed to having a certain outlook on life, and this may affect uncertainty levels. Upbringing, life experiences, culture and other factors can be influential. It would be difficult to explain how a risk manager might affect these influences on risk and uncertainty – although it is arguable that a risk manager has a responsibility to make an organisation's management team more self-aware of the influences of these factors on its decision-making.

The more obvious and tangible uncertainty reduction efforts can be directed at 'information management' – a term used here in a broad and general sense and not connoting its more specific information technology meaning.

The increase in knowledge of a particular risk often results in a reduction of uncertainty. If more is known about the causes of motor vehicle accidents, for example, it is likely that judgements and decisions regarding driving behaviour will be sounder. Notably here, the actual underlying risk is not changed, but the driver's understanding is changed for the better. The cloud of uncertainty is thinned, allowing the decision-maker to act with greater clarity.

This example can be extended broadly to the organisation exposed to risks. If an effort is made to understand systematically the environment in which the organisation exists, overall uncertainty can be reduced and better – and more consistent – decisions may be made. Thus, part of the risk manager's role is to ensure that the organisation can systematically gather and analyse information relevant to the organisation's life.

Information management comes with some caveats. First, information-gathering is not costless. Second, more information does not automatically reduce uncertainty, as that information may be contradictory, unclear, highly technical or difficult to analyse. Third, the information may be inaccurate, which may lead to incorrect conclusions. Fourth, additional information does not solve all the contributing factors underlying uncertainty. Previously, the notion of genetic and psychological influences was mentioned, and it is easy to imagine that the interplay of 'more information' with subtle psychological factors may produce unexpected results. For instance, some psychology of risk studies suggest that attitudes towards risk are influenced by the form in which information is obtained, when it is obtained (recently or long ago) and whether it resonates with private fears and apprehensions. Nevertheless, it probably is a safe proposition to state that more information usually is better than less information, at least up to a point.

## Loss prevention

Loss prevention involves all techniques and strategies that reduce or eliminate the likelihood of losses occurring. Readers should note here that outright elimination of losses – while the preferred outcome – is not commonly the expected outcome in risk management. Rather, loss prevention is seen as a concentrated attack on loss frequency with the intended outcome of reducing losses to some tolerable level.

The discussion of risk analysis in Chapter 3 suggests how the study of risk might give rise to the solutions necessary to manage the risk, and almost automatically such analysis will point most directly to loss prevention measures. For example, a thorough study of the causes of lower back injuries among road maintenance gangs may pinpoint improper lifting activities, physical fitness factors, time of day considerations and inadequate equipment as contributing factors. In turn, each of these factors can be controlled through a variety of interventions – from teaching proper lifting techniques, to lumbar support belts, to training and conditioning programmes, to changes in management techniques – resulting in a lowered frequency of injury.

Chapter 3 also introduces the risk chain concept, and it is helpful in isolating the points of intervention. Loss prevention can attempt either to alter or eliminate the hazard, the peril, or the exposure to a particular risk. So, for instance, the following loss prevention measures may be undertaken to address each link in the chain.

## Hazard-based prevention actions

- *Hazard*: untidy, improperly maintained equipment storage facility. *Action*: cleaning and maintenance protocols.
- *Hazard*: flooding. *Action*: water resource management.
- *Hazard*: overweight local government employees. *Action*: counselling and exercise opportunities.
- *Hazard*: Wastewater management. *Action*: properly maintained treatment facilities.
- *Hazard*: icy and/or deteriorating roadways. *Action*: snow removal, salting, regular maintenance and repair schedules.

## Peril-based prevention actions

- *Peril*: fire. *Action*: fire-resistant construction materials.
- *Peril*: subsidence. *Action*: strengthened foundations.
- *Peril*: hot pursuit practices. *Action*: hot pursuit policy and training.
- *Peril*: poorly lit parking facility. *Action*: lighting, escort and security services.
- *Peril*: slippery town hall steps. *Action*: installation of non-skid surfaces.

## Exposure-based prevention actions

- *Exposure*: road maintenance gangs. *Action*: proper training, adequate equipment.
- *Exposure*: vehicle fleet. *Action*: regular maintenance and inspection schedule.

- *Exposure*: computers. *Action*: year 2000 evaluation and resolution.
- *Exposure*: accounts receivable records. *Action*: backup records with off-site storage.
- *Exposure*: honesty (fidelity) of employees. *Action*: financial accounting, auditing and management procedures.

In a sense, the allocation of certain loss prevention measures to particular elements of the risk chain is arbitrary – often it is difficult to understand whether a particular measure addresses the hazard or the peril. However, such fuzziness is of little concern to the practising risk manager, and the previous discussion is intended mainly as an illustration of concepts, not a blueprint for action.

One final word is necessary regarding loss prevention. While loss prevention largely focuses attention on measures that prevent bad things from happening, it should not be forgotten that reducing loss frequency improves the prospects of good things happening (in risk situations where upside risk exists). For example, if an authority were able to cut employers' liability losses by 40 per cent, funds normally used to finance these claims would be available for more productive investment. Loss prevention often can be seen as 'gain enhancement', which may be an important element in persuading elected members to allocate resources to prevention measures.

## Loss reduction

Bad things will happen to a local authority, even when risk management is practised. Loss reduction includes those measures taken to limit the impact – direct and indirect – of losses once they have occurred.

Chapter 3 cites an important observation about losses – that the indirect and consequential impact of a loss can outstrip the obvious and direct impact. If interventions can take place after a loss to limit or prevent indirect and consequential losses from arising, such losses – even very large ones – become much more manageable. Rapid response measures, fire suppressant systems, seat belts, cardiopulmonary resuscitation training, lifeguards at swimming pools and catastrophe management plans all represent techniques and tools that can contain loss costs. Even when an event has progressed to court, as, perhaps, in a police liability case, litigation management strategies can be used effectively to intervene and limit losses. Occasionally, subrogation opportunities arise in court settings where an authority may seek to recover damages it has paid to a plaintiff by seeking redress from some other responsible party.

Risk managers extend loss reduction to the level of salvage strategy. Since losses rarely are total in actuality, the ultimate cost of loss can be offset by efforts to salvage damaged property.

One aspect of loss reduction has become so important that it demands separate attention – contingency or catastrophe planning and management. Recent history has done much to enable catastrophe management to be seen as a distinct area of management, which certainly is good in that it represents an important aspect in overall management planning. However, readers must recognise that catastrophe planning really only becomes effective if it is done in an organisation that has an established commitment to risk management. There are philosophical and practical reasons why this is true. But for purposes of this book it is sufficient to argue that the failure of most catastrophe-planning efforts is due to the absence of a 'champion' within the organisation who can advocate and advance catastrophe-planning efforts – and of course, oversee the execution of such a plan. Naturally, a strong case can be made that a risk manager is the appropriate individual to perform this role.

With the preceding qualifier in mind, this section turns briefly to the subject of catastrophe planning.

## Catastrophe planning and management

This chapter's 'Read More About It' section develops the structure of both a catastrophe-planning process and the resulting plan itself. Thus, the discussion here is limited.

A catastrophe (or contingency) plan is a document that establishes an organisation-wide, integrated, and co-ordinated effort to manage emergency or large loss events. What constitutes a catastrophe is determined by the organisation; it most certainly is not an absolute concept. In any event, the planning process closely follows strategic planning models as it requires top management/elected member direction and support, but will also require development efforts at all levels of the organisation.

In brief, a catastrophe plan requires an organisation to develop a disaster scenario and then to create a co-ordinated series of actions, plans, responses and measures to control the effects of that disaster. In its broadest sense, it is a risk reduction initiative in that it assumes the disaster has already occurred and that the principal objective is containment. However, that simplification is misleading because individual measures taken to control and minimise the loss may exhibit a wide range of characteristics. In other words, a successful catastrophe management plan will include avoidance, prevention, transfer, reduction, and neutralisation elements.

Finally, as was the case with loss prevention, readers should consider the upside risk aspects of loss reduction. It could be argued that measures taken to specifically enlarge positive outcomes might be related in some way to loss reduction measures. For instance, capitalising on an opportunity to purchase land for a park at a windfall price might be characterised as the mirror image of a situation where a loss is limited through measures to reduce costs of loss. Risk management also entails (or can entail) efforts to maximise the positive possibilities that risk presents.

## Risk neutralisation

The final risk control tool considered here is risk neutralisation. Neutralisation refers to those measures taken to reduce the effects of risk to zero (or near zero) through arrangements to offset one risk with another. While in most technical senses, risk neutralisation practices (often called 'hedging') fall under the heading of risk-financing, the idea is broad enough to include in a discussion of risk control practices.

Neutralisation differs from avoidance in that the risk still exists and is directly borne by the organisation. Neutralisation differs from prevention in that no efforts necessarily are made to influence the frequency of loss; nor is neutralisation like loss reduction because no direct actions are taken to affect the magnitude of loss (or gain).

Hedging arrangements (see Chapter 5) are the obvious illustrations of neutralising efforts, but numerous examples of techniques exist where taking the 'opposite' position on a risk does not fit traditional financial hedging practices. Resource pooling often can be construed as a type of hedge position – mutual aid agreements being good illustrations. Neighbouring organisations sometimes enter into commitments with one another to neutralise particular risks. An agreement to share certain resources does not eliminate the risk of a resource-taxing loss, nor is the risk transferred. But, the co-operating organisations have packaged together their exposure to predetermined eventualities in such a way that no member will have insufficient resources if and when they are needed.

Finally, another – somewhat lesser – risk control tool should be mentioned here as it is related conceptually to neutralisation and pooling. 'Separation' is a strategy whereby the resources of one entity are physically separated to minimise the risk of total destruction of assets. Storing equipment in multiple locations illustrates this, and occasionally authorities will strike agreements whereby they separate assets among participating authorities. This does not 'neutralise' the entire risk, but it does tend to reduce or eliminate the chance of catastrophic loss.

An important modern variant on separation is 'duplication'. Backing up computer records and storing them off-site provides an important type of separation that virtually eliminates or neutralises the chance of total loss.

## Mandated risk control

Although management of risk, and particularly the controlling of risk, is a practice that serves the interests of a public body, there are many circumstances in which risk control is not merely a good idea – it is the law. This phenomenon, called mandated risk control, offers some ironies for readers interested in public sector risk management. Mandates almost invariably arise from regulatory or administrative sources (and less often, from the courts), which means that public bodies are being required by other public sector bodies to practise risk management. Or to add even more confusion to the observation, as a matter of social risk management policy, one level of government is creating an organisation risk management requirement for other levels of government.

The intergovernmental aspect of risk control (i.e., a government department requiring a local authority to practise risk control) is a largely unexplored subject in risk management. It is, however, one worthy of considerable study. For instance, in some respects the central and local government systems might be well suited to a structured risk management strategy whereby risks and responsibility for risks are allocated to levels of government best positioned to manage, control and finance them. To an extent, this happens – by design or accident – but, equally, problems are apparent in many areas of public policy where programmes are not integrated and rational risk allocation decisions are not made.

For practising risk managers, compliance with mandated risk control is a challenge. Depending on the range of the risk manager's responsibilities, the monitoring of present and new requirements can consume a great amount of time and effort. Central government legislation may generate risk control requirements across a wide spectrum of a public body's operations. Court decisions, particularly those emanating from the Courts of Appeal or House of Lords, can give rise to new risk control considerations or can overturn previously accepted views of risks and exposures. Another source of mandated risk control requirements has opened up following the UK's membership of the European Community in 1973 and the push towards the harmonisation of community-wide legislation, particularly, but not exclusively, in relation to employment risk. And, importantly, intergovernmental transfers (such as grants) often arrive with requirements attached – many of which are risk control in nature.

## APPLICATIONS

### Playground safety

Many of the core concepts of risk control can be illustrated through the example of playgrounds in public parks or schools.

Playgrounds represent a convergence of risks in a single physical space: physical assets can be damaged or destroyed, employees and visitors can be hurt, even financial assets (e.g., capital budgeting projects) can be jeopardised. Further, playgrounds and parks have a symbolic community value, which suggests that elements of subjective risk (i.e., the perception of safety) play an important role in the overall exposure the local authority faces.

In order to show briefly how risk control works, this section provides an overview of the nature of the basic risks and the risk control applications that address these risks.

### *A comment on playground injuries*

Statistics collated through the Leisure Activities Surveillance System and published by the Department of Trade and Industry suggest that in 1997 some 31 000 accidents occurred in the UK in public playgrounds resulting in the need for accident and emergency treatment. Of the accidents reported 31.2 per cent involved climbing frames, 23.5 per cent involved slides and 21.8 per cent involved swings.

The Health and Safety Executive's interest in playground accidents has heightened since the successful prosecution of Mendip District Council in 1998. A girl was playing on a set of swings in a playground situated in a housing estate. Her necklace caught in the chain, the chain broke and the girl struck her head on an area of ground where impact-absorbing tiles were missing. She subsequently died from her injuries. Mendip were successfully prosecuted on two counts:

- failure to maintain the impact-absorbing surface under the swing involved in the accident
- general failure to maintain impact absorbing surfaces in a number of their playgrounds

and were fined £50 000.

## Mandated risk control requirements

Mandated risk control requirements surrounding the operation of playgrounds include the requirement under Section 3 of the Health and Safety at Work Act 1974 to ensure so far as is reasonably practicable the safety of non-employees using the equipment and facilities. Moreover, the Management of Health and Safety at Work Regulations 1992 require all activities to be risk assessed and for suitable controls to be implemented.

The European Standard on Play Equipment (BSEN 1176), implemented fully in January 1999, requires playground operators to:

- set up an appropriate system for the safety management of playgrounds
- assess at least annually the effectiveness of all the safety measures used and to alter them if it is found necessary on the basis of experience or altered circumstances
- maintain records of all actions taken in respect to safety management.

## Risk control solutions

The risk control solutions should require the introduction of more forgiving surface materials under playground equipment, perhaps replacing asphalt with shredded bark, mulch, or other loose materials, such as sand. Other measures might also be necessary or effective, such as the layout and design of the equipment, the relationship of the equipment to other activity areas, training of playground supervisors and implementing maintenance protocols.

---

# TOOLS YOU CAN USE

## Human Rights Act 1998

The Human Rights Act 1998, implemented in the UK in October 2000, gives legislative endorsement to the following Convention Rights:

- right to life
- prohibition of torture
- prohibition of slavery and forced labour
- right to liberty and security
- right to a fair trial

- no punishment without law
- right to respect for private and family life
- freedom of thought, conscience and religion
- freedom of expression
- freedom of assembly and association
- right to marry
- prohibition of discrimination.

Of particular relevance and concern to public bodies is Section 6 of the Act which makes it unlawful for a public authority to act in a way that is incompatible with a Convention Right. There are certain exceptions, notably in circumstances where the public authority could not have acted differently by virtue of primary legislation or where the powers granted to a public authority by primary legislation are not compatible with Convention Rights. For public bodies such as police authorities, whose powers granted by primary legislation are primarily discretionary rather than duties, the implication is that they need to act in a way that is compatible with Convention Rights.

The range of potential victims of breaches of Convention Rights is wide. A complainant need not show that their rights have been violated; it is sufficient to show that they run the risk of being directly affected by the action being complained of. Moreover, it may be sufficient to demonstrate that the complainant is an indirect victim of the action being complained of, for example, a close relative of the person affected. Governmental organisations themselves cannot be victims but corporations might be, although not their shareholders.

A victim has one year to make a claim and the time period commences from the date on which the action being complained of occurred. This limitation period may be varied at the court's discretion in certain circumstances.

Where a public body has been found guilty of acting in contravention of the Human Rights Act 1998, the court or tribunal has the authority to grant such relief or remedy within its powers as it deems to be just and appropriate. So a court which has the power to award damages may award damages but, before doing so, it must satisfy itself that the award is necessary to award just satisfaction.

It is too early to say what the impact of the Human Rights Act will be on public bodies. Given the increasing litigiousness of society and the breadth of scope of the Act, it is reasonable to suppose that there will be an increase in claims against public bodies. This, however, could be tempered with the reflection that the period for making a claim is relatively short (particularly in comparison with limitation periods for property damage claims (three years) and personal injury claims (six years)) and that the level of damages likely to be awarded, if any, are uncertain.

What is clear, however, is that the implications of the Human Rights Act impinge very heavily on the risk assessment and risk control exercises of a public body. The Human Rights Act dimension must be considered in the assessment process. The control mechanisms need to ensure, as much as is possible, compliance with the Act and documentary evidence needs to be maintained of such compliance.

---

## READ MORE ABOUT IT

## Contingency/crisis management plans

The Risk and Insurance Management Society, Inc. (RIMS, the world's largest professional association of risk managers), offers an excellent half-week seminar on crisis management planning. The following paragraphs draw from key highlights of that seminar as well as other contingency planning materials.

### *The purpose of a crisis management plan?*

By definition, crises occur rarely, if at all, so experts in crisis management argue that managers need to recognise that the crisis will impose unusual and hard to anticipate conditions on a local government. Decisions take on a life or death dimension, pressure is enormous, public scrutiny is heightened, uncertainty is high and the 'playing field' is fluid and changeable. Further, a local government's structure and operations are not naturally configured to manage a crisis, which means that completely different resources and processes may be necessary. And changing in and out of crisis mode is not easy.

A crisis management plan should be detailed enough to guide the local authority. It should 'do some of the thinking' for the organisations so that managers can focus on other issues when an actual crisis arises. The plan should be flexible enough to allow for adjustments as events unfold, and it should be comprehensive enough to provide substance to the wide range of activities that will constitute a crisis management plan.

Additionally, a plan should specifically account for at least the following:

- measures to facilitate the quick commitment of resources to the crisis
- a detailing of duties, responsibilities, and lines of authority

- unequivocal upper management support
- creation of lines and means of communication
- audit and testing mechanisms
- involvement of the entire organisation
- interfaces with other organisations
- media management.

## The crisis management team

Most experts advise the creation of a cross-functional, multilevel crisis management team (CMT) to supervise the development of the plan as well as actual implementation of the plan should a crisis arise. Although circumstances may occasionally dictate otherwise, most teams will have an emergency director who is responsible for management of the team and its work on the development of a plan as well as the management of the team in the event of a crisis. The following discussion is based on the emergency director model.

## Setting the terms of a crisis

Oddly enough, one of the more difficult matters in crisis management is defining 'crisis'. Occasionally, the term will be statutorily determined, as is the case with environmental crises. In most instances, however, an early challenge for the CMT will be to specify the kind of events that will trigger an emergency response and the scope and scale of such events that will trigger the declaration of a crisis.

Not surprisingly, most communities might be exposed to numerous environmental or human-made conditions that could qualify as a crisis: terrorism, flooding, fire, explosion, toxic chemicals, excessive snow, and so on. Thus the process of defining a crisis may require either that the definition is keyed to the scale of exposure ('when events put such and such a level of community resources at risk, we have a crisis') or that an overall crisis plan may need to be modularised to recognise that different types of events may require unique measures (e.g., use of the town hall as a command post may be possible in a terrorism situation but not in a flood).

## The makeup of the crisis management team

The team should be organisation-wide in its makeup, but the authority should consider whether outsiders should also be involved. There might be a tendency to think that a local authority should close ranks in an emergency and keep crisis management in-house, an instinctive response perhaps motivated by the fact that the government is likely to be held responsible for emergency response and therefore needs to impose its control.

While there is an element of truth to the control concern, crisis management probably needs to include outside involvement. For example, a large chemical plant that may be the potential source of an environmental disaster probably should have involvement in the community's planning and response efforts. Likewise, emergency services may have important roles to play, as could the media, other communities, non-profit organisations, hospitals and others. Logic probably dictates outside participation on crisis planning, and the instinct to circle the wagons should be considered with care.

## The emergency response policy statement

The CMT should develop a policy statement that declares both the defining characteristics of a crisis, the makeup of the CMT and the overall governing philosophy of the initiative. This statement should be widely communicated.

## The crisis management plan

In a brief introduction like this, it probably is not possible to present a crisis management plan in too much detail since all plans will be unique. In general terms, such plans likely will include at least the following elements:

- the creation of an emergency operations centre
- the creation of a media operations centre
- the establishment of core policy and procedure plans.

The emergency operations centre concept is based upon a command-post model and is central to the actual management of a crisis. Staff at the centre should include the emergency director, the risk manage-ment co-ordinator, the media operations centre liaison, the human resources co-ordinator, the security co-ordinator, the information services co-ordinator and the logistics co-ordinator.

The media operations centre should be physically separate from the emergency operations centre for obvious reasons. Staff likely to be involved would include a media operations centre director, a spokesperson, an emergency operations centre liaison, a statement writer, a media liaison, an audio/visual co-ordinator and others as necessary.

The procedures and protocols plans will vary widely, but among the more commonly seen are things like:

- emergency phone and communications lists and protocols
- facility setup plans and procedures
- guidelines for media statements and briefings
- data hot site activation and operation plans and procedures
- resource lists and protocols
- facilities and equipment maintenance and inventories
- training, drill and exercise protocols and plans.

Readers who would like more information on crisis management planning can find numerous resources to support the development of such a plan. For individuals whose thinking is still at the conceptual stage, Laurence Barton's *Crisis in Organizations: Managing and Communicating in the Heat of Chaos* (South-Western, Cincinnati, 1993) is an excellent starting point for developing a more sophisticated understanding of the crisis management process.

# Asset exposures
# to risk

## EXECUTIVE SUMMARY

Chapter 3 first identified the typical public body's exposures to risk: physical assets, financial assets, human assets, legal liabilities and moral responsibilities. The first three asset exposures to risk are important to understand and manage as they represent an organisation's productive resources.

Physical assets include the obvious things like buildings, computers, motor vehicles and leisure complexes. However, this category also includes indirect and consequential risks too, things like disruptions in revenue flows, extra expenses related to rebuilding after a loss and reductions in the productive values of assets.

Financial assets refer to cash, bonds, securities, notes and other financial instruments that a local authority might possess. Importantly, though the physical safeguarding of these assets may be of some concern, the main focus of risk management in this area is the defence of the economic value of these assets.

Human assets are the people who make up the organisation. They are powerful contributors to the work the public body undertakes, but they also are exposed to important risks that can bring harm not only to them and their families but to the local authority as well.

## PRINCIPLES AND CONCEPTS

Chapters 3 and 4 discuss the subjects of risk assessment and control. Various methods of identifying, analysing, measuring and treating risks are explained – but the nature and character of the risk exposures themselves are not. A more thorough discussion of the risk exposure begins in this chapter and extends through Chapter 6.

The discussion of assessment in Chapter 3 introduces the idea of exposure to risk, and notes that exposure is a key ingredient in the concept of ORM. Unless there is exposure, an organisation risk manager mainly is unconcerned about risks and uncertainties.

Understanding the nature of exposure is important. In a broad sense, an entire public body is an exposure, but this notion provides little technical insight into the nature of particular exposures to risk. A much more meaningful approach is suggested in Chapter 3, and this approach relies on a categorisation of exposures into asset and liability groupings. The five categories are:

1   Asset exposures:
    (a)   physical asset exposures
    (b)   financial asset exposures
    (c)   human asset exposures
2   Liability exposures:
    (a)   legal liability exposures
    (b)   moral liability exposures.

This chapter introduces asset exposures, while Chapter 6 deals with liability exposures. Readers should note that some imprecision will arise in the use of these classification systems. For instance, is workplace safety a human asset issue or a legal liability issue? The practical answer, of course, is that it is both; but it only really matters that an assessment methodology identifies workplace safety as a risk management issue. The fact that it would arise both in the context of human asset exposure analysis and in legal liability exposure analysis only reinforces the notion that workplace safety is an important issue.

The intent of Chapters 5 and 6 is to provide a broad frame of reference with respect to organisational exposures to risk and to have readers develop an appreciation for two key aspects of risk exposure: the fundamental nature of each exposure to risk, and the matter of exposure valuation.

## Physical asset exposures

Traditional risk management has concerned itself with the protection of physical assets, particularly with regard to risks leading to direct physical harm of those assets. Not surprisingly, traditional risk management practices in this area have been shaped by the notion of 'insurable risks'. Nowhere else in all of risk management is insurance more influential in forming the concepts, terminology and parameters of discussion than in the area of physical asset management.

Terms like 'direct, indirect and time element losses' are important to an understanding of physical asset exposures, as are the valuation methods that have arisen from insurance practice. However, the insurance-based frame of analysis does have limitations, especially regarding the nature and character of speculative risks. There is not a widely accepted language in the risk management field to discuss physical assets in the context of their contribution to productivity or profitability. This is not to say that such language does not exist else-where – it does – but it is to say that concerns about upside potential have not been part of the traditional risk management world.

Of course, consistent with all other changes occurring in the public sector, the barriers that exist between pure and speculative risk management also are falling. For instance, when a local authority considers its participation in the development of a new sports facility, it is limiting to look at the facility only with respect to its ability to attract hazard-driven risks (e.g., fires, vandalism, windstorm, subsidence). Risk-factor driven risks also attach to the facility, and the distinctions seemingly fail to warrant separate examination. For example, size, location and capacity – which have direct profitability impacts – cannot be separated from physical safety and premises security considerations. They all are part of a single decision.

Because risk managers are concerned about all risks, the discussion that follows seeks to reorient traditional language in a way that opens full consideration of the wide range of effects of risk on physical assets.

## How are physical asset exposures classified?

The wide range of physical assets a public body can possess or have responsibility for can be categorised at least four ways:

- by physical asset type
- by cause-of-loss (gain) type
- by loss (gain) type
- by interest.

### By physical asset type

The simplest form of categorisation is by property classification type. Physical assets are classified broadly as either real assets or personal assets. Real property refers to land, fixed structures on that land, and – more or less – attached appurtenances of those structures. Personal property basically is everything else.

A slightly different wording would characterise property as fixed or movable, and this slight change in the language more plainly reveals a core risk management concern. That is, although exposure to risk is changeable, a fixed asset's exposure to risk is more constant and knowable than that of an asset whose physical location changes. Mobility introduces a new dimension to the nature and character of risk.

The fixed and movable property concepts do belie a strong insurance influence. Historically, underwriters were uncomfortable with assets that moved from one place to another because it was more difficult to ascertain the likelihood of harm. Because insuring movable property required specialised knowledge, the development of the insurance industry followed two parallel tracks: one dealing with fixed property (e.g., fire insurance) and one dealing with movable property (e.g., marine insurance). Although the separation between the two tracks is nearly imperceptible to the outsider today, the problematic distinctions are still manifested in policy language, exclusions, pricing and, even, claims management procedures.

## By cause-of-loss (gain) type

This classification is based on the nature of the peril or opportunity that affects or may affect a physical asset.

There are a number of ways that perils might be broadly classified. Consistent with the language Chapter 3 (Risk assessment) introduces, we might describe peril categories as 'natural-hazard based' or 'behavioural-hazard based'. Perils arising from natural hazards are generally obvious to most readers – fires, subsidence, freezing, gales and storms. Behavioural-hazard based perils have intuitively obvious examples (vandalism, riots, assassination, theft), but also include a range of broad social, political and economic phenomena that arise from collective behavioural influences. Changes in social preferences for, say, government services certainly is the result of individual changes in preference, but it is the accumulation of changes in behaviour and preference that create the risk for a local authority. Likewise, investment behaviour of an individual may be linked to the overall behaviour of the investment marketplace, but the aggregated behaviour is distinct from individual behaviour. Thus, behaviour-hazard based perils include phenomena that are not directly traceable to a single individual's behaviour, but are nevertheless the result of it.

The same argument can be made about 'risk-factor based opportunities'. An authority located on a beautiful lake with recreational potential may find that natural risk factor opportunities can be exploited to improve the economic well-being of the community. Behavioural risk-factor based opportunities might be seen in the voting preferences of the electorate.

## By type of loss (or gain)

Physical assets might be typed by the nature of the impact of peril/opportunity on the asset. These impacts would be direct, indirect and consequential. Direct impacts would be an actual physical result – a police car is damaged in an accident, heavy snowfall might improve the skiing season for a publicly owned recreational facility in the Highlands of Scotland. Indirect impacts are those that influence the 'value' of an asset without directly or physically affecting that asset, for example, the destruction of one part of a building might lead to the tearing down of the undamaged portion, or the re-routing of traffic due to highway construction might have a favourable impact on a publicly-owned asset that was previously off the beaten track. Consequential impacts (often called net income or time element impacts) refer to effects that occur as a result of a direct or indirect impact – a fire to the town hall means that the authority has to rent a temporary facility while the new town hall is built or heavy snowfall may generate higher revenues for a publicly owned skiing facility over an extended period of time.

## By interest

It certainly is in keeping with the COCA view of organisations to observe that the best perspective of physical assets is not obtained by considering their tangible characteristics alone, but by understanding the enforceable interests that attach to physical assets. This is especially important when considering the matter of exposure because in a practical sense, a public body's exposure to risk is dictated by the enforceability of its interests. Put plainly, the loss of a vehicle is defined as much by whether an authority owned it or was borrowing it, as by the physical nature of that asset or the manner in which it was lost.

Ownership interest obviously is a key interest in property, and the law clearly delineates the rights and obligations owners have with respect to physical property. However, lenders, tenants, vendors, lessors, contractors, franchise holders and licensees also may have enforceable interests in some property. The important insight here is that the contract-, obligation-, commitment- or agreement-based nature of risk can inform one's thinking about physical asset exposures to risk and (as Chapter 3 mentions) can provide the means to managing exposure to physical asset-related risks.

## How are physical asset exposures valued?

At first, it might be assumed that the valuation of physical assets is straightforward. The value of a particular asset is a function of its purchase price – or so it might seem.

However, readers should realize that the purchase price of an asset has very little to do with its value to the organisation. The value of replacing the asset is more likely to reflect the economic impact of a loss or gain on a local authority. Naturally, replacement value is the coin of the realm for insurance companies, and this is no accident. The insurance indemnification promise is to restore loss, so the valuation challenge is to determine the cost of restoring, replacing or rebuilding a physical asset. To put it in a slightly different context, the generally accepted method for valuing physical assets is to set a value on the asset at the moment after it has been damaged, destroyed or lost. There are several approaches to determining a value for replacement – but the idea of replacement cost is important to introduce here.

A significant extension of the valuation question must be considered. The valuation challenge really has to be addressed on two levels. The basic level, as discussed above, is the replacement value – the 'intrinsic' value of the asset. The cost of replacing a police car is, say, £30 000. The secondary valuation level is the economic value – or 'contributory' value of an asset.

The contributory value of an asset is the value it adds to the organization. For example, the intrinsic value of the police car is £30 000, whereas the contributory value would be judged by the value that car adds to the policing performance of the police force (naturally, this valuation has a quantitative and qualitative component). Assets that generate a revenue stream would perhaps be a slightly more obvious illustration of this point. For instance, council housing can be measured based on its cost of replacement but, equally, that facility could be measured by the present value of rental income streams. Which is the right value?

Both are right, but both serve different purposes. The contributory value, although represented as a secondary value above, probably is the first consideration in determining an asset's value. If the asset does not have a contributory value to the organisation, the determination of intrinsic value is moot. For example, an authority's vehicle repair shop may contain old or damaged vehicle parts that would or could not be used in any way. Do those assets contribute to the value of the authority and the services it provides? No, and because that is the case, the intrinsic value of those assets is immaterial, unless, of course, salvage opportunities exist.

## Financial asset exposures

In a very general sense, financial assets are a subset of physical assets, inasmuch as a share certificate or bank notes are exposed to the same perils as are motor vehicles, computers and buildings. Indeed, conventional insurance can be purchased to protect against 'physical losses' (fires, thefts) of financial assets. However, financial assets are further exposed to a set of risks that fall beyond traditional insurance and risk management boundaries – those risks being characterised as 'financial risks' (price, credit, interest rate, currency, counterparty, and so on).

With only a little reflection it is easy to realize that the management of financial risks could be extremely important to an organisation. After all, a diminution in value to some asset as a result of a physical peril such as fire is not any more (or less) real than a diminution in value due to turns in the economy. Indeed, further reflection might yield the observation that financial risks and traditionally insurable risks probably share common features (more on this below), and that from a public body's perspective the principal risk management concern is *that* an asset might be diminished in value and not so much *how* that diminution would occur. Risk managers want to undertake measures to assure that value is retained within an organisation, regardless of the potential cause of loss.

The observation that the management of financial risks is important and shares some common features with insurable risks is interesting, but until recently it was an observation of abstract rather than real concern. This is because financial tools were not widely available to manage many of these financial risks. Of course, the risks themselves existed for hundreds of years and methods existed within the banking and investment community to limit risk. But, it has been the advancing sophistication of derivative contracts (forwards, futures, options and their various permutations) that has allowed greater access to the tools of financial risk management and the formation of markets for pooling and distributing financial risks. This has led, in turn, to the steady erosion of boundaries between capital markets and the insurance industry. The result has been the emergence of 'alternative risk financing', a phenomenon that is meant to suggest tools and products that combine financial instruments with insurance (or insurance-like) contracts.

While in a way 'assets are assets', financial assets possess an important feature distinguishing them from physical assets – their value is derived from some other asset (and that other asset may or may not be possessed by the holder of the financial asset). Certainly this is obvious if we think about, for example, a fuel oil futures contract. The contract offers the right to buy or sell oil at some future date. The price of that contract is based upon the price of an 'underlying' asset, the fuel oil itself. A less obvious example is currency, which at one time had its value based upon the price of gold. In a sense, currency's value today is still derivative, in that it is based upon the full faith and credit of the national government.

The notion of financial assets as 'derivative' creates a further important distinction when comparing physical and financial assets. In a traditional insurable risk, the notion of insurable interest is critical. It means that the policyholder has a legal interest in the exposed asset (if a loss occurs, the insured suffers an economic loss). Insurable interest is important in controlling moral hazard. Policyholders are somewhat less likely to cause losses intentionally to assets where they possess an insurable interest. In the case of financial assets, the moral hazard question is not quite as clearly addressed. Certainly, an investor/owner in a company has little interest in that company suffering from negative performance. However, two things can happen that introduce potential moral hazard: if investors hold a well-diversified portfolio of investments, they may be much less concerned about the fortunes of any one particular share and, in some instances, certain financial instruments enable an investor to take an 'opposite position' on a particular asset (indeed, this is the particular genius behind most derivative products). In extreme instances, investors even may be hoping for a loss to occur.

Another interesting distinction between physical and financial assets is that the latter are both sources of risk and – possibly – risk management tools. So, the purchase of an options contract presents financial risks to the buyer, but (in conjunction with other assets) also might be an effective risk management tool.

We can conclude here that physical asset risks and financial asset risks have important distinctions, but also have common features that might be amenable to risk management treatment. However, with the bewildering array of financial instruments available, is it possible to generalise about the nature of the exposure?

Yes. Exposure to financial risk arises from either holding financial assets or issuing them. The holding of financial assets is the result of investment policy, while the issuing (bonds, for instance) is more commonly the result of capital budgeting policy. This is an important insight in the context of the COCA concept as it suggests risks arising from arrangements entered into to serve the broader purposes of the public body.

The 'Physical assets' and 'Human assets' sections of this chapter present discussions on asset valuation – but, unfortunately, a similar discussion here will take the book far afield from its central purposes. Indeed, pricing financial assets is a theory-driven business that would require a high degree of technical knowledge among readers before even beginning such a discussion. Let it suffice here, then, to say:

1   Financial assets have a value determined at issuance that
2   may nevertheless vary widely during the asset's life due to the market's assessment of its value at any given point in time and that
3   will be influenced by a range of outside factors such as the state of the economy and governmental monetary policy, which produce risks that
4   may be managed within the market through the use of sound investment management or risk management strategies.

To a degree, the courts in recent years have rather constrained the ability of local authorities in the UK to avail themselves of some of the more sophisticated financial instruments commonly available in the marketplace. In a landmark case in 1991 the use of interest rate swaps by the London Borough of Hammersmith and Fulham was ruled to be unlawful and financial institutions were unable to recover any losses accumulated by the council (see 'Read More About It' section). On the other hand, the collapse of BCCI in 1991 resulted in substantial losses being incurred by a number of local authorities. This in turn reduced the appetite of public bodies for high-yield returns, engendering a more conservative investment strategy, but also brought into sharp focus the risks and exposures associated with the holding of financial assets and emanating from investment strategies.

# Human asset exposures

Humans – whether stakeholders, managers or employees – constitute the third asset exposure area. Risk produces outcomes that can either diminish or enhance this particular asset in ways that are not dissimilar to physical and financial asset exposures. However, the particulars of this exposure are unique and deserve special attention.

Several perspectives are possible in thinking about human asset exposures. The approach employed in this book is to characterise the key human asset risks as:

- premature death
- disability and poor health
- old age and retirement
- unemployment
- poverty
- productivity.

Poverty and productivity are unique among these risks in that they may be the result of the other five risks, but also may be viewed as risks in their own right. A brief discussion of each human asset risk follows.

## *Premature death*

Most of us believe that our own death will always be premature, but the concept of premature death has a widely accepted interpretation. It is a death 'where outstanding obligations remain'. Some experts further refine this definition and focus on outstanding economic obligations (debts, dependent children and spouse, other financial commitments), but this book adopts a broader view to recognise that these obligations may be emotional or psychological, or in other ways 'non-economic'. Certainly, the death of a popular figure within an organisation can affect the morale of surviving members, even when economic impacts are either absent or small.

## *Disability and poor health*

The rise in importance of the risks of disability and poor health is partly due, perhaps surprisingly, to society's improved ability to prevent premature death. In the past, accidents resulting in injury to individuals often resulted in the death of those individuals, mainly due to the unsophisticated nature of medical care. Advancements in public health and sanitation indirectly and directly influenced mortality as well. Illnesses and injuries were caused by poor public sanitation, and this squalor also contributed to heightened mortality rates.

In contrast to premature death, disability and poor health reveals a number of dimensions that contribute to the complexity in managing the risk. A person is either alive or dead, but disability and health exist along a spectrum. Further, there are parallel subjective and objective elements to health (or its absence). A person objectively could be in very poor health but feel that they are doing well. The converse equally can be true.

## Old age and retirement

Old age brings with it the heightened possibility of death, disability and poor heath, but also presents the economic challenge of retirement – or to put it more broadly, economic security. The nature of the challenge currently is confounded by the fact that people generally are living longer and preferring to retire earlier. Supporting retirees once was the exclusive responsibility of younger family members, but the mobility of modern society has limited the practical ability of families to meet this challenge, which in turn has given rise to various social insurance and security programmes that are intended to (mainly) supplement private saving and support efforts.

Current demographic trends conspire to create an enormous 'ageing challenge' for societies and organisations. The post-Second World War populations within developed nations all have variations of the 'baby boom', and so the major economic powers all must struggle with the challenge of managing an increasingly numerous and long-living elderly population. Uncertainty limits society's ability to fully comprehend the impact of this phenomenon since it has never really been seen before in the modern age.

## Unemployment

People may suffer unemployment or underemployment as the result of poor health and disability, but this may be due to broad economic and social factors as well as to individual attributes like ambition, education and ability.

Like disability and poor health, unemployment differs from premature death because it is a complex risk. Duration is an issue of importance in understanding unemployment, as is cause of loss, nature of the economic environment in which the unemployment is occurring, and contributing social and political factors.

From an organisation perspective, why would a risk manager choose to be concerned about the risk of unemployment to other employees? While the dismissal or laying off of employees reduces costs and can permit an organisation to manage its way through economic difficulties, it can have significant effects on organisation performance and effectiveness. Certainly, morale can suffer significantly and may engender a higher level of litigiousness among the departing employees than would otherwise be anticipated.

## Poverty

Poverty may be due to premature death, disability, poor health, old age and unemployment but, importantly, it also is the result of human capital factors. Lack of or level of education can contribute to poverty and the inability or unwillingness of individuals to invest in their own development can lead to inadequate resources.

One must plainly state that sloth and indolence are contributing factors – and indeed, social critics today seem to characterise poverty as being largely the result of laxity of morals, laziness, moral hazard and a failure to take responsibility for one's own life. While this criticism is partly fair, students of risk management also must recognise that random events, uncontrollable factors and misfortune often play a part. A challenge for risk managers is to sort through the poverty issue and understand or appreciate the complexity of causes behind poverty.

As a final note, it is worth remembering the previous discussion of unemployment. Organisations might reasonably not believe themselves concerned with poverty, since most of their employees will not be poor. However, this is wrong because many people in poverty are 'working poor', and inadequate resources are a day-to-day issue for many employees. Additionally, like unemployment, central government mandates interest in poverty inasmuch as taxes support numerous public assistance programmes.

## Productivity

Productivity might be broadly construed as the 'investment risk' associated with human assets. Training and personal/professional development are investments made in employees with the expectation that they will become more effective, efficient and useful.

In a sense, reducing the other human asset risks might dramatically influence productivity. This preceding statement reveals a traditional risk management orientation in that it suggests that human asset risk management is best practised in controlling bad things in the hope of indirectly enhancing good things. However, the ORM idea gives voice to the notion that risk management should include efforts that directly contribute to the likelihood of gains or even contribute to the magnitude of gains. Certainly, training and education are tools that might be properly construed as upside risk management techniques.

## Valuing human asset exposures

Development of a single method for valuing human life simply is not possible – at least not in any generally accepted sense. Clearly, life does have an economic value and most risk management measurements of the human asset exposure to risk incorporate fundamental economic considerations. For instance, a widely adopted valuation approach is to estimate the lost earnings of an injured or killed individual and to produce a present value by discounting future lost earnings.

Readers readily will recognise the flimsiness of the assertion that human life is fully measurable in economic terms. Unfortunately, most management books weakly make this point and then wave off the trickier discussion of what the non-economic value of human life might be. But not here!

Public bodies have legally enforceable duties and, of course, the possibility of civil or criminal penalties might be factored into the human life value equation. However, the real concern for risk managers is judging the moral values associated with human well-being. Western societies have universally embraced the idea of the sanctity of life and, although contrary behaviour abounds in day-to-day life, this general valuation assumption mainly is uncontested. Therefore, risk managers should be cognisant of the fact that:

- although total life value may not be quantified, that indeterminate value is nevertheless extremely high
- although the moral value is extremely high, it is non-comparable in the sense that people will reasonably disagree with the value at the margin
- although the moral value is high and non-comparable, efforts to come to terms with these characteristics are important.

An absolutely key point in understanding moral valuation is the recognition that individuals have a fundamental right to contribute to moral valuation of their own life. As a practical matter, this means that individuals should have a role in the evaluation of and subsequent management of risks to which they are exposed. Certainly, individuals should be made aware of risks to which they are exposed and, ideally, should have some say in decisions that affect those risks.

# Concluding comments on asset exposures

Physical, financial and human assets represent a rich diversity of exposures to risk and the challenge of managing them in an integrated fashion is not an easy one. However, the preceding discussion has produced a few central themes that must be carried forward. First, these assets all are 'speculative' in Chapter 1's sense of the word. These assets are susceptible to loss or diminution, but also may prove to be productive. The goal in managing asset exposures would seem to require a focus on maximising the productivity of assets through a concerted effort to minimise possibilities of loss and to enhance the likelihood of gain. This proposition, while seemingly simple, shows that the purpose of risk management is not simply (or only) to prevent losses from occurring, but rather to find a philosophical balance between reasonably controlling the downside of risk while not unnecessarily muting the chance of gain. This point is more fully discussed in Chapters 10 and 11.

Second, 'interest' in assets matters. Whether it is an enforceable ownership interest in some building, a legally assertable right that is protected by the Financial Services Agency or the interests we necessarily have in our own persons, an appreciation of risk and the management of risk needs to incorporate recognition of the relevant interests in play.

Third, morality matters. While certainly true with respect to human assets, morality also matters with the physical and financial assets of the government. These assets are public resources held in trust and public bodies have a moral as well as a legal obligation for the responsible use of those assets.

Fourth, measurement of asset values is problematic. In a very narrow sense, the benchmark valuation of any asset is its apparent value after a loss has occurred. However, this statement fails to incorporate a number of salient issues. For one thing, it fails to reflect a value of upside risk and, for another, it does not clearly suggest the effect of indirect and consequential losses on the total cost of loss. Additionally, the 'post-loss' measure does not address the contributory value issue: an asset may have a determinable replacement value, but not really contribute anything to the overall value of the local authority. Thus, it seems that an asset's value to an organisation is – first – a function of its contributory value. Only secondarily, then, is its replacement value relevant.

Finally, readers can begin to see the point of risk interdependency, which is first raised in Chapters 1 and 2, and developed further in Chapter 3. The holding of assets is a strict violation of the concept of independence of exposure to risk if for no other reason than there is a single holder (the public body) of those assets. On a more practical level, a local authority, for example, could easily be characterised as clusters of assets – a school building filled with books, computers, desks, students and staff; a vehicle depot filled with lorries, vans, street sweepers and all the equipment necessary to support public works activities; a police station filled with officers, suspects and prisoners, records and files, computer equipment and police vehicles. Additionally, Chapter 5's brief tour of asset exposures reminds readers that risk's possible impact on assets is complicated and challenging to comprehend – and these possible effects must be considered in any plan to manage the asset exposure to risk.

## APPLICATIONS

## Underground storage tanks: a problematic asset

Although hazardous waste management issues tend to focus on legal liability and mandated risk control matters, it is possible to look at this issue as a physical asset concern. This applications section discusses property asset exposures in the context of underground storage tanks.

Many local authorities possess underground storage tanks, primarily to hold vehicle and heating fuels. Often they have been underground, placed there originally to manage against the risk of fire and explosion, for twenty to thirty years. Due to turnover in government management and the passage of time, some authorities may not even be aware that they possess such assets.

Estimates vary, but experts suggest that as many as half of all storage tanks are leaking – due to corrosion, chemical incompatibility, improper installation and maintenance, or other design problems. Naturally there are legal liability concerns with leaking underground storage tanks, since the Environmental Protection Act will require that polluters (regardless of their awareness of the pollution) clean up damaged sites. With pollution site clean-up costs potentially high, the legal liability dimension of this problem is worrisome.

Consider the asset side of this issue. Functioning tanks have a contributory value to a local authority, so the development of maintenance protocols and overall management procedures can help maximise the productive value of the tanks themselves. The presence of leaking tanks can degrade property which otherwise might have a significant value to the local authority. The land might produce revenue by being leased to a private organisation, or it might be used for a city park or stadium, or it might have more prosaic, but productive, uses.

Underground storage tanks also offer some insight into the multiple dimensions of assets and their valuation. For instance, if such tanks are looked at as physical assets, their value might be measured by the cost of replacing/repairing them. Alternatively, one could look at the contributory value, that is, the impact on the community if they cannot be used. This asset is interconnected to other assets like motor vehicles and buildings, and it influences the value of the real property it occupies. It also can influence human assets.

There might even be a financial asset dimension to underground storage tanks. Leasing this asset to private parties might produce a revenue stream that converts the tanks from tangible, non-productive things into financial assets.

---

## TOOLS YOU CAN USE

## How local government is financed

Local government expenditure is broadly subdivided between capital expenditure and revenue expenditure.

### *Revenue expenditure*

Revenue expenditure can be defined as the day-to-day expenditure required to keep the authority's services running. Revenue expenditure is financed from four main sources:

- central government grants
- non-domestic rates (NDR)
- Council Tax
- fees and charges.

The reasons why central government funds local government expenditure are:

1   Some local government services such as education and social services are of national importance and so part of the cost should be met from national taxation.
2   To ensure that local authorities can provide a similar level of service at broadly the same cost throughout the country.

3      The full cost of providing local government services is too large to be met solely by the local taxpayers.

4      To influence local government spending on some services.

5      To encourage local authorities to implement central government's policy initiatives.

6      To act as a pump primer for development works.

7      To redistribute resources from one part of the country to another.

The starting point in the local government financing process is central government's determination of *total standard spending*, the amount of local government spending it is prepared to support through grants.

*Central government grants* – and non-domestic rates are largely outside the control of local authorities and represent 68 per cent of revenue financing in England and 79 per cent in Wales This funding is known as *aggregate external finance*. The difference between total spending standard and aggregate external finance is the approximate amount local authorities need to generate by way of Council Tax if they were to spend at the level of total standard spending. Council Tax income represents 17 per cent of gross expenditure in England and 12 per cent in Wales.

*Specific and special grants* – central government covers another part of total standard spending through specific and special grants which fund particular services. For example, there is an Under Five Education grant that local authorities can apply for if they plan to increase the number of places available for children under five in pre-school education in their area.

*Standard spending assessment* (SSA) – central government calculates a SSA to work out each council's total share of total standard spending, apart from specific and special grants. Separate formulae, taking into account of the population, social structure and other characteristics of each authority, have been developed to calculate the amount to be allocated to the following major service areas:

- education
- personal social services
- police
- fire
- highway maintenance
- environmental, protective and social services
- capital financing.

The total that the SSA formulae give for each major service is normally slightly different from the amount central government allocates to each major service area (the *control totals*). To make the figures match, the SSA for each major service area is either scaled up or down, as appropriate.

## Non-domestic rates

Non-domestic rates are payable on non-domestic properties, such as shops, factories, offices and warehouses. The amount of NDRs is set by central government on a national scale rather than at an individual authority's discretion. One authority in an area will have responsibility for collection and for payment of the collected rates into a national 'pool'. Central government distributes the collected NDRs between all the authorities.

Before the start of the financial year, central government estimates the amount in the pool, the *distributable amount*. This is fixed, irrespective of the amount actually collected in the pool and is shared out between the local authorities according to the number of residents each authority has.

## Revenue Support Grants

Every financial year central government provides a Revenue Support Grant (RSG), which is simply the part of the aggregate external finance which is not provided for by NDRs and special and specific grants. The RSG system is designed so that if all the local authorities were to set their budgets at the SSA level, then the Council Tax for a band D property would be the same at taxpayer level throughout the country.

The RSG calculation for each authority is relatively straightforward. It is simply:

- its standard special assessment *less*
- the amount it will get from the national pool of NDRs *less*
- the amount it would get if it set its Council Tax at a national standard rate.

The primary intention of the RSG system is to:

- equalize for differences in spending need and taxable capacity within an authority
- keep down Council Tax to a politically acceptable level.

If central government were to reduce the RSG the consequences would be to:

- increase the proportion of local government spending financed from Council Tax
- reduce the gearing of the Council Tax (see below) so that a change in an authority's overall spending level would lead to a relatively smaller change in the Council Tax rate than it does now
- increase the level of the Council Tax for all authorities and all properties
- increase resources available from national taxation for central government to spend elsewhere or to give back by way of tax cuts.

## Council Tax

Once an authority knows its level of funding from central government, it can make final decisions on:

- how much it expects to spend in the coming year
- what income, other than from the government, it expects to raise in the coming year through fees and charges
- how it can use its financial reserves to fund spending or to keep down its Council Tax.

Table 5.1 shows the calculation of the Revenue Support Grant.

**Table 5.1** Calculation of Revenue Support Grant

|  | Authority X | Authority Y |
|---|---|---|
| Population | 540 000 | 540 000 |
| SSA | £310 million | £360 million |
| Council Tax base | 190 000 | 140 000 |
| Council Tax for standard spending | £635 | £635 |
| Distributable amount per capita | £250 | £250 |
| Population × Distributable amount per capita = Income from redistributed NDRs | 540 000 × £250 = £135 million | 540 000 × £250 = £135 million |
| Council Tax base × Council Tax for standard spending = Income from Council Tax if set at standard rate | 190,000 × £635 = £120.65 million | 140,000 × £635 = £88.90 million |
| SSA | £310 million | £360 million |
| Less income from redistributed business rates | £135 million | £135 million |
| Less standard Council Tax income | £120.65 million | £88.90 million |
| RSG | £54.35 million | £136.10 million |

A local authority's planned spending, after deducting any funding from reserves and income it expects to raise, other than from general funding from central government and Council Tax, is known as the *budget requirement*. Each local authority then sets its Council Tax at the level necessary to raise its amount.

**Table 5.2**  Calculations of actual Council Tax

| Assuming budget requirement set at SSA | Authority X | Authority Y |
|---|---|---|
| Budget requirement | £310.00 million | £360.00 million |
| Less income from redistributed NDR | £135.00 million | £135.00 million |
| Less RSG | £54.35 million | £136.10 million |
| = Actual Council Tax needed | £120.65 million | £88.90 million |
| Divided by council's estimate of Council Tax base, assuming 97 per cent collection | ÷ 184,300 | ÷ 135,800 |
| Council Tax level for band D | £654.64 | £654.64 |

| Assuming budget requirement set at SSA plus 5% | Authority X | Authority Y |
|---|---|---|
| Budget requirement | £325.50 million | £378.00 million |
| Less income from redistributed NDR | £135.00 million | £135.00 million |
| Less RSG | £54.35 million | £136.10 million |
| = Actual Council Tax needed | £136.15 million | £106.90 million |
| Divided by council's estimate of Council Tax base, assuming 97 per cent collection | ÷ 184,300 | ÷ 135,800 |
| Council Tax level for band D | £738.74 | £787.19 |

| Assuming budget requirement set at SSA less 5% | Authority X | Authority Y |
|---|---|---|
| Budget requirement | £294.50 million | £342.00 million |
| Less income from redistributed NDR | £135.00 million | £135.00 million |
| Less RSG | £54.35 million | £136.10 million |
| = Actual Council Tax Needed | £105.15 million | £70.90 million |
| Divided by council's estimate of Council Tax base, assuming 97 per cent collection | ÷ 184,300 | ÷ 135,800 |
| Council Tax level for band D | £570.54 | £522.09 |

# Gearing

Table 5.2 shows the effect of a phenomenon known as gearing which is consequent upon the relative dependence of English and Welsh authorities on revenues from central government. A decision made by Authority X to spend at a level of 5 per cent above the SSA results in an increase in Council Tax for band D of 12.85 per cent. Authority Y's decision to budget at 5 per cent above its SSA results in a 20.25 per cent increase, because its income from central government is 75.30 per cent of its budget requirement set at the SSA level. Conversely, gearing means that if an authority decides to budget at less than its SSA, then the percentage reduction in Council Tax will be greater than the percentage by which the budget requirement is set below the SSA.

## Capital expenditure

Capital expenditure can be defined as spending on assets such as the purchase of land, improvement of housing stock, etc. Borrowing has hitherto been the most important source of financing capital expenditure but in recent years there has been a central government push for capital projects to be financed by means of private finance initiatives and public private partnerships.

The general power of a local authority to borrow comes from Section 43 of the Local Government and Housing Act 1989, which states that a local authority may borrow:

- on overdraft from the Bank of England or any other bank authorized under the Banking Act 1987
- from the National Debt Commissioners or the Public Works Loan Board
- by means of a loan instrument including bills, bonds, mortgages, debentures or annuities.

Other forms of borrowing are acceptable provided that they conform to the criteria for valid loan instruments specified in Section 43 of the 1989 Act. In May 1993 general consent was issued allowing authorities to borrow from any institution outside the EU or in any currency without the consent of the Treasury.

However, Section 44 of the 1989 limits the amount a local authority may borrow to its *aggregate ceiling limit* (ACL). This is calculated as the sum of:

- its credit ceiling as at 1 April of the current financial year
- its temporary revenue borrowing limit

- its temporary capital borrowing limit
- any credit approvals used during the financial year
- the difference between approved investments and cash added together when compared with usable capital receipts.

Local authorities must take formal decisions on the following in relation to each financial year:

1   Transferring any credit approval to any other authority (an authority cannot carry forward any unused credit approvals to the next financial year but can enter into an arrangement with another authority to exchange any credit approvals).
2   The use it makes of credit approvals.
3   Whether or not it intends to set aside voluntarily any part of its usable capital receipts as provision to meet credit liabilities (PCL) – i.e., to set aside a greater proportion of total capital receipts than it is required to do by legislation.
4   Its use of capital receipts to finance capital expenditure.
5   Its use of revenue resources to finance the capital programme.

Under Section 47 of the Local Government and Housing Act 1989 any borrowing by a local authority using a loan instrument falling under the Act's definition is secured as a charge against an authority's revenues in perpetuity. The costs of repaying or servicing such a loan has first call on any current or future sources of revenue generated by the authority and should assure lenders that all authorities enjoy a high degree of credit worthiness. Section 44(6) also underpins the issue of creditworthiness: 'A person lending money to a local authority shall not be bound to enquire whether the authority have the power to borrow the money and shall not be prejudiced by the absence of any such power'.

This only relates to borrowing. The spate of cases concerning *ultra vires* (see Chapter 6 for a discussion on this important concept) led to the passing of the Local Government (Contracts) Act 1997 confirming local authorities' powers to enter into a wide range of contracts for the provision of assets or services. It is intended to protect the integrity of parties to a contract so that the contract can stand whether or not it is judged to be *ultra vires*.

# READ MORE ABOUT IT

## Financial risk management

Treasury or financial risk management has been an area of significant expansion in the 1990s as organisations have become more sophisticated in their investment strategies in the financial instruments they use and more aware of the upside and downside exposure their trading activities present. It has not always been thus, and the Hammersmith and Fulham interest swap tale represents a salutary reminder of why a financial risk management process is necessary. Equally instructive is the Orange County, California case.

## Hammersmith interest swaps[1]

### *Some background information and motivations*

The early 1980s saw the central government impose severe spending restrictions on local authorities in the UK. The more a local authority spent, the less financial support it received from the government. Local authorities that were loath to reduce their levels of expenditure were forced to look for new sources of revenue, particularly sources that were outside of the remit of central government's regulations.

City institutions in the UK were looking to develop a British swaps market in sterling but there was little interest in the corporate market. Interest rates were very volatile making the taking of any view on their future direction too risky a venture for most corporations to contemplate. The few corporations that were interested in interest rate swaps had poor credit ratings.

By 1983 Hammersmith had seen a strategy of selling options on shares in the pension fund – giving the purchaser the right to purchase the shares at some specified price in the future – not only as a way of generating additional income, but also as a way of circumventing central government's regulations. From the City's perspective, other than central government itself, a local authority represented 'blue chip' security.

### *Trading pattern*

The first swap deal Hammersmith entered into was signed in December 1983 and switched a fixed rate loan into a floating rate, the authority anticipating that interest rates would fall.

Between 1983 and 1987 seven swaps had been sold with the express intention of reducing the council's debt. This activity escalated between May and November 1987 when twenty-eight swaps were sold, primarily giving the buyer the right to exchange their floating rate debt payments for Hammersmith's fixed rate debt payments at an agreed rate. The council's position required that interest rates stayed below 8 per cent. In the following nine months a further 390 new transactions were entered into.

By July 1988 Hammersmith had a notional principal risk of £3.5 billion and by the end of the 1980s its swaps were worth £5 billion and represented about 75 per cent of the sterling interest swap market.

In part to dissemble its activities, Hammersmith transacted interest swap deals with at least fifteen different banks through some ten different brokers during its period of trading, making it very difficult for any one bank or any regulatory authority to measure the extent of their activities and/or exposure.

## Trading strategy and risk exposures

Hammersmith's aim in transacting interest rate swaps was to generate income for the local authority. Its trading strategy was to be a seller of swaps. Indeed its projection of option premium income from these transactions was £700 000 for 1988 and £2 million per annum for the next three years.

Its strategy meant the use of any premium income generated from lapsed options to cover any losses from exercised options such that if the exposures from exercised options exceeded income from lapsed options, the result was that more swaps were sold. Inevitably this strategy increased the authority's overall risk.

Moreover, the concentration on premium income meant that Hammersmith would often only deal when option premiums were rising. Unfortunately, the classic condition for a rise in option premiums was when the risk of interest rate movement was at its highest. Consequently, when entering into their deals the authority was often taking the maximum amount of risk.

Most deals that Hammersmith transacted assumed that interest rates would fall. However, by the end of 1987 interest rates were rising and in the first half of 1988 had risen by 2 per cent to 11 per cent. A hedging strategy was not considered because to do so would have resulted in a diminution in the flow of premium income.

## Regulatory response

Although this section has focused on the activities of the London Borough of Hammersmith and Fulham, they were not the only local authority transacting interest swap deals at the time. The only difference was the volume of trading transacted by Hammersmith.

By the middle of 1988 authorities were sufficiently concerned about the level of trading and exposures that the controller of the Audit Commission which oversees local authority finances, declared that in conducting these interest swaps authorities may be acting *ultra vires* (see 'Read More About It' in Chapter 6). The legal consequence of the deals being *ultra vires* was that they were null and void.

Despite the Audit Commission's insistence that Hammersmith cease its trading activities, the authority transacted new deals until some time in 1989, by which time it had accumulated losses estimated, conservatively, at £400 million.

## Legal view of local authority interest rate swap deals

Hammersmith relied on the Audit Commission's view that these transactions were *ultra vires* and so null and void, refusing to meet their debt obligations and challenging the financial institutions to sue them in the courts if they wanted their money back.

Some financial institutions took up the challenge and sued. In the ground-breaking case Hazell *vs*. Hammersmith (1991) the courts backed the Audit Commission's view that the transaction of interest swap deals was *ultra vires*, that the deals were null and void and, therefore, the authority could escape the financial consequences of the transactions.

The ratepayers of Hammersmith were thus spared by this judgement from paying the consequences of their authority's failure to recognise, understand and manage the risks and exposures emanating from their treasury management strategy. The residents of Orange County, California were not so lucky.

## Orange County, California

### Some background information

Orange County, located just south of Los Angeles County, is one of the wealthiest counties in California and, therefore, one of the wealthiest counties in America. The county was responsible for the management of an investment pool that combined funds from Orange County with those of 187 other local governments. Investment pools are not uncommon in the USA, and certainly are a visible feature of California state and local government.

The motivation to participate in an investment pool is somewhat self-evident (lower transaction and management costs, economies of scale), but other environmental factors contributed to the attraction of the Orange County pool in the early 1990s, notably:

- state legislation that capped local authorities' ability to raise revenues through taxation
- a faltering (at that time) state and national economy that further limited revenues and also increased demands for public services
- increasing expectations that investment management practices could produce additional revenues for local governments
- a gradual relaxing of statutory limitations on government investment practices, which allowed governments to assume greater investment risks
- local demographic pressures that added to overall demand for public services
- that the Orange County pool was producing higher returns than other pools.

In general, these factors contributed to an environment where local governments were earnest about maximising the efficiency and productivity of all assets (physical, financial and human). Focus, naturally enough, was placed on financial assets because increased productivity was more easily attainable through more aggressive risk-taking in the investment marketplace. Higher returns are more quickly and easily seen in financial assets, so there is a political value in relying on financial assets as a demonstration of improved government performance.

If one focuses only on the preceding elements of the story, certain conventional risk factors emerge: the tricky relationship between risk and reward, the stress of political risk, broad and interrelated environment perils and risk factors, even changes in the social environment. However, there are other dimensions of the story that could stand alone as risk management lessons in their own right.

For example, the Orange County story could be viewed as a purely financial risk management matter. The Orange County treasurer, Robert L. Citron, had worked closely with financial advisers to devise an investment strategy that, while diversified, pivoted around a belief that interest rates would stay low. While in a broad sense the investment portfolio was diversified and therefore seemingly immunised from startlingly unexpected results, there was an exposure to a worrisome systematic risk – interest rates.

The specifics of the investment strategy are rather straightforward. The fund strategy was to buy higher-yielding long-term securities by borrowing short-term money, with pool funds pledged as collateral. This strategy was sound enough as long as interest rates remained stable and low but, as interest rates rose, the cost of short-term borrowing increased and the market value of the long-term securities fell. In the face of these conditions, the Wall Street investment houses demanded more collateral, even though the full value of the bonds held had not changed.

Notably, a sizeable number of the investment instruments were derivatives. Derivative securities are not, in and of themselves, culpable in this story. Derivatives are financial instruments that derive their economic characteristics by combining the characteristics of other instruments (an example would be a contract whose value is based upon currency exchange spreads; a simpler example would be a futures contract that is based upon the price of oil at some predetermined date). Their value to an investment portfolio lies in their ability to allow the purchaser to limit or hedge risk, or to speculate on a specific type of risk.

The fallout of the plunge in portfolio value was a dramatic belt-tightening among the pool participants (layoffs, deferrals of capital projects, library closures, etc.) and, in the case of Orange County, bankruptcy.

In addition to classic financial risk management lessons, like the importance of true investment diversification, the Orange County case also presents an interesting risk management audit and controls moral. While there has been debate and speculation about the treasurer's motives, expertise and values, there is much clearer agreement that the county had insufficient oversight and control, especially relative to the exposures at risk. So while fraud and political corruption likely were ingredients to the story, readers should reasonably wonder how the institution performed its supervisory role in making sure that an employee did not singularly jeopardise the county.

In the Spring 1995 *Insight*, a University of California-Irvine magazine, noted financial management and derivatives expert Philippe Jorion offered a commentary that captures many elements of the previous discussion. What follows is an extended excerpt:

> The Orange County fiasco may lead to renewed calls for regulations to control derivative products. This is misguided. At fault are the risk management guidelines (or lack thereof) and professional incompetence, not derivatives.
>
> The £1.7 billion loss in Orange County represents a fall of about 22 percent in the £7.4 billion investment pool. To put things in perspective, a passive investment in the bond market would have lost only about 4 percent of its value since the beginning of the year. The

abnormally large loss reflects the fact that the County's portfolio was leveraged up to three times its value. 'Leverage' involves borrowing funds to invest in additional risky assets. The fund also invested in 'structured notes', special bonds issued by government agencies such as Fannie Mae, that can be viewed as derivative products. But the main factor in the losses was leverage and exposure through market risk, not derivatives.

In the bond market, exposure to interest rates can be achieved through investing in longer-maturity instruments, or through leveraging, or through derivatives. Derivatives are only a means, albeit particularly efficient, to manage market risk. But it should be noted that investing in a 30-year zero coupon bond could also have led to a 20 percent loss. In my view, the loss was due to two problems.

The first problem is that County Treasurer/Tax Collector Bob Citron implemented speculative positions with substantial downside risk, which were inconsistent with the responsibilities of running a public fund. Also, exposure to market risk was increased as an attempt to make up for losses incurred at the beginning of the year (the well-known 'doubling up' strategy in poker). Essentially, the pool operated as a 'hedge' fund. Investing in private hedge funds should be allowed as long as investors realise that their capital is at substantial risk. The resulting exposure, however, was highly unusual for this type of fund and was clearly unexpected.

The second problem is that investors who have benefited from the superior performance of the fund over 1990–1993 should have suspected the strategy was risky. How else would the fund have been able to perform much better than the industry average? In financial markets, there are no free lunches.

Investors share part of the blame because they benefited from the superior performance and turned a blind eye to risks. In particular, the board of supervisors unabashedly supported this strategy, and failed to understand potential losses.

For a private corporation, such as Procter and, guess what, Gamble, such speculative activities may be condoned by shareholders, who ultimately risk their own capital. In the case of a public fund, it is not clear who bears the residual risk of such losses.

To address this control failure, I would suggest establishing a risk management system setting limits on market risk, including leverage and positions in bonds and derivatives. Instruments that cannot be priced easily or fully understood should be avoided. Once in place, these guidelines should be monitored by an independent party. Portfolios should be valued at prevailing market prices, and disclosed to investors.

Provided they are used prudently, derivatives are useful risk management tools. In particular, futures and options traded on organized exchanges in Chicago are simple to understand, fairly priced, and easy to value.

Overall, this loss can be squarely blamed on an inadequate risk management system and professional incompetence. In any business, this combination would be deadly.

Professor Jorion touches on most of the key points and emphasises the value of controls, oversight and risk management. What is, perhaps, missing from his analysis is the extraordinary pressures that have come to bear on local governments, especially the limitations on resources and the increasing demands for service. Management in a public organisation, even financial management, is not just a matter of science and systems. Ultimately it involves human beings making decisions on complicated issues where information is at a premium and the environments are constantly changing. In the case of Orange County, greed or even fraud may have been ingredients, but readers should recognise that lack of clarity, absence of information, high levels of uncertainty, and subjectivity are characteristics of management life that can negatively affect those with even the best of motives.

For readers interested in financial risk management and particularly the Orange County case, Professor Jorion has produced an excellent analysis entitled *Big Bets Gone Bad: Derivatives and Bankruptcy in Orange County* (Academic Press, Orlando, FL, 1995, ISBN: 0-12-390360-2).

# Note

1    For a more detailed analysis of the history of derivatives in general and the Hammersmith and Orange County stories in particular, the reader is encouraged to read *Apocalypse Roulette* by Richard Thomson (1998), published by Macmillan, priced £20.00, ISBN 0333664574.

# Liability exposures to risk

## EXECUTIVE SUMMARY

Liability exposures and moral responsibility exposures are related liability exposures to risk. Legal liability arises from the system of law that is applicable to public bodies. In the main, risk managers concern themselves with the broad area of common/civil law, that is, with the assertion and protection of individual rights. In this context public bodies may find themselves on the defensive for actions that may have resulted in bodily harm to others, damage to their property or less tangible personal injuries or financial losses.

The challenge of liability management is that the law is very complex and the range of exposures is quite broad. Some areas of the law, like premises liability, are fairly straightforward, while others, like Employer' Liability, are enormously complex and difficult to understand.

The issue of moral responsibility is more important than one might think. While moral lapses occur and usually result in no obvious or direct punishment, it is nevertheless true that a systematic consideration of the moral or ethical dimensions of risk is an important element of overall organisation risk management. Risk management, in many respects, is concerned with the consequences of the decisions and actions of the public body, especially their impact on the community.

## PRINCIPLES AND CONCEPTS

Chapter 6 turns to the liability side of the exposure balance sheet. The term 'liability' is broadly construed here to encompass moral responsibility as an exposure issue.

The subject of legal liability is extremely wide and complex, and a full treatment of the legal environment for public bodies would dwarf the other chapters of this book. Therefore, the focus in this chapter is to establish a basic understanding of the English legal system with a specific orientation towards the practical implications for public bodies. To that end, the chapter begins with a short overview of the legal system, with particular emphasis on civil law. Notable risk management related characteristics of the legal system are identified and discussed. Key liability problem areas are explained in some detail.

The chapter concludes with an introduction to and exploration of the moral and ethical responsibility dimension of liability exposures to risk. A central topic of this section is the challenge of framing moral and ethical issues in a broader risk management context.

## Legal liability exposures

There are three legal systems operating in the UK, one for England and Wales, one for Scotland and one for Northern Ireland. Unless stated otherwise any general reference in this discussion to a legal system will refer to that which pertains in England and Wales.

The key attributes of the English legal system are that:

* it is a system based on common law, equity and statute
* in matters of European Community law the Court of Justice of the European Communities has ultimate sanction over it.

### *A system based on common law, equity and statute*

Although the statement is a simplification, it could be said that there are two broad forms of law practised throughout the world – codified law and common law. The distinctions are obvious and subtle, but probably it is sufficient here to state that code law is based on a fairly explicit set of laws and rulings (the Ten Commandments can be seen as the prototypical code law illustration). France and countries with historic ties to France tend to follow a code-based system. Common law is based on judges' rulings and is generally seen as more flexible and adaptable in concept and application.

Equity grew out of a reaction against the rigidity of the common law and the harshness of its application in medieval England. The equity system operated in parallel to the common law system and where the two came into conflict the rules of equity prevailed. The primacy of equity over common law was incorporated into legislation with the passing of the Judicature Acts of 1873 to 1875.

Common law only recognised the remedy of damages or financial compensation. Equity, however, introduced a range of other remedies, including injunctions and specific performance, considerably enhancing a court's options in circumstances where monetary compensation was deemed not to meet the claimant's needs.

Statutes are an important source of law and much of the caseload of the courts involves the interpretation and clarification of legislation passed by Parliament.

Underpinning the English system of common law is the doctrine of precedent. Under certain circumstances a court is bound to follow a decision of its own or of a higher court, even though it may believe that decision to be wrong. From a risk management perspective, there are several inherent benefits in following a system of precedent:

1    It creates a level of certainty. In other words, claimants, defendants and their respective legal advisers are better able to ascertain the likely outcome of any litigation which, in turn, facilitates settlement of a case before it comes to trial.

2    It reduces the number of cases coming to trial. If courts in certain circumstances were not required to follow earlier judgements, each case would have to be decided upon its own merits, thus increasing the number of cases going to trial.

3    It means that a person or organisation can act in reliance upon a statement of law.

However, it would be wrong to give the impression that because of the doctrine of precedent the English legal system is ossified. The law is constantly changing with new interpretations of earlier established points of law and new judgements in areas where hitherto there had been little or no established precedent.

What enables this dynamism and fluidity to exist side by side with the doctrine of precedent is the appeals system that pertains in England. Courts are divided between those dealing with matters of criminal and civil law. As we are concerned with the liability exposures of public bodies we will concentrate on the courts dealing with civil law. Exhibit 6.1 represents the hierarchy and appeals structure of courts dealing with civil law courts in England and Wales.

At the bottom end of the hierarchy sit the County Courts and the Magistrates' Courts dealing with smaller cases of civil litigation and the High Courts of Justice which deal with the more serious cases. Sitting above these courts is the Court of Appeal (Civil Division).

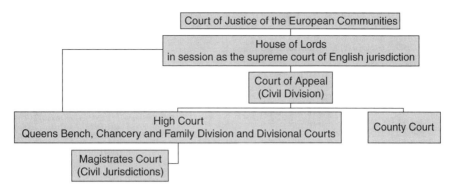

**Exhibit 6.1** The hierarchy and appeals structure of courts dealing with civil law courts in England and Wales

Above that the House of Lords. Ever since the UK's entry into the European Community in 1972 the Court of Justice of the European Communities (European Court) has sat above the House of Lords.

While, on the one hand, the doctrine of precedent requires that a court is bound to follow an earlier decision of its own or a higher court, on the other hand it means that a court higher up the hierarchical structure is not bound to follow a decision made in a lower court. On appeal, the Court of Appeal (Civil Division) can overturn a decision made in the High Court, County Court or Magistrates' Court, the House of Lords can overturn a decision made in the Court of Appeal and, in certain cases, the European Court can overturn a decision made in the House of Lords.

It is possible that the doctrine of precedent could be eroded by the Human Rights Act. First, all statute law must be interpreted in accordance with the European Convention on Human Rights; therefore any previous case law interpreting statute will not be binding. Second, as public bodies, courts must follow the European Convention in making any decision. Arguably, the court may ignore any case law that is inconsistent with the convention with the implication that lower courts could ignore the decision of higher courts. However, it is the writers' view that a lower court will not be able to overrule a previous decision of a higher court, even if it is inconsistent with the convention.

From an organisation risk management standpoint, the hierarchy of courts and the appeals procedure introduces a level of uncertainty that would not – perhaps – exist to quite the same degree if a codified system were used.

## The supremacy of the European Court

One of the consequences of the UK's entry into the European Community in 1972 is that in matters of interpretation of community law any court may, and the final court of appeal in a member state must, refer the case to the European Court for a ruling. As a result, in certain circumstances the House of Lords is no longer the ultimate arbiter in a case of English civil litigation and, conversely, a European Court judgement on a civil case originating in another member country can create a precedent binding on English civil courts.

To date, European Community law has mainly impacted on employment related issues, health and safety, employment protection and working conditions. The European Court rules on community law and should not be confused with the European Court of Human Rights. The implementation of the Human Rights Act in October 2000 means that citizens of England and Wales can seek a remedy for breach of the convention in domestic courts instead of taking their case to the Human Rights Court in Strasbourg. With the growing trend towards harmonization of member states' legislation, the areas where the European Court is the ultimate court of sanction will increase as will the implications of their rulings on the operations of member states' judicial systems.

## Legal liability problems and issues

Public bodies are diverse in size and responsibilities. In many respects their differences vastly exceed their commonalities. Certainly, the issues facing an inner city authority can differ radically from those faced by a rural district council. Yet, their publicness does give rise to some common concerns, and they do share many management-related problems and issues – though clearly of differing scope.

Despite this diversity, there are a set of legal liability problems and issues that are widely observed:

* nature and purpose of tort law
* contract law as a foundation problem
* premises liability
* products and services liability
* environmental impairment/public nuisance liability
* professional liability
* elected members and fiduciary liability
* bailment liability

- employment liability
- agency liability
- motor vehicle liability
- social services and education liability.

The discussion below of each topic is intended to be general in nature rather than a detailed review of particular judgements impacting the liabilities of public bodies. Readers requiring a detailed account of the liabilities of public bodies are directed to *Local Authority Liability*, edited by John Morrell and Richard Foster and published by Jordan Publishing of 21 St Thomas Street, Bristol BS1 6JS, (ISBN 0-85308-509-9).

## Nature and purpose of tort law

The English legal system can be categorized in several ways – public v. private law, civil v. criminal law, and so on. And, depending on the type of public body in question, one or the other of these approaches might be suitable. However, since the focus of this book is on the management of risks in public organisations generally, the main concern for readers will be the impact of risks on public bodies. Thus, treatment of criminal law is not essential (although it certainly could be of concern with respect to employee actions), nor is an extended discussion of distinctions between public and private law (again, from time to time the issues could be important, but not on an ongoing basis). Indeed, the best use of time here is to focus on civil law and the key categories in it.

Civil law is that part of the common law system that pertains to the relationships between individuals (and organisations). A civil action is one that is brought by one party against another for alleged wrongs. These actions are taken at the litigant's own expense, and the awards that are granted under the civil system are determined by a judge or, in certain circumstances, by a jury under a judge's direction. Those awards might include indemnity for loss, punitive damages, restitution or injunctive relief.

In a civil action the burden of proof differs from criminal law. Civil liability is based on the preponderance of evidence (as opposed to 'beyond all reasonable doubt' in criminal law). This standard is a comparative standard, meaning a party must have more credible evidence supportive of its position than the opposing party presents on its behalf. They must win on the balance of probabilities.

Civil law is classifiable into several categories: contract law, torts, equitable actions and certain actions that fall outside the other categories. A claimant – that is, the party alleging that harm was done

– need not necessarily name the type of civil action being pursued, and thus an action may proceed until a determination of its status is established. Of course, the claimant does need to satisfy a judge that a theory of recovery exists before a case proceeds very far.

The parties of a civil action must comply with the rules and requirements that are set forward by each jurisdiction. These include things like the form and procedure for initiating an action, the methods by which evidence is gathered, the nature of communications between parties, and so on. Ordinarily, the claimant carries the burden of proving the case although, from time to time, the evidence of wrongdoing is sufficiently obvious that the doctrine of *res ipsa loquitur* ('the thing speaks for itself') is applied. In such cases the defendant must carry the burden of proving it is not liable.

Part of the difficulty of facing the legal liability exposure rests in the complexity of the process. Almost inevitably the pursuit of legal redress requires expert legal counsel and additional expertise in the technical matters relevant to the case. This is expensive, but more importantly, it puts the risk manager in a situation where there is a reliance on outside advisers. Further, conflicts of interest can arise between counsel and client.

Most civil actions are settled between litigants well before the case comes to trial. Other actions are discontinued or thrown out for lack of sufficient support – but they all cost the defendant money and time. This supports the general view that the real risk within the realm of legal liability is not losing a case but simply being named in a case, as this sets in motion a commitment of resources regardless of its merits. In the past claimants suing public bodies often had the benefit of legal aid. This meant that if the public body won, they could not recover their costs from the claimant. While the legal aid regime put the means of obtaining justice in the hand of the poorer members of society, it also had the effect of increasing the number of speculative claims against public bodies. The tightening of the legal aid regime and the introduction of a no win/no fee protocol for personal injury cases may well reduce the number of speculative claims and reduce the overall costs of the litigation process for public bodies.

Those few cases that do go to trial and do end in a court decision will likely have gone through the process of filing pleadings, pre-trial disclosure and case preparation, the trial itself, a possible appeal to a higher court and the final enforcement of the verdict. The awards that are granted fall broadly into the categories of special damages, general damages and punitive damages. Special damages are compensation for indirect losses suffered by the prevailing party – medical expenses, lost wages, lost or damaged property. General damages refer to tangible losses including pain and suffering. Punitive damages may be awarded in situations where the defendant's actions are deemed to be grossly negligent or sufficiently outside the bounds of acceptable behaviour as to warrant an economic punishment.

## Tort law

The word 'tort' means a civil wrong other than a breach of contract. Broadly speaking, torts are either intentional or unintentional (negligence) actions. Intentional torts, which are not discussed further here, include such things as trespassing, conversion of property, assault and battery, false imprisonment and defamation of character.

Negligence cases typically involve alleged personal injury or property damage. A claimant will be expected to demonstrate (with a preponderance of the evidence) that:

- the defendant had a legal duty to act or not act in a particular way
- the defendant breached that legal duty
- the breach of duty was the proximate cause of the loss sustained
- there were damages sustained by the claimant.

Defendants have numerous defences available. Obviously, they may be able to demonstrate that any one of the four ingredients listed above is not true. But if circumstances permit, they may also invoke a contributory or comparative negligence or an assumption of risk.

Contributory or comparative negligence may be invoked when it is permitted and when it can be shown that the claimant contributed in some way to the damages sustained. In some circumstances, even a 1 per cent contribution on the part of the claimant is sufficient to allow the defendant to prevail. More commonly, a degree of contribution limits but does not eliminate a defendant's liability. The assumption of risk defence asserts that the claimant was aware of the risks and assumed responsibility for the consequences.

The tort system has recently come under attack. Among the criticisms levelled against it have been that negligence is too difficult to prove, that the cost of pursuing a claim is prohibitive for those who do not qualify for legal aid, that litigation is too uncertain and that the whole process is too lengthy. In 1978 the Pearson Commission recommended that for personal injuries arising from road accidents a scheme of automatic no-fault compensation should be established and that it should be administered alongside the social security system and financed by a levy on the price of petrol. This recommendation has not been implemented to date. However, the Woolf reforms, implemented in April 1999, were designed to accelerate procedures for settling certain types of personal injury claims. Clearly any attempts to alter the existing tort system will introduce new areas of risk and uncertainty for the public sector risk manager.

## Contract law: a foundation problem

Contract law is a fundamental concern for risk managers, and this is so because the COCA view of organisations bases much of its power on the insight that organisations are collections of COCAs. Since COCAs are the principal means by which organisations become exposed to risk, the legal issues surrounding these arrangements are central to managing risks.

Contracts become legally enforceable when four elements are present:

1   There is offer and acceptance by the parties involved.
2   There is consideration offered by the parties involved.
3   The parties are legally competent to enter into the contract.
4   The contract serves a legal purpose.

From an exposure standpoint, any one of these elements might prove to be problematic for a public body. Further, parties may be unable to perform, the intent of the contract may be disputed, inherent risks may not be identified in advance (and thus not planned for) and a contract may come to cross purposes with other arrangements.

Public bodies have always had to address contract-related risk issues, meaning that, apart from the risks that pass through the contract, the management of the contract itself may generate problems and issues. What has changed in the last ten to fifteen years is the level of contracting for services. Broad pressures to privatise, to seek greater performance efficiencies, and to downsize organisations has led to new and extended uses of private-sector service and non-profit providers. The management of these arrangements has expanded the scope of risk management activity, so much so that many risk managers complain that contract risk management has generated a paperwork blizzard in the form of certificates of insurance (verifying that vendors have purchased appropriate coverages), performance bonds, warranties, and credit assurances.

# Premises liability

In a practical sense, premises liability is the most common liability exposure any organisation will face. The law imposes certain expectations on property owners (or those controlling property) with respect to the duties they owe visitors to those premises. Although the duty varies depending on whether the visitor is lawfully or unlawfully on the premises, it generally is true that visitors have a right to a degree of safety and to reasonable warning about hazards that may exist.

For a local authority, for example, the practical challenge of managing this exposure is daunting, as it could extend from the town hall steps, to streets and roads, to parks and playgrounds, to sporting arenas and fairgrounds, to marinas and ski slopes. Premises liability – in addition to being the most common exposure – is the broadest liability exposure an authority will face.

It is easy to imagine disaster scenarios in premises liability situations – the collapse of a publicly owned sports stadium, children trapped in a school fire, and so on. However, well over 90 per cent of legal claims arising from premises liability are classic 'slip and fall' claims, each troubling enough but not individually catastrophic from the organisation's perspective. This observation offers hope to risk managers inasmuch as it suggests that reasonable steps may be taken to prevent or avoid such accidents from occurring.

# Products and services liability

It might be thought that public bodies have no exposure to product liability (or services liability), since they are not commonly in the business of selling products – at least not in the private-sector sense of the buy-sell transaction.

However, this is no longer true, and for certain public bodies (e.g., public utilities) it never has been true. Public bodies can and do sell products or services and do fall under the area of civil law that addresses product and service liability. Further, as pressures continue to exist to impose more private sector practices and market disciplines on public sector operations, the presence of product liability claims can only grow.

Two key aspects of product or service liability warrant highlighting here. First, liability for defective products or services may be the result of a range of legal approaches. For example, claimants might pursue a legal remedy under a breach of warranty doctrine, of which there are several possible types – breach of an express warranty, breach of an implied warranty of fitness, breach of an implied warranty of merchantability, and breach of an implied warranty of title. Breaches of warranty are problematic, at least relative to a claim of negligence, because the claimant has only one challenge, and that is to prove that a warranty was breached (whereas a negligence case requires the claimant to prove duty, breach of duty, proximate cause and damages sustained). Warranties hold a special status in the eyes of the law, and they are valuable if held, and worrisome if issued.

Second, product liability claims that are pursued as negligence actions are largely subject to strict or absolute liability standards. Although the two words (strict and absolute) have slightly different technical connotations, the general meaning is that the standard of care or duty is so high that it is assumed the defendant is unlikely to meet that duty. One might see a case occasionally where a defendant is able to demonstrate attainment of the standard, but the history of absolute liability shows an evolution towards the notion of an unattainable standard. To explain this in a different way, readers might recall that a conventional tort action requires the claimant to establish duty, breach of duty, proximate cause and damages sustained. In an absolute liability action, the duty is so high that breach is assumed; thus, the claimant really need show only that the assumed breached duty directly lead to the claimant's loss.

## Environmental impairment/public nuisance liability

Maintenance of a public nuisance is seen as the area of exposure when the actions of a wrongdoer affect the public in general (there is such a thing as a private nuisance as well). Historically, legal actions falling in this area include complaints about sirens or whistles disturbing the peace, disturbances due to blasting during construction and unsafe construction of roadways. Over the past few years, however, this area of civil law has become transformed by the specific public nuisance of 'environmental impairment'.

Numerous factors behind the growth of the environmental impairment (EI) exposure can be cited. The 'green' movement, governmental activism, the complicated nature of many polluted sites – all have contributed to heightened activity in this area. While the courts have played an influential role in the evolution of environmental impairment law, government and EU sponsored legislation has been particularly important.

Public sector risk managers commonly cite environmental impairment as one of the most significant problems they face. This is due, in part, to the increasing complexity of the law (and, indeed, the environmental impairment problem itself), the fact that strict and absolute liability standards are widely applied in such cases and, of course, because a public body is unlikely to evade or avoid responsibility for environmental problems that fall within its general purview.

## Professional liability

Professionals, however they are defined, possess a legal status that is different from the ordinary person on the street. In short, professionals are held to a higher standard of care – more is expected of a professional in terms of knowledge, competence and judgement in the scope of professional expertise.

What constitutes a professional in the eyes of the law? Unfortunately, the concept is somewhat open-ended and there is something of a trend in expanding the concept to include more individuals. Certainly, physicians, lawyers, architects and others for whom advanced training is essential would fit into the general category of professionals. Somewhat less clear would be managers within an organisation, like financial managers, operations managers and others with fairly specialised expertise. Additionally, a survey of professional liability claims would reveal individual cases where a wide range of occupations are deemed to be professionals in the context of a particular case.

Professional liability cases are frequently referred to as malpractice cases and, although these cases extend beyond the bounds of what the general public would consider a malpractice situation, the word does convey one important element of professional liability cases. Personal/professional reputation is closely bound up in a malpractice case, and this upsets the equilibrium that might otherwise prevail. A hospital, for example, might be willing to settle a case against a surgeon because the economic uncertainty of the case outweighs the benefits of litigation – whereas the surgeon is likely to include loss of reputation in the cost-benefit calculation and, therefore, is more motivated to litigate the case.

Readers should note here that insurance companies offering professional liability coverage deem the risk to be sufficiently different from others that they tend to either specialise in it or exclude it from broader coverages. And, the nature of the coverage offered tends to differ in important ways from other liability coverages (e.g., professionals are permitted greater participation in their defence under professional liability coverages).

## Officials' and fiduciary liability

Although officials' and fiduciary liability have distinctly different technical implications in the world of insurance, they have some conceptual connections that make a common discussion appropriate.

Officials might be held legally liable for any number of things mentioned previously or in subsequent sections of this chapter. An official might drive a council motor vehicle in a negligent fashion and be subject to the laws that pertain to that situation. An official might also fall under the scope of professional liability if, for instance, actions or decisions taken by the authority are influenced by that official's professional training (say, engineering). However, the term 'officials' liability' refers to an exposure arising from errors and omissions – as opposed to negligent acts – that a person commits in the scope of duties. A classic example is a planning decision that demonstrably is the result of a failure to exercise the due care expected.

The errors and omissions of an official might be thought of as an issue of general negligence law (and, as will be seen later, of general liability insurance), but this is incorrect for at least two reasons. First, general negligence matters tend to focus – though certainly not exclusively – on events that lead to physical damage to assets or physical harm to individuals (reckless driving damages the car of another and injures its driver). The world of officials' liability contemplates economic damages that are generally distinct from direct physical harm (a planning decision deprives a business of sales to customers) – though, again, not exclusively – and are not the result of deliberate or negligent acts but of oversights, errors, mistakes, misinterpretations, and so on. Second, officials' liability refers to an area of public law where officials might be held responsible individually for the errors and omissions they commit. A public employee will be named in an action but it is the organisation that is the principal party to an action due to the concept of agency.

The second point suggests that officials' liability is similar to directors' and officers' liability in the private sector, where boards of directors can be sued as individuals for mismanagement, among other things. In both the public and private instance, a particular problem arises because many legal actions pursued under this area of law will come from shareholders or citizens. If the organisation promises to insure or indemnify the board member or official, it means that the organisation is expending resources to protect that individual against suits filed by the 'owners' of the organisation – clearly a troubling conceptual and practical problem.

This concern was highlighted in the ruling in *Burgoine and Cook* v. *Waltham Forest LBC* (1996) which was ground-breaking to the extent that it challenged the validity of indemnities given to their employees by public bodies. Where the activity in which the employees are engaged is deemed to be *ultra vires* (that is, outside the statutory powers of the public body) any indemnity provided to an employee in respect of any personal liabilities they may incur will be null and void (see 'Applications' section). This decision has forced employees and members to consider seriously their position with respect to personal liabilities they may incur while acting in an official capacity.

The matter of fiduciary liability is related to officials' liability in the sense that a fiduciary responsibility refers to the legal duty one party has in managing or controlling the assets of another. In that sense, boards and officials have a broad fiduciary duty to those parties that provide the resources necessary to run the organisation.

However, it is true that fiduciary liability tends to refer to managers who have specific responsibilities for the management of distinct assets, say, an employee-funded pension scheme. Generally, the finance or treasury function of an authority will have pockets of fiduciary responsibility for certain funds or pools of assets, and that responsibility is to parties outside the organisation. It is enough here to say that the general legal expectation is that managers behave as if the assets within their trust and care are their own.

## Bailment liability

Bailment liability is somewhat related to fiduciary liability in that it refers to assets that are temporarily in the care, custody or control of another. An example of this may be the impounding of stolen goods by a police officer or of goods in lieu of unpaid Council Tax liabilities by a bailiff acting on behalf of a local authority. In the broadest sense, the police or local authority has a certain duty to safeguard the goods while under their control. A council-owned car park would have – again, broadly speaking – a similar duty.

The two examples above are obvious, but they also are equivocal, because laws frequently modify the exposure a public body might have in bailment situations. In the case of the car park, the parking ticket may be viewed as a waiver of the authority's duty to safeguard the motor vehicle while in its care, custody or control.

## Employment liability

Unlike many countries, the UK does not have a no-fault workers' compensation system. This is in part due to the existence of a comprehensive state provided health and social security system whereby employees as a right have access to free medical treatment and to income assistance in the event of absence through sickness or injury. As a consequence, in order to obtain redress for injuries sustained in the workplace an employee must prove negligence against the employer. For their part, the employer can rely upon the normal defences to a charge of negligence.

When a public body enters into an employment agreement with an individual, the terms and conditions of that contract raise fundamental risks that would exist in any contract – the ability of the parties to perform, the strength of guarantees, and the risk-bearing capacity of the parties. These risks, while important, are not the key risks of the contract. The key risks are not necessarily expressed in the contract but include the array of common and statutory laws that pertain to employment relationships. These include such thing as the Equal Pay Act, minimum working hours, protection of the employment rights of pregnant women and their right to work after child birth, health and safety legislation, protection against unfair dismissal and many others. Moreover, a range of anti-discrimination measures have been introduced over time to protect minorities, women and other groups.

As has been noted above, the European Community has been very active in introducing employment-related legislation and regulations that have a binding effect on all member states. These measures include directives imposing extra obligations upon employers to provide safe working environments for their employees, protecting employment benefits accrued with previous employers when staff are transferred from one employer to another in certain circumstances and imposing maximum weekly working hours on certain types of employee. The human rights legislation introduced into the UK during the course of 2000 enhances, *inter alia*, employees' protection against harassment and discrimination at the workplace.

Most employers in the UK are required to insure their legal liabilities for injuries sustained by employees at work under the terms of the Employers Liability (Compulsory Insurance) Law 1972. In 1999 the minimum limit of cover per occurrence required by this legislation was increased from £2 million to £5 million. While local authorities and many other forms of public bodies are exempt from conforming to the requirements of this legislation most buy some form of insurance protection.

In recent years the boundaries of injury and illness for which employers can be held to be liable have been subjected to legal challenge. It is now accepted that the duty of an employer in taking reasonable care for the safety of their employees can in certain circumstances include the providing employees with proper support if they show signs of suffering stress at work. Equally, employers can become liable if in the course of an employee's duties he or she is exposed to circumstances that give rise to post-traumatic stress disorder. The continual testing of the boundaries of an employer's duty of care towards its employees creates considerable risk and uncertainty in the management of employment-related exposures.

## Agency liability

In light of the increasing reliance on private or non-profit providers of public services, a word about the area of law pertaining to agency relationships is appropriate.

Principal–agent relationships abound in the public sector. Certainly, public sector managers act as agents of the body that employs them, and the general rule is that – while in the performance of their duties – employees and the body are the same. Knowledge of the employee is knowledge of the organisation, an employee's acts are the organisation's acts, and so on.

The principal–agent relationship is problematic within the organisation, but there is a degree of control present due to the nature of reporting relationships and natural oversight that occurs. However, a degree of control separation occurs when activities are outsourced and when the day-to-day supervision of agents is not possible. An agent providing outsourced services is still an agent, and the principal is under the same legal expectations.

In truth, the concept of agency liability offers one of the key conundrums faced by public sector risk managers today. Privatisation or outsourcing of public services may make considerable sense in a broad economic context, but for the risk manager it means that the organisation retains ultimate responsibility for the activity, but has loosened its ability to control the activity itself. In principle, outsourcing is likely to make the management of risk even more difficult than it already is (this subject is discussed more thoroughly in Chapter 10).

## Motor vehicle liability

Despite the positive recommendation of the Pearson Commission in 1978 for the adoption of a no-fault compensation scheme in relation to injuries sustained as a result of a motor accident, in general in the UK the rules of ordinary negligence apply in cases involving motor vehicles. If a council employee negligently causes harm to another person, that person may sue the council, and will prevail if the tests of negligence are met.

Most owners of motor vehicles are required by law to insure their legal liabilities arising from their use of a motor vehicle. While public authorities are technically exempt from conforming with the requirements of this legislation, most buy some form of insurance protection.

## Social services and education liability

The latest reorganisation of local government in the UK effected between 1995 and 1998 has created more local authorities with responsibility for the provision of social services and education. Both areas of responsibility have and continue to produce significant risk exposures for the public sector risk manager.

The abuse, physical sexual and mental, of inmates of council-run social service establishments has been an increasing and distasteful tale over the last fifteen or so years. The greater openness in bringing such cases to light is to be welcomed. However, from a public sector risk manager's standpoint, the fact that the victims are often minors and that the perpetrators are often clever at covering up their activities means that many years pass before these exposures become apparent.

Section 47 of the Children Act 1989 imposes duties on local authorities to investigate cases where children are thought to be at risk and, where appropriate, to provide protection to children perceived to be in danger. The care in the community legislation has devolved responsibility for the care of certain categories of vulnerable people from central to local government. By their very nature these individuals, who are minors, elderly and mentally unstable, present very real and uncertain risk exposures to the receiving authority.

The provision of educational services has become a growing and fruitful area for emerging legal liability exposures. Individuals' growing awareness of their rights, their heightening sense of expectation, their increasing litigiousness and central government's campaign to improve the quality of education delivery by developing national benchmarks have all served to bring to a sharp focus an education authority's obligations to its student population. An authority's failure to recognize a pupil's special educational needs, its failure to provide an appropriate standard of education and its failure to protect a pupil from bullying by other students have all been recent claims made against education authorities. This trend is likely to continue.

# Moral responsibility

We often hear public officials justify an unsavoury action or decision by noting that no laws were broken. While it always is wise to avoid breaking the law, the statement carries with it a whiff of impropriety. We would hope that human behaviour is not governed solely by the standards of the courts. Other standards of conduct prevail in public matters, and it is important for risk managers to recognise that the ethical domain is an exposure area for public organisations.

Following the format discussed in this chapter and Chapter 5, the moral responsibility exposure should be defined (identified and assessed) and measured. The difficulty for risk managers is that standards of ethical behaviour are not fully agreed upon in a democratic society. This is not to say that people do not believe in absolute or nearly absolute standards of behaviour – it is only to say that government has chosen to tread carefully in imposing a single standard of morality on society. How would we come to consensus on that standard? Who would enforce it? What would the consequences be?

This does not mean, however, that risk managers cannot think about the exposure area and cannot incorporate analysis into overall risk assessment efforts. At the very least, a risk manager should consider the moral dimensions of particular considerations and articulate the implications of being deemed 'wrong' in some action. For instance, a government decision to build a road extension through a neighbourhood should incorporate recognition of the ethical dimension of relocating home owners as well as recognition of the consequences of that decision.

This illustration does, however, suggest the difficulty in measuring the exposure to moral risk. Unless one is privileged to gaze upon the 'heavenly ledger', it is impossible to gauge the impact. On a more temporal plane, surrogate values might occasionally be appropriate. For instance, loss of political support can sometimes be measured fairly precisely, and sometimes can be linked to ethical performance. While this line of reasoning can be every bit as troubling as the 'we didn't break any laws' defence (e.g., the voters do not mind, so why should we?), it does show that there are ways to think about the impact of ethical risks on individuals and organisations.

In many respects, risk management is all about consequences. If a public body does something, intended or unintended outcomes may occur. Some of the consequences naturally will be moral and ethical and they may weigh as heavily on the local government as does damage to property or a threatened liability suit. This means that risk managers must be conscious of their role in assessing moral risks and taking measures to manage them. Perhaps another way of putting it is to say that risk managers serve the role of the chorus in a Greek tragedy, reminding fellow managers of the consequences of their actions, the fickleness of fortune and of human fallibility.

# APPLICATIONS

## *Ultra vires* and indemnities to employees

### The concept of ultra vires

*Ultra vires* is a fundamental concept in local authority law in the UK, determining the basic ability of local government to act and its powers and responsibilities. Local authorities are created by statute and have no existence outside the statutes that created them. Consequently, they draw their powers and responsibilities from these statutes and the statutes clearly delineate the extent of their powers and responsibilities.

Much case law relating to the concept of *ultra vires* originated from the nineteenth century and many concern railway companies, who, like local authorities, were also creatures of statute. The nineteenth century saw the development of the railways in the UK and, as more dynamic and entrepreneurial organisations than their Victorian municipal counterparts, the railway companies tested more often the boundaries of what was permissible and what was not.

The landmark case was *Attorney General* v. *Great Eastern Railway* (1880), (5)App Cas 473 HL(E), where it was held that the *ultra vires* doctrine had to be applied reasonably so as to permit whatever is fairly incidental to the specific powers authorised by the creating statute. This view of *ultra vires* was echoed in Section 111 of the Local Government Act 1972 which states that local authorities may do anything calculated to facilitate or that is conducive or incidental to the discharge of any local authority function.

### The redefinition of ultra vires

Over the last decade there has been a narrowing of the view of what is *intra vires*. In particular, the ruling in *Hazell* v. *Hammersmith and Fulham LBC* (1991) 2WLR 372, demonstrated the strictness of the interpretation and the consequences of acting *ultra vires*. In the famous interest rate swaps case (see Chapter 5's 'Read More About It' section for a fuller discussion) the House of Lords ruled that the swaps were not conducive to or incidental to the local authority's ability to borrow, were consequently outside the scope of Section 111 of the Local Government Act 1972 and so *ultra vires*. As the swap deals were *ultra vires*, they were void and unenforceable.

*Credit Suisse* v. *The Borough Council of Allerdale* (1996) 3WLR 894, was another important case. The council set up a company to carry out recreational developments in order to circumvent certain restrictions imposed by central government on local authority spending and borrowing. The company borrowed monies from Credit Suisse and the council provided guarantees that the bank sought to enforce when the company encountered financial difficulties.

It was held by the courts that the deal was *ultra vires* on two counts, namely that the council did not have the power to guarantee the borrowings of a separate entity and, as the objective was to avoid government controls, that in itself was unlawful. The guarantee, consequently, was unenforceable.

## The position of indemnities to employees in circumstances which are ultra vires

Over the last twenty years it has been normal for the employment contract that local authorities provide to their employees to contain an indemnity to protect an employee in the event of that employee assuming any personal liability from activities carried out on behalf of or at the request of the authority. Until the *Burgoine* v *Waltham Forest LBC* case in 1996 it was generally assumed that the contractual indemnity held good in all circumstances.

Waltham Forest entered into a joint venture with a private sector company to run a leisure centre. The company borrowed monies from financial institutions using a guarantee from the council. Burgoine and Cook, two employees of Waltham Forest, were directors of the joint venture company. The company encountered financial difficulties and the banks sought to enforce the guarantees. Following the Allerdale decision it was agreed that the guarantee provided was *ultra vires* and, therefore, unenforceable. The liquidators sought to recover losses resulting from the wrongful trading directly from the directors who in turn sought to rely upon the indemnities provided by their employer. The court took the view that everything stemming from an *ultra vires* act was null and void and, consequently, the indemnity could not be relied upon.

An incident in South Herefordshire, reported in the *Local Government Chronicle*, further eroded confidence in the value of the indemnity. The Director of Finance was one of a number of council appointed representatives who sat on a charitable trust. The trust was involved in legal proceedings concerning some employment related issues and ended up having to pay substantial legal fees. The council had purported to give an indemnity to its representatives in respect of any personal liabilities they may incur in respect of such expenditure but the District Auditor ruled that such an indemnity was unlawful.

## The implications of the rulings

The consequences of the rulings have been significant, particularly for employees of local authorities who by dint of their position with the council serve on the boards and committees of organisations external to the authority. It appears that where an authority has acted *ultra vires* the employees are not protected by any indemnity offered within their contract of employment.

The remedies available to employees participating on outside bodies are to ensure that the body has its own directors' and officers' cover, or to effect cover to protect their own personal liabilities or to withdraw from participation in the organisation. The latter course of action would, of course, be regrettable from a community and public relations standpoint.

---

# TOOLS YOU CAN USE

## A quick guide to the Woolf reforms

The Woolf reforms were introduced into the English legal system on 26 April 1999 with the express intention of reducing the cost of litigating and speeding up the process. Given that in the majority of cases public bodies will be taking the role of defender rather than claimant the following notes highlight the implications of the reforms from a defendant's perspective.

### Pre-action protocols

The pre-action protocols are intended to apply in respect of all claims involving personal injury and involve a set of actions to be completed within a set timetable, as follows:

1    The claimant must send a letter of claim before commencing action. For the first time the claimant must detail at the outset what allegations are being made, provide adequate details of the location of the accident so that an investigation can be carried out and give details of any injury sustained and an estimate of any financial loss incurred.
2    The defendant must reply within twenty-one days identifying any insurer if applicable.
3    The defendant will have a maximum of three months from the date of acknowledgement of the initial letter to investigate the matter and state whether liability is denied.

4    If liability has been denied, the defendant must enclose with the letter of reply any documents in their possession which are clearly relevant to the subject of the claim. Certain documents have been identified as being required in published Standard Disclosure Lists for certain types of cases.

5    Before either party appoints an expert to assist with the claim they should give a list of names to the other side who, in turn, has fourteen days in which to register any objection. If the parties to the dispute cannot agree on experts, they can both, separately, appoint their own. However, if the second party does not register an objection to an expert, they cannot subsequently rely upon their own expert witnesses. Where an expert has been agreed upon, either party can send them written questions.

6    The claimant must disclose medical records.

## Penalties for failure to follow the protocols

If there has been a failure to comply with the protocol the court may order a party to pay a sum of money into court. Moreover, the court should, in exercising its discretion over the allowance of costs, consider whether the parties have followed the pre-action protocols. If costs have been incurred because the protocols have not been followed, the party failing to follow the protocols will be liable for the costs, probably on an indemnity basis. Additionally, if evidence is not adduced during the protocol stage, it will normally be excluded from any subsequent defence.

## Fast-track

Personal injury and housing disrepair claims valued between £1000 and £15 000 and non-personal injury claims valued between £5000 and £15 000 will be allocated to the fast-track system. Claims with a valuation greater than these bands will be allocated to the multi-track system.

   Below is a typical timetable applicable to the fast-track system, although it may vary from case to case:

1    File Acknowledgement of Service within fourteen days of service of Particulars of Claim.

2    Defence is due fourteen days after service of Particulars of Claim unless an Acknowledgement of Service has been filed, in which case defence is due within twenty-eight days.

3    A twenty-eight day extension of the time for service of Defence may be agreed between the parties. Any further extension requires the permission of the court.

4    Where a defence has been filed, the court will issue an alloca-
     tion questionnaire to both parties who have fourteen days from
     service to respond.
5    Following responses to the allocation questionnaire the court
     will issue a notice of allocation and may issue directions.
6    Disclosure of documents is to take place within four weeks of
     notice of allocation.
7    Witness statements are to be exchanged within ten weeks of
     notice of allocation.
8    Experts' reports are to be exchanged within fourteen weeks of
     notice of allocation
9    The court issues a listing questionnaire within twenty weeks
     of notice of allocation.
10   The completed listing questionnaire is filed within twenty-two
     weeks of notice of allocation.
11   Hearing occurs within thirty weeks of notice of allocation.

## Multi-track

This is basically a continuation of the existing system although the
courts will exercise greater control over case management conferences to accelerate the litigation process.

## Offers to settle

Under the Woolf reforms a claimant may now make an offer to settle
at a given sum and the defendant has twenty-one days in which to
respond to such an offer. If the offer to settle is rejected, the case
subsequently goes to trial and the claimant is awarded more than
the original offer to settle, the court may order interest to be applied
at 10 per cent above the base rate on the sum awarded, order costs
on an indemnity basis or order interest to be applied at 10 per cent
above the base rate on the costs.

The defendant can also make an offer to settle. If this is done
before proceedings are issued, the amount offered must be paid into
court within fourteen days of service of the claim form.

## Defence

If the defendant denies an allegation, the reasons for so doing must
be stated. If the defendant intends to offer an alternative version of
events, they must state this. If they fail to do this, the court can
strike out the defence on their own initiative or on the application
of the claimant.

# Disclosure

There is a requirement to disclose all documents upon which reliance is placed, which affect adversely either party's case or support either party's case. In addition there is a duty to search but it must be reasonable. In determining reasonableness the factors that will be taken into consideration will include the number of documents involved, the nature and complexity of the proceedings, the ease and expense of retrieval and the significance of the documents. The List of Documents must include a disclosure statement identifying the documents searched for and a statement of the documents not searched for signed by an appropriate person. If a statement is signed without an honest belief, proceedings for contempt of court can be brought. These revised disclosure procedures mean that claimants need to be clear in their specification of the types and categories of documentation to be searched for. If there is a failure to give disclosure or produce witness statements in time, a court will probably:

- strike out the defence or
- order that the defendant cannot rely on that evidence at trial.

## Statements of truth

All statements of the case, the defence, witness statements, experts' opinions, responses to requests for further information and any application where the applicant wishes to rely on matters set out in the application must contain a statement of truth to the effect that facts stated in the document are true. Proceedings may be brought for contempt if a statement of truth is made in the absence of honest belief.

## Implications of the Woolf reforms for public bodies

The intention of the Woolf reforms is to reduce the costs of and accelerate the litigation process and, to an extent, the initiative rests with the claimant. In order to be in a position to offer the best possible defence and be compliant with the fast-track timetable, where it applies, public bodies must be able to:

- identify and retrieve all documents named in the pre-action protocols, and other discoverable documents, well before proceedings are issued

- identify witnesses and take witness statements before proceedings are issued
- take an early view on liability to reduce costs and to make and respond to offers of settlement
- call upon reliable experts quickly
- identify when to object to an expert and the sort of standard questions to put to an agreed expert.

---

# READ MORE ABOUT IT

## Managing litigation: a brief introduction

Chapter 4 makes a brief allusion to the concept of litigation management as a type of risk reduction tool. In that context, litigation management was meant to conjure up the notion of measures that would minimise the extent of damages that an existing loss event might impose on a public body.

While litigation management is a loss reduction technique, it is a sufficiently complex and advanced subject that this book would be doing readers a disservice by failing to develop further the explanation of litigation management.

### Litigation management: what is it?

Managers often are tempted to conclude that litigation is something far beyond their control, and it is true that the technical complexities of the law are difficult to fathom without the assistance of competent legal counsel. However, there is much about a legal case that is within the control of the organisation, and it is the systematic and planned measures to exert that control that are the basis for litigation management.

In a sense, litigation management is two different but related things. It is the organised philosophy and plan a public body might develop as a type of strategy for a particular case or cases. (What are our objectives? When might we settle?) Litigation management also includes the means by which a public body manages its relationship with its legal counsel. Often, this latter concern is of minor importance when legal counsel is in-house, but frequently the services of outside law firms are retained, so the matter can be of great importance.

### What are the elements of litigation management?

There are four major elements that constitute a basic litigation management plan.

## Development of a litigation management philosophy

Although the philosophy a public body might adopt could evolve over time, in an introductory discussion it is useful to highlight the importance of litigation management's broader strategic dimensions. An organisation's litigation persona is one of the faces by which it reveals itself to the world. Care should be given in recognising that a logical and consistent philosophy not only provides guidance to counsel and to managers, but it also sends a signal to the community. For instance, there may be a range of circumstances and a range of reasons for a local authority to establish a highly aggressive stance towards litigation, as it may warn off less serious claims and it may signal to the broader community the authority's seriousness in safeguarding public assets. Equally, there may be certain situations where a more open and charitable approach might be appropriate.

## Establishment of written procedures and policies

Flowing from an overall philosophy, actual policies and procedures should help provide a degree of practical consistency across all legal cases a public body encounters. Among the many things that such statements should include are:

- who is responsible for litigation management
- steps to be taken when a lawsuit is served
- process by which legal counsel is selected
- who manages legal counsel (especially if outside) and how those services are evaluated
- a reporting format for providing information on a case's progress
- who is responsible for gathering information and co-ordinating with legal counsel
- who is authorised to make policy decisions and to settle cases
- who is responsible for carrying out remedial actions that may be the result of a legal case.

## Creation of a process for the selection of legal counsel

The previous paragraph indicates that the selection of counsel should be subject to set policies and procedures. Among the types of information a public body would wish to gather about a potential counsel are:

- qualifications and experience of lawyers, especially litigators
- areas of expertise represented by the law firm
- local, regional, and national reputation, where relevant

- availability of the lawyers
- personality of the lawyers
- fees, expenses, and costs
- other resources or services offered by the law firm
- location and accessibility
- intangibles or other specific issues.

Part of the process involved in retaining counsel is to communicate clearly the philosophy and policies the public body has established and to be clear that the law firm can work within those parameters.

With respect to specific cases that arise over time, the actual litigation management philosophy and process will be discussed at the commencement of legal actions, with attention paid to the strategy of the case in hand, staffing, billing procedures and expectations regarding reporting and communications.

## Articulation of the specific risk management role in litigation management

Within the context of risk management, a litigation management plan will have to address the specific duties that fall to the risk manager (or whomever assumes the general role of a risk manager).

Naturally, an effective risk manager might be the key interface between the organisation and outside counsel, though often they are one of a team that is responsible for overseeing litigation. The risk manager's general technical knowledge may be useful from a strategic or tactical sense, but there are certain areas where specialised knowledge is likely to be particularly relevant. One is in the area of insurance expertise, especially with respect to coverage issues but also in situations where the insurance company provides (under the terms of the insurance policy) the legal counsel for the case. A second area of importance is in the development of the legal defence, especially with respect to organising information regarding the loss event and measures that may have been taken to prevent or respond to such an event. After a legal action is closed, mandated remediation or even common sensical remediation may need to be undertaken to prevent future similar cases, and risk managers are well-positioned to assume such responsibilities.

# 7

# *Risk-financing principles*

## EXECUTIVE SUMMARY

The second broad area of risk management action is risk-financing. Risk-financing involves measures to finance the cost of loss, of risk and of uncertainty. Historically, risk-financing virtually has been synonymous with buying insurance. Over time alternatives to insurance have evolved – self-insurance, pools, large deductible programmes, finite insurance programmes, banking arrangements and capital-market based solutions. The concept of risk-financing has extended to include products that address a range of financial risks like interest rate and credit risk. These products include derivatives and some new and innovative securities.

The rapid evolution of the risk-financing market has created a number of practical problems today. Notably, regulatory and legal structures have not kept pace with change, and this has resulted in a great deal of confusion about risk-financing products. Many products look and perform in an almost identical manner with others, and yet history and custom have dictated very different treatments by regulators, taxing authorities and others. There is growing pressure for significant legal and regulatory adjustment to occur.

For newcomers to the topic, risk-financing measures might be thought of as existing on a continuum, ranging from pure retention (all losses are paid directly out of pocket) to pure transfer (where a third party accepts and bears fully the costs of risk). A key insight of the risk-financing continuum is that no products are fully retention or transfer, but rather a varying blend of the two approaches. Hedging of risk, for example, is a near perfect blending of a retention and a transfer of risk.

# PRINCIPLES AND CONCEPTS

Risk imposes costs (and benefits) on organisations. As Chapter 1 suggests, those costs come in two broad forms – loss costs and the costs of uncertainty. The concept of risk-financing refers to those measures and methods taken to finance the costs of risk.

Chapters 7, 8 and 9 provide an introduction to risk-financing in the public sector. This chapter focuses on the development of an overall framework for understanding the array of financing mechanisms now available. Key terms and concepts like insurance, self-insurance and pooling are defined and compared, as are emerging methods for handling financial risks. General goals and objectives of risk-financing also are discussed.

Chapters 8 and 9 provide an in-depth presentation of insurance (Chapter 8) and intergovernmental pooling (Chapter 9). Each of these financing tools has technical, legal, and institutional aspects that must be explained and developed separately.

## Risk-financing defined

As noted above, risk-financing is defined as measures and methods taken to finance the cost of risk. While this definition is adopted by this book, it is worth noting that this view is not without controversy.

Historically, the concept of risk-financing has been influenced by insurance, which in turn is viewed as a mechanism associated with financing losses. Therefore, most traditional definitions of risk-financing have focused on measures that directly relate to paying losses.

Paying losses is an important risk-financing purpose, but financing arrangements also exist to address the costs of uncertainty. Ironically, insurance serves as an example here too, inasmuch as insurance premiums are paid whether there are losses or not. In the absence of uncertainty about the future, these financing arrangements would not be necessary. However, extending the definition of risk-financing to include costs of uncertainty forces us to consider that risk-financing includes expenditures for safety programmes and equipment, risk management information systems, research, consulting services and the risk manager's salary.

Further, the importance of the extended view of risk-financing is that the financing of the cost of uncertainty measures is intertwined with the loss-financing measures. In a straightforward example, the hiring of a risk manager might be seen as ultimately related to the cost of loss-financing because an effective risk manager will drive down loss costs. In a strategic sense, these two expenditures cannot be evaluated independently. Some insurance companies are recognizing this and are directing part of the premium to those insured specifically to finance broader risk management costs (e.g., development of safety manuals, purchase of safety equipment, purchase of training programmes).

Additionally, the method of financing risk influences the signals sent to those who might control the risk. Incentive programmes, for example, can influence safety behaviour. By realising the relationships between the risks and all costs associated with those risks, an organisation can begin to approach risk-financing in a co-ordinated fashion, the result being greater financing efficiency, greater risk communication and signalling, and stronger links between risk control and financing.

Finally, we should note in passing that while – in a very loose sense – all financial arrangements might warrant the label 'risk-financing', it probably does not advance our understanding to apply the term that way. Certainly, acquiring a blue chip stock (and thereby being exposed to a speculative risk) could be construed as risk-financing inasmuch as the financial commitment to that risk could produce a positive return. However, there is a usefulness in maintaining some distinction between making investment decisions and making decisions that focus on financing the mainly 'downside' dimension of pure and speculative risks. Readers should note, though, that limiting the use of the term 'risk-financing' does not mean that investment decisions are not part of an organisation's risk *management* efforts.

Since there are core technical aspects of risk-financing, readers should be clear that the following discussion focuses mainly on measures that are both loss-financing and uncertainty-reducing. Thus, scant attention is paid to the financing of risk assessment, control, and administration efforts – they are risk-financing concerns, to be sure, but require little additional explanation.

## The risk-financing grid

Traditionally, risk-financing has been subdivided into two categories: insurance and not insurance. And, despite the revolutionary changes that have occurred in the past twenty years, that distinction still influences the thinking of many managers and regulators.

The mismatch between historical categories and current practices creates confusion and limits the chance of grasping admittedly complex topics. Additionally, the mismatch creates very practical problems in matters like regulation of financing products and financial analysis of alternatives. A reoriented approach to discussing risk-financing is necessary.

For the purposes of this book, readers might organise their thinking about risk-financing by first imagining how a public body might pay for risks. The answers have two dimensions – how financing occurs and when financing occurs.

## How financing occurs

Intuitively, one might view this dimension as straightforward; either an organisation finances risks directly or it gets some other party to finance risk. And, in fact, those methods represent two core financing strategies – risk retention and risk transfer.

Risk retention refers to methods of self-financing. The risk is borne by the organisation and if risk-related costs arise, the organisation directly bears those costs. The various ways in which this happens are discussed shortly.

Risk transfer refers to methods of transferring the cost of risk (or more properly, the direct responsibility for bearing the risk) from one party to a non-related party. Insurance serves the purpose of illustrating risk transfer. Through the purchase of insurance, a public body has transferred the cost of the risk of, say, fires to an insurance company.

For newcomers to the subject of risk management, the distinction between transfer and retention can create confusion. In an important sense, risk is not being transferred in an insurance contract. Certainly the actual risk of a fire still resides with the organisation; only the economic impact is being transferred. Further, as Chapter 8 shows, the pricing of insurance is undertaken in such a way that over time an insured is paying for all its losses (and that is because the premium is based on a calculation of average expected losses). What, therefore, is actually being transferred is the timing risk associated with the fire. In other words, most conventional risk transfer vehicles are structured to facilitate a smoothing process whereby the insured is protected from the risk of not having sufficient resources at the time a loss occurs. In facilitating that arrangement, however, the insurance company is requiring the insured to make payments over time that will – on average – ultimately equal and exceed the cost of benefits paid out.

An important feature of the retention/transfer concepts has been suggested indirectly by the previous paragraph – they are neither discrete methods nor are they absolutes. Rather, measures to finance risk involve varying degrees of retention and transfer. No single approach to financing is either completely one or the other.

Later in this chapter when the subject of financial risk management is presented, the concept of neutralisation is raised as a third financing method. Neutralisation involves the hedging of risk, which is effected by offsetting one risk with another. In a sense, insurance is a type of hedge in that an insured possesses a risk of loss (e.g., a fire to a building) and a possible gain (e.g., the proceeds from a fire insurance policy) that offset one another. While this observation is only roughly true, the notion of insurance as a type of hedge provides a useful insight here, which is that neutralisation is a financing strategy that is both retention and transfer.

The advent of sophisticated tools for hedging financial risks (e.g., derivatives) has heightened attention to the hedging phenomenon, and it is true that the technical complexity of these products has spawned an area of financial risk management all of its own. From an ORM perspective this is all to the good, because the control of such things as interest rate, currency exchange, credit and price risks is critical to effective management. However, it also should be noted that financial risk management is not a separate (or even superior) matter to organisation risk management. It is a part of an overall approach to managing an organisation's risk and, despite technical complexity, involves fairly conventional notions regarding risk and its management.

## When financing occurs

The second dimension relates to the timing of the financing approach. The financing of risks could occur before, during or after resources are needed. More formally, certain financing tools are prospective and involve arrangements to accumulate resources in advance of a particular need. Other tools are contemporaneous, meaning the financing of a risk occurs as the resources are needed. Yet other tools are retrospective in the sense that they are structured to provide financing after events have occurred giving rise to a need for resources (see Exhibit 7.1).

The risk-financing grid in Exhibit 7.1 provides a useful method for organising thinking about risk-financing tools and techniques. Risk-financing tools can be categorised as to who is paying directly for the risk (and how) and when the financing occurs. Later, this chapter shows various tools that might fit into the various cells of the grid, but an important caveat should be offered here. The cells in the grid are inserted for instructive purposes, but really the axes of the grid are continuous and not discrete. As a consequence the cell walls are not firm. The various tools and techniques might fall anywhere along either axis and are not confined by the boundaries of the grid cells.

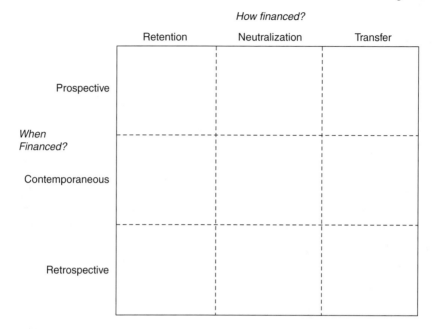

**Exhibit 7.1** The risk-financing grid

# The retention/transfer demarcation line

While it is true that no tool or technique is solely transfer or retention – at least not conceptually – readers reasonably should wonder
what distinguishes retention from transfer measures. In other words,
what are the characteristic differences by which one technique is
construed as transferring a risk, while another is seen as a retention measure? The question is more relevant than might be thought,
as it bears on a host of legal and regulatory concerns that plague
risk management today.

   Previously in this chapter, transfer was distinguished from retention by noting that an unrelated party assumes responsibility for
the timing and economic consequences of a risk. But what makes
a transfer a transfer? Insurance law and regulation provide an
important insight here. Among other characteristics that define
an insurance contract as a risk transfer are:

• the legal validity of the contract
• the nature of the consideration of the parties
• the pooling of risks and resources.

The first point is self-explanatory. A risk transfer agreement, both
practically and conceptually, must meet the test of legality and

validity. This means that it must serve a legal purpose, that the parties must be legally competent to enter into the agreement, that there must be an identifiable offer and acceptance and that each party must give some consideration. A key feature of valid risk transfer contracts is the degree of separation between transferor and transferee. Considerable litigation has occurred over the question of what constitutes parties to a transfer agreement. For instance, imagine two companies owned by a holding company. Is transfer of risk from one of those companies to the other a legal transfer? In general, the courts have concluded no. A legally valid risk transfer contract must involve non-related parties. If the risk does not escape the corporate family, the risk is not transferred.

The nature of the consideration given by each party is significant in the case of insurance, particularly, and in risk transference generally. The transferor of risk is generally expected to make an economic commitment to pay for the benefits of transfer. The transferee (acceptor of risk) offers consideration in the form of an aleatory and conditional promise – that is, a promise to perform (e.g., pay a claim), conditional on some further chance event such as a loss.

The third feature, the presence of pooling, is important in the history of insurance law and regulation but is a criterion that is under some pressure today. Traditionally, pooling referred to the notion of a risk bearer (insurer) accepting many similar risks and pooling those risks together to accumulate funds sufficient to cover expected claims as well as fluctuations from expected levels of claims. The mathematical notion behind pooling is the law of large numbers, which essentially establishes that the claims experience of an accumulating pool of risks becomes more stable and predictable as it grows.

Recently, some revision in thinking has been made regarding what is actually happening as a pool of risks grows. While historically the view has been that it is the actual accumulation of risks that leads to stabilisation, a current proposal suggests that it is the accumulation of funds – not risks – that is the logic behind pooling. Put plainly, as a pool obtains more and more funds, the funds accumulate to a level where they are not only adequate to meet expected payments; they also overwhelm the most probable variations that might occur.

For the uninitiated reader this may appear to be a purely academic matter, but this changing view has very important implications. Traditionally, risk transference was closely associated with insurance and this meant that the distinction between retention and transfer could be (and was) based on evidence of a pool of risks. Is a risk-accepting party offering a similar arrangement to many other parties and are those accepted risks being pooled together for financial purposes? The newer way of looking at transference requires only that a pool of resources be available to cover the promises made under the contract. In other words, it is the ability to financially bear the risk that matters, more so than the presence of other similarly constituted risks.

As Chapter 8 discusses, regulation of insurance companies is based on the notion that insurers have special obligations worthy of separate oversight. This chapter is asserting that transference is transference, whether it is a traditional insurer selling standardised coverages to hundreds of public bodies or a bank offering a one-off risk transference arrangement to a single customer. All risk transference arrangements – under this line of reasoning – should be regulated, if at all, under a common structure.

That consistent regulation presently is not the case is evident to anyone examining the world of risk-financing. Many of the products discussed later in this chapter will appear to be indistinguishable from one another, but they are treated differently from a tax, legal and regulatory perspective because some fit the traditional test of insurance and some do not.

## Risk-financing methods in overview

In a sense, the risk-financing matrix is an open field and the combinations of transference/retention and prospective/contemporaneous/retrospective characteristics are limitless. However, for introductory purposes, it may be useful to characterise a set of alternatives that will represent the distinctions that exist between the prototypical approaches to financing. The grid shown in Exhibit 7.2 offers a possible placement of the tools, most of which are discussed below.

### Transfers

Perhaps the best starting point for visualising the nature of risk transfers is traditional insurance arrangements. Conventionally, insurance companies issue contracts that meet the legal tests of risk transfer. Further, these contracts meet the less tangible criteria one might expect to see. In exchange for the premium paid, the insured is confident that a risk is fully and completely covered. When a claim occurs, the loss is fully restored.

Within conventional insurance coverages, however, the degree of transfer will vary, and this is due to the pricing approach employed and the degree to which the contract represents a reduction in uncertainty as well as risk. Perhaps the best way to illustrate this

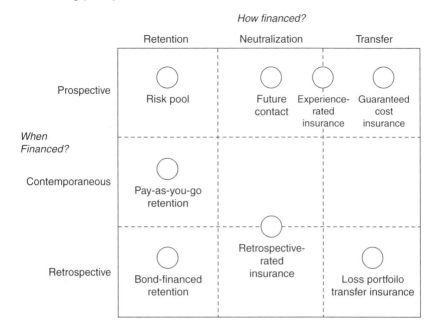

**Exhibit 7.2** Example of a risk-financing grid (one possible placement of financing tools)

is to draw the distinctions between guaranteed cost insurance, experience-rated insurance, and retrospective-rated insurance.

## Guaranteed cost insurance

Most insurance sold is priced based on a classification rating scheme, which means that the insurer develops risk groupings and computes the average expected losses for such groupings – which in turn serves as the basis for the premium. Additionally, that premium is guaranteed, meaning it cannot be adjusted to reflect the actual loss experience during the coverage period.

So, for instance, an individual buying motor insurance will pay a premium based on the average expected losses of people like that individual (e.g., twenty-one to twenty-four year-old men, living in rural areas, driving a certain kind of vehicle for business only). The rate does not specifically correspond to the individual, and indeed it cannot. A single person cannot provide an insurer with sufficient driving history to enable that insurer to develop an individualised rate.

Classification rating, which serves as the principal rating method for personal lines insurance (motor, house and contents, individual life and health insurance) as well as for small businesses and organisations, differs fundamentally from the rating approaches discussed below, and it is important to underscore that difference. All other rating methods are based (at least in part) on the actual experience of the insured, whereas classification rating is not. Therefore, the earlier discussion that, over time, policyholders pay for their own losses really only directly applies to rating schemes other than classification rating. Certainly, an individual house owner might discover that claim payments roughly correspond to the premiums paid, but this is a very rare circumstance. House owners will mainly pay premiums and never suffer losses. Occasionally, a house owner will receive far more in benefits than has been paid in premiums, but this also is not common.

Thus, when discussing the role of classification-rated insurance, it probably is more appropriate to say that the principal benefit being purchased is uncertainty reduction (no matter how rarely losses occur, the insured is certain that benefits will be paid). Indeed, it is the diminishing role of uncertainty reduction in the following rating schemes that signals the movement towards retention.

## Experience-rated insurance

Organisations that are large enough to produce a consistent volume of claims typically are subjected to a form of rating known as experience rating. This means that the organisation's own loss experience is used, at least in part, to develop the premium that is paid. The degree of statistical credibility assigned to the loss experience will vary depending on the amount and quality of the data, but the key feature here is that a direct link is established between the actual risk and losses and the amount paid. This feature, in turn, evokes the concept of control, meaning that efforts expended to prevent or reduce losses will translate more or less directly into the ultimate cost of risk-financing. The degree of correspondence between risk and rate is positively correlated with a move away from transference. Increasingly, the insured is paying its own losses. However, because the experience-rating approach factors in other loss data from similar organisations, it still is a transfer and still provides benefit against timing risk and against uncertainty.

## Retrospective-rated insurance

For very large organisations, with highly credible loss data, insurers may employ a third form of rating. Retrospective- or retro-rating is based on an insured's own current loss experience. In the sense that it is the insured's loss experience only that sets the price, transference is low. The fact that it is based on current losses means that the timing risk transference also is low. Certain transference protections remain, but while this is legally viewed as an insurance agreement, it does not present much evidence of transference.

The preceding discussion demonstrates that one factor that moves transference arrangements towards a retention posture is the relationship between the actual risk and the amount financed. The discussion also implies that the movement from transference to retention does not precisely correspond with the temporal distinctions between insurance and retention.

Other risk-financing characteristics are evident in the preceding discussion. Notably, the timing of the financing mechanism can vary. Guaranteed cost insurances tend to be paid for proactively, as are experience rated coverages. Retrospective coverages, naturally, are retrospectively financed (to a significant degree, anyway). Some types of contemporaneous financing also may be seen in certain products.

The introduction of features like deductibles, co-payments, or other cost-sharing provisions can further shift a classic transference contract towards retention, as can the limits of coverage in the contract. If the exposure to loss is £1 million, but the coverage limit is £100 000, much of the risk is retained.

The financial solidity of the insurer would also be a dimension of the transference. For instance, a complete coverage of some risk under a guaranteed cost plan might pass the basic test of transference, but if the insurer is of dubious financial quality, the degree of transference must be questioned.

## Neutralisation

The risk-financing grid suggests an environment where risk neutralisation serves as an intermediate point between retention and transfer. This is not an uncontroversial view. Some observers would argue that neutralisation is the 'third point' of a risk-financing triangle – that is, neutralisation is something distinctly different from the other two risk-financing methods.

In a sense, the model we accept is less important than is an appreciation of the basics that underlie the neutralisation concept:

1   Neutralisation is defined as a financial method for offsetting risks principally through taking opposite positions on a given risk.
2   In a perfect neutralisation arrangement, the pre- and post-event financial position of the party exposed to the risk is unchanged.
3   The risk itself is not treated directly and so the exposure is retained; however, the use of financial instruments allows

aspects of the risk to be transferred to a counter-party or distributed into financial markets. In this sense neutralisation is both 'transfer' and 'retention'.

4    Instruments that are used to neutralise risks can also be used to speculate on risks.

Risk neutralisation serves an intermediate role (between retention and transfer, that is) in another way as well, which is that it allows risk managers to address a range of risks that are not traditionally insurable, but are not risks on which an organisation may wish to speculate. Those risks are speculative in the Chapter 1 sense of the word, but they are not risks that are directly related to the central purposes of the organization. For example, fuel oil prices are a key input cost for local authorities, and the fluctuations in oil prices present a real speculative risk. However, betting on fuel oil price swings is not (or should not be) a concern for most local authorities as they are not in the commodity investments business. The authority's main concern should be to neutralise the impact of price changes – that is, to make the input cost more predictable.

Alternatively, there are risks that a local authority may willingly undertake (building a leisure centre) for which neutralisation of the overall risk is nonsensical. The financial risk should not be neutralised because it is the 'upside' potential of generating revenue that makes investment an attraction in the first place.

The idea of a risk-financing continuum makes some sense *within* the world of risk neutralisation too. Some techniques exhibit higher levels of transfer than do others, and an explanation of that point can be offered by briefly discussing the two most common forms of neutralisation – futures and options contracts.

A futures contract is an arrangement for securing the future purchase or sale of goods/services and a predetermined price. 'Forward' contracts do much the same thing, but tend to be customised to specific buyers and sellers, whereas futures contracts are traded in markets and can be bought and sold anonymously. The purpose of a futures contract is to allow the buyer of that contract to neutralise the risk associated with some particular asset that the buyer will be acquiring or selling at some future point in time.

For example, an organisation might be concerned about fixing the price of heating oil it will purchase the following winter. As a basis for discussion, imagine that a supplier is willing to guarantee oil at £20 a barrel for that future delivery date. This arrangement presents a risk to buyer and seller – that the price on the market at that future date will be different. If, say, the market rate of oil at that future date of delivery is £14, the buyer is overpaying by £6 a barrel and the seller is earning an extra £6 a barrel. Obviously, the opposite could occur as well. The seller may choose to speculate on price fluctuations, but the organisation may want to neutralise the risk, which it could do by purchasing a heating oil futures contract that would permit it to sell oil at £20 on the delivery date. Thus, at that future date it could buy oil at £14 and – via the futures contract – sell at £20, thereby offsetting the £6 per barrel 'loss' it incurred on the under-lying purchase. Newcomers to the world of futures should note immediately that the opposite risk is neutralised as well; the organ-isation could not come out ahead if prices go up.

An options contract is one in which the holder has a right to buy or sell some asset at a specified time and amount. In this case, however, an options contract may or may not be exercised (futures transactions must occur at an agreed date). So, in the previous heating oil exam-ple, the option contract ('put' options allow the owner to sell an asset, 'call' options allow the owner to buy) would enable the organisation to exercise the option if the price rises – thus assuring that the price will be no higher than £20 a barrel. However, if the price of oil drops, the organisation will choose not to exercise the option, meaning that it can take advantage of the lower £14 a barrel market price.

From a slightly different perspective we might say that options contracts and insurance contracts have a great deal in common. If an authority buys an insurance policy, it has purchased an option that it may choose to exercise (by filing a claim when a loss occurs) if it is in the authority's interests to do so. Of course, the policy does not lapse if no claim is filed – which occurs with an options contract – but the similarity is important to observe because it shows how, like an insurance policy, an options contract can transfer risk – to financial markets rather than to an insurance company – while still retaining the more attractive features of the risk.

As a final and separate note, the phenomenon of 'risk securitisa-tion' should be introduced here as it reveals a different risk-financing method that is emerging from the convergence of capital and insurance markets. Securitisation, of course, is not a new idea. Mortgage-backed securities are a fairly common example of non-traded contracts being bundled together and sold as securities (the security allows its buyer to earn a revenue stream that is based on the collective cash flows generated by the mortgages). Today, many insurance companies are turning to capital markets to package asset and liability exposures to risk and to sell the risk into the market. For example, insurers can package together insurance contracts and sell securities based on the cash flows generated by the policies. For risk managers, the real interest here arises from the growing application of insurance securities to alternative risk-financing uses. One example would be the weather bonds discussed in the 'Applications' section of this chapter.

## Retention

In a sense, the concept of retention requires little specific discussion. If an organisation makes no arrangement to transfer/neutralise a risk, it will continue to possess sole responsibility for the risk and is practising retention. Inevitably, all organisations practice some degree of retention by virtue of the fact that some risks are not identified and handled in advance.

Allowing for the fact that unconscious retention occurs, the principal concern here is with the planned and conscious retention – what widely is referred to as self-insurance.

The particular means by which an organisation can self-insure are varied. Much self-financing is undertaken on a pay-as-you-go basis, without any special provision for pre-funding. This is contemporaneous financing in its most basic form. Some organisations extend this approach to a type of pre-funding, lines or letters of credit that allow an organisation to draw on its credit line to finance losses. Other more formal self-financing approaches can be employed – captive insurance companies (an insurance company that insures only one policyholder, its parent organisation), risk retention groups and pools (see Chapter 9) or finite risk insurance (a banking arrangement where the risk manager can accumulate funds and obtain certain financial management – even transference – services from the financial institution), among others.

Perhaps more important here than the means behind self-financing risks is the matter of why risks should be financed in such a manner. Although this is discussed in Chapter 11, it does deserve some attention here.

Broadly, the decision between transferring and retaining a risk is governed by the following factors:

- the degree of control over the risk
- the cost of financing options
- the quality/value of services
- the opportunity cost
- the tax issue (where relevant).

### The degree of control over the risk

In general terms, the more the organisation can control a risk, the less necessary transfer appears. Control implies predictability, knowledge of the risk, and the means to manage it. In such circumstances, it commonly is more effective and less costly for an organisation to retain the risk and manage it, paying directly for losses when and if they arise.

## The cost of financing options

In its most basic sense, an insurance premium is made up of the insurer's estimate of average expected losses to be paid out (plus the costs of adjusting and settling those claims) and the overhead costs of selling the policy (commissions to agents, taxes, profit, etc.). Depending on the degree of risk predictability, the retention decision is governed by the size and value of the insurer's margin. If, for example, a local authority pays £1 million in premiums to an insurer and both the insurer and the local authority believe average losses are about £700 000 a year, the question becomes whether it is wiser to simply set aside £700 000 to pay for losses and forgo many (but not all) of the overhead costs.

Interestingly, since the mid-1990s, the commercial insurance market has been so competitive that premiums offered, in some instances, are below the average expected loss costs (naturally, the insurers are hoping to make up the loss through investment returns on those premiums while in their possession). This has made it difficult for risk managers to argue for increasing their retention practices, at least on purely economic grounds. Thus, the decision to retain must be judged more on matters of control, quality of services, politics and public relations. Of course, the competitive market may change.

## The quality/value of services

This factor is suggested above in the discussion of cost comparisons. Certainly, the overhead costs of insurance are not dead-weight costs to the buyer. They include the technical expertises necessary to manage many risks (claims management, actuarial, loss control) and these have an economic value.

While in the past the quality and value of these services has weighed strongly against a decision to self-finance, this is no longer the case. Most insurers now unbundle their services. Thus, a self-financing public body could acquire an insurer's claims services without purchasing the insurance itself. Indeed, the emergence of unbundled services has produced an explosion in the risk management services industry. Today, it is possible to purchase any type of risk management service from insurers, brokers and other third-party providers. More is discussed on this point in Chapter 10.

## The opportunity cost

Previously it was observed that insurers consider the investment income earned on premiums as an important economic factor in their pricing. Note that this is a lost opportunity for the insured. Thus, for a public body, part of the decision to retain is governed by the lost opportunity associated with possessing the funds.

The nature of this cost is directly related to whether the risk in question is a long-tail or short-tail risk. Long-tail risks are those where a significant amount of time elapses between the loss-producing event (or notice of that event) and the eventual settlement of the claim. This is a notable feature of liability-related losses where a claim is filed and litigated, appealed, and ultimately closed, perhaps five to seven years after the case has begun.

Short-tail risks are those that open and close quickly (e.g., a fire loss, a theft claim). Short-tail risks present little in the way of opportunity costs, while the long-tail variety might present a benefit that more than offsets a degree of uncertainty associated with the actual ultimate outcome.

## The tax issue

For public bodies, tax considerations in risk-financing are not as profound as is the case in private sector firms. For private firms, the taxation authorities generally recognise insurance as a deductible business expense. Self-financing is treated differently and, for the most part, losses are only deductible when they are paid. This creates a general advantage for insurance over self-insurance. Set against that, however, is the fact that insurance premiums now attract Insurance Premium Tax, currently set at 5 per cent but widely anticipated to increase over time.

Generally, public bodies are tax exempt so far as the treatment of insurance premiums and self-insured loss is concerned. They are also exempt from Value Added Tax, currently set at 17.5 per cent, which is payable on services which may be bought to support a risk retention programme. However, they are not exempt from paying Insurance Premium Tax. So there are some fiscal advantages for a public body to consider risk retention ahead of risk transfer.

## *General observations on risk-financing*

Readers wading through this discussion for the first time may still remain a bit unclear on the distinctions between products that are mainly transfer, that neutralise risk or that retain risk. They should not feel alone! The risk-financing market is in a high state of flux and transformation, and many expert observers have difficulty in keeping straight in their minds the extraordinary range of new methods for financing risk. It probably is sufficient at this point for readers to remember the following:

1   Risk transfer, retention and neutralisation arrangements are not mutually exclusive in practice. Most risk-financing arrangements involve varying combinations of these approaches.
2   The emergence of banks, capital markets and investment management firms in the risk-financing business now presents a number of arrangements for managing financial risks, and these providers are beginning to offer products for more traditional, non-financial risks. The entry of these new providers is stirring up the industry.
3   Regulation and the law have not kept pace with these changes, meaning that traditional definitions of transfer and retention now – as often as not – confuse, rather than clarify, the situation.
4   The degree to which retention is attractive to a public body is related to the control that government can exert over the risk, the degree of predictability regarding that risk, the financial capacity of the public body to bear the risk and to withstand variations from the expected.
5   For reasons stated in item 4, most public bodies in the UK will continue to seek transfer and mostly transfer-financing arrangements (insurance), or will participate in a pool. Chapters 8 and 9 provide an extended discussion of those topics.

## APPLICATIONS

## Protecting snow removal budgets from extreme weather

Investment banks have committed significant resources in trying to develop financial products that can supplement, substitute for or replace conventional insurance products. Success has been limited thus far due to the experimental nature of these products, the complexity of many of these products and some of the more visible financial risk management problems (e.g., Orange County, see Chapter 5).

One area where rapid advancement has occurred is in weather-related financial products. The interest among public authorities, particularly in North America, has been high because these are arrangements that compensate public bodies for economic impacts related to a variety of weather-related phenomena – excess snowfall, drought, extended low or high temperatures. Traditional insurance does not address weather-related losses unless they produce direct physical damage, but weather can affect budgets, disrupt revenue streams and produce myriad effects.

A good illustration of this innovation is tied to the risk of excessive snowfall. Most public entities in the northern states of the USA budget for snow removal and, on average, they tend to be reasonably accurate. However, on a year-to-year basis, average does not count and wild swings in costs can occur. Since budget stability is a purpose of risk management, a risk manager might wonder whether it is possible to protect the snow removal budget from the risk of excess (meaning greater snowfall than is budgeted for). Ideally, the risk manager might like to arrange a risk-financing contract that would produce additional revenue to support snow removal if the existing budget is imperilled by unusual snowfall amounts. How might this happen?

It could occur in a number of ways. First, the risk manager might consider a weather hedge. This would be a derivative contract that would tie payout to an agreed schedule (so much per excessive inch of snowfall). The premium and the payout are both tied to snowfall rather than to loss, so in this sense a government could receive payouts with little in the way of claims investigation and negotiation.

The first stage of designing a weather hedge would be to quantify in financial terms the public sector organisation's exposure to excessive snowfall. For example, the government may indicate that it budgets for 25 inches of snowfall between October and April of each year. Further analysis may reveal that cumulative snowfalls of up to 30 inches would not excessively tax the government's budgets. So the realm of concern would be those years in which snowfall exceeds 30 inches.

In such a scenario, other elements will influence the determination of the contract price. Certainly 30 inches of snow in one storm has a different impact than thirty 1-inch snowstorms, so time concentration may be a variable. Ambient temperature can also influence the impact of a particular snowfall. Heavy snowfalls can occur with temperatures near 30 °F, but snow-melt occurs quickly, whereas snow falling in subzero temperatures may remain on the ground for weeks.

In any event, the government will want to understand the level of snowfall it is willing to tolerate and the likelihood that this level will be exceeded. Further, a measurement of the impact of excessive snowfall will occur (for every inch of excessive snowfall, it costs the authority an additional £15 000).

Through the intermediation of an investment bank or an insurance company, a financial contract can be designed. For instance, an options contract could be purchased where the public body pays a premium up front and then receives payments up to some agreed level. A swap contract might be used where the government spreads the payment for the contract over time with a series of fixed payments in return for receiving protection up to some limit. A collar might be used, where the government pays smaller amounts up front and specifies a coverage range (e.g., payments will be made if snowfall is 6–10 inches above the acceptable level).

The purported benefits of derivatives over conventional insurance include:

1   These arrangements can be set for multiple years at a time.
2   Since most payouts are set by official statistics, payouts occur quickly with little difficulty.
3   Insurance taxes are not applicable.
4   Unlike insurance, a government will almost invariably receive a benefit from the financial arrangement.
5   Certain revenue flow benefits may occur, even when no losses occur.
6   These contracts can deal with numerous risks that traditional insurance does not.

Newcomers often find derivatives confusing, and a quick reading of the preceding description easily could lead to an important question. Who would want to sell such a thing? After all, weather catastrophes tend to have a broad impact, so if an investment bank sold hundreds of these contracts, they could be wiped out in a single event (indeed, this is why traditional insurance would be so wary of such risks). The answer is that an investment bank would seek to balance this risk against contracts covering the opposite exposure. For example, there are many potential buyers that face the opposite risk (too much snow is good, too little snow is bad – a ski resort for example). Ideally, an investment bank would like to sell enough counterbalancing contracts to minimise its overall risk and generate sufficient fee income to make the efforts worth its while.

A second generic approach to weather risks is a weather-backed bond. Like mortgage-backed bonds or securities, an investment bank could issue a bond whose proceeds might be tied to snowfall rather than to interest rates. These bonds would present a default risk that is not present at the same level in traditional bonds but, equally, the return paid presumably would be higher.

# TOOLS YOU CAN USE

## A glossary of risk-financing techniques

*Administrative services only (ASO) plans.* An arrangement whereby
a third party provides risk-financing administrative services but
not the risk-financing. Commonly used as part of a self-insurance plan, ASOs also may be used in conjunction with the
purchase of some types of commercial insurance.

*Captive insurance companies.* An insurance company that is owned
by the insured and operates for the benefit of that owner/
insured. Some types of captives do permit non-owners to insure
under such a plan.

*Consumer proprietaries/co-operatives.* Two types of risk-financing
mechanisms whereby the members form a for-profit or not-for-
profit arrangement to finance jointly the costs of a particular
risk exposure. A significant characteristic of these arrangements
is that they usually are incorporated as an insurance company.

*Derivatives.* A financial asset whose value is derived from some other
underlying asset. *Forwards* and *futures* are derivatives in which
parties agree to exchange an asset at a future time at a predetermined price. *Options* are a derivative contract providing the
holder with the right to buy (call) or sell (put) an asset at a
stated price. Unlike forwards or futures, which must be acted
upon and closed at the end of the period, options can be allowed
to lapse if the action is not favourable to the option holder. A
*swap* is an agreement to exchange a series of payments such
as loan repayments, where the two loans may be denominated
in different currencies. *Collars* are agreements that hedge or
offset risk within a limited range.

*Experience-rated insurance.* An insurance arrangement whereby the
insured's own past loss experience directly affects the premium
charged. The degree of influence this loss experience has is tied
to the statistical credibility of that insured's loss experience.

*Finite risk insurance or reinsurance.* A risk-financing arrangement
whereby the policyholder spreads the cost of risk over time but
does not transfer the risk to any other party. Sometimes gener-
ically referred to as banking arrangements.

*Guaranteed cost insurance.* An insurance arrangement whereby the
insurer agrees to reimburse the losses of the policyholder in exchange for a premium that is fixed at the time the contract is signed.

*Hedging plans.* A financial transaction in which gains on one contract
are used to offset losses on another transaction. Usually hedging
involves two bets whose outcomes are opposite in sign.

*Loss portfolio transfers.* A contract where an insurance portfolio or a portfolio of self-insured losses is transferred from one party to another. While historically such products were used by insurance companies to sell off books of business or blocks of loss reserves, these contracts now may allow a self-insured organisation to package up past and current losses and reserves, and transfer them to an insurance company. The insurance company is betting that it can close out losses less expensively than can the transferring organisation.

*Reinsurance.* Coverage purchased by an insurer to transfer part or all of the financial burden associated with a group of insurance contracts it has written. *Proportional risk-sharing* contracts are most common, with a reinsurer agreeing to either a part of each loss or a part of losses when they exceed some predetermined level. *Excess of loss* arrangements tend to apply when cumulative loss experience across many insurance contracts rises to a predetermined level. Above that level, the reinsurer pays all loss costs.

*Retrospective-rated insurance.* An insurance arrangement whereby the premium is based on the losses of the insured during the policy period. Subject to maxima and minima, the premium is based entirely on the insured's own experience.

*Risk retention groups.* Risk retention groups are financing mechanisms where organisations in a common industry jointly finance the costs of product liability or employment-related risks, either through an organised retention programme or through the group purchase of commercial insurance.

*Self-insurance plans.* A rational and planned programme whereby the organisation retains the costs associated with the bearing of risk.

*Self-insurance pools.* A type of risk-financing arrangement often found in the public sector. Pools are arrangements whereby public entities enter into a contract for jointly financing the costs of losses and the administrative costs of pool operations.

---

# READ MORE ABOUT IT

## Some perspective on the risk-financing marketplace

Readers of this chapter will possess an abstract understanding of risk-financing, but what does the risk-financing marketplace really look like? The purpose of this section is to give readers more of a real-world feel for risk-financing practices.

Relatively modern practices of insurance date back to the 1600s (Lloyd's of London was formed in 1688), but the history of insurance in the Western world could be characterized as the constant rise and assimilation of alternatives to insurance. Invariably new coverage problems would arise that were not addressed by the existing insurance industry, at which point buyer-led groups would form co-operative mutual arrangements. This arrangement would serve as an alternative until the time came when the alternative would be absorbed into a new and expanded insurance industry.

This historical reference is useful for readers to understand, because the current world is full of alternative risk-financing arrangements and there is evident disorientation in the marketplace. Some observers think we are in the death throes of the insurance industry, some see financial services becoming a single monolithic industry. History might suggest that the turn of the twenty-first century is a period of transition and that a new and expanded risk-financing (insurance?) industry will emerge.

But what about today? The concept of self-insurance (as it is defined today) has been around for most of the twentieth century, although most of the serious growth in this alternative has occurred since 1950. The advancement of self-insurance heralded a measurement problem that has existed ever since. It is difficult to measure the risk-financing marketplace when a sizeable portion of the expenditure remains internal to the users.

A second early alternative to insurance was the offshore captive, which has been around since the first ones were formed in the 1950s. Captives are insurance companies that insure one client, the parent corporation. The benefits of captives are tied to tax treatment, ability to control worldwide programmes, and access to reinsurance markets. Captives, in turn, have spawned their own alternatives – rent-a-captives, protected cell companies, co-operative mutuals, financial and finite reinsurance, and catastrophe reinsurance.

Other macro-trends in the insurance industry have influenced the shape and state of the current industry. They include:

- the globalisation of the insurance industry and the larger organisational buyers of insurance
- several waves of mergers that have created a group of very large global insurers and reinsurers
- increasing pressures to diversify and broaden coverages
- more knowledge of insurance by organisational buyers and their advisers, which has strengthened the demand side of the marketplace

- emergence of banks and capital markets as competitors in the risk-financing industry.

These forces have led to many new needs that traditional insurance has been unable to address. Naturally, the older alternatives (self-insurance and captives) picked up much of the initial demand, and risk retention groups and pools have also absorbed much of the new demand. At this time it is unclear how much demand diverts to derivatives and other capital-market based products, though interest in weather-related arrangements has been considerable.

## The size of the risk-financing market

A major industry study estimates that the global risk-financing market (for organisation property and liability risks) is about $220 billion, of which about one-quarter is self-insured or insured through a captive.

In 1997, A. M. Best indicated that 30 per cent to 40 per cent of the US commercial property and liability risk-financing market, which itself was estimated at $80 billion, was engaged in self-insurance or captive programmes. Although this study focused on very large organisations (mainly Fortune 1000) businesses, a key finding was the extension of alternative risk-financing practices into medium-sized organisations.

Conservative estimates value the size of the UK local authority market at around £600 million of which probably some 50 per cent is retained within the local authorities by way of self-insurance. Central government itself in the main self-insures its risks and exposures. The National Health Trusts have recently moved their property and liability exposures from the commercial insurance market to an entirely self-insuring position. Clearly, it could be argued very plausibly that considerably more than half of the risk-financing market that is dedicated to public bodies involves the use of self-insurance.

## A key trend to watch

The financial services industry is undergoing significant change, and it is difficult to predict the outcome with much accuracy. The key trend for public bodies to watch is the rapid globalisation and integration of financial institutions that provide risk-financing products. With increasing frequency, public bodies are likely to encounter sales offers from foreign insurers and even large international investment management firms and investment banks. The general interpretation of this trend is that these institutions will look to offer a wide range of risk-financing products to deal with traditional hazard-based risks, as well as financial risks and other organisational risks. Though this could bode well for public bodies to have greater choice and lower prices, it does create greater complexity for the public body in judging the financial solidity of these new players in the marketplace.

# 8

# *Insurance*

## EXECUTIVE SUMMARY

Insurance is a contract whereby one party (the policyholder) promises and makes a payment or series of payments in exchange for the second party's (the insurance company) promise to indemnify the policyholder for losses that are covered under the terms of the policy. Perhaps an easier way to view insurance is that the policyholder is trading small regular losses (the premium paid) for large and irregular gains (claims proceeds).

Insurance contracts vary widely, as they are written to address many different risks. However, there are general similarities to the contract structure, and analysis probably is not as difficult as popular impressions would suggest.

In the UK the insurance industry is largely self-regulated, at least as far as commercial insurances are concerned, although the Department of Trade and Industry does oversee the financial solidity of insurers as well as their business practices. Personal and individual policyholders enjoy much more protection, particularly in the event of insurer insolvency. The fact that organisational buyers of insurance (corporations, public bodies and the like) have less regulatory protection than individual consumers puts great pressure on risk managers to investigate thoroughly the financial security of any insurance company before they purchase insurance from that insurer.

## PRINCIPLES AND CONCEPTS

The subject of insurance is important for both conceptual and practical reasons. Conceptually, much of our understanding of risk and its management derives from insurance theory and practice, and so an appreciation of insurance and insurance institutions provides valuable insights into the management of risks in organisations. In a practical sense, insurance is a financing arrangement of profound importance to most public-sector risk management programmes.

The 'practical' point above should be underscored here. The expanding definition of risk management has pushed the role of insurance somewhat to the side – at least this is happening in professional and academic discussions. Unfortunately for the uninitiated, this might leave the false impression that insurance is of marginal importance to risk managers. Insurance remains a critical feature of risk-financing programmes.

Chapter 8 provides an overview of insurance – a tall order indeed. The chapter begins with an introduction of the concept of insurance and its principal characteristics. This discussion is followed by an analysis of the insurance contract – its forms and functions, its content, its pricing, and the contract law that supports it. The chapter concludes with an institutional look at insurance, which touches on legal forms of organisation, functions within the insurance operation, and relevant financial and regulatory issues.

# Insurance in overview

Insurance is a mechanism by which the *financial* responsibility for a risk is legally transferred from one party to another. Insurance is distinguished from other types of contractual risk transfers by the following features:

- the nature of the consideration given differs from most contracts
- performance differs from most contracts
- the financial basis for insurance differs from most contracts.

## The nature of the consideration

The consideration given by an insurer and insured takes a distinct form. For the insured, the consideration is a payment or promise of payment (the premium). This payment is expected to bear some financial relationship to the underlying risk in question. For the insurer, consideration is a promise to perform, a promise that is conditional on a chance event (a loss) covered by the contract.

## Performance

Insurance is a conditional and aleatory contract, meaning that the performance of at least one party is based on a chance event. By implication, insurance contracts are not commutative; they are not exchanges of equal value.

## Financial basis

Insurance further distinguishes itself by virtue of its 'pooling' of risk. Legal disputes centring on whether a contract is insurance or something else often pivot around the question of whether risks have been pooled together so that the funds of the many finance the losses of the few. The mathematical basis of insurance rests on the notion that the gathering together of similar risks allows the insurer to estimate future losses with greater accuracy, and this ability affords funding stability and predictability, as well as certain economies of scale.

Theory demonstrates that the act of pooling produces a social good in the sense that pooling reduces the aggregate cost of risk that otherwise would be paid by society. A minor debate has arisen in recent years regarding the thing being pooled (see Chapter 7). Traditionally, the view has been that it was the aggregating of the risks (e.g., a number of motor vehicles) that served to improve predictability. Recently, the observation has been made that it is the pooling of 'resources' that is the key issue. By accumulating premiums, an insurer can overwhelm possible variations in loss experience, thus providing stability and predictability.

Notably, insurance is a mechanism that addresses both aspects of the cost of risk. Obviously, insurance manages the cost of losses by indemnifying the insured against the economic impact of loss. Less apparent is the impact on the cost of uncertainty. The presence of insurance can reduce the uncertainty an insured feels about the possibility of loss – which, in turn, lessens worry and stress and frees the insured to concentrate on matters of greater importance.

Insurance can reduce the cost of risk, but insurance can impose costs as well. The insurance premium is based in part on the insurer's estimate of average expected losses; thus, over time an insured is paying for its own losses. This means that the cost of losses ultimately is paid by the insured and that the insurer mainly is providing a means by which risk of sudden, large and unexpected losses are traded for the certainty of steady, small, and budgetable 'losses' (the premiums paid).

The more difficult to appreciate cost of insurance is moral hazard. Moral hazard is defined as illegal or irresponsible behaviour prompted by the presence of insurance (this is not a characteristic exclusive to insurance, as other contracts and arrangements may have the same effect). The purchase of insurance, while clearly a risk management action, might also change the behaviour of individuals in such a way as to promote the very losses the insurance was intended to address. A common example of this is arson, which in many respects is motivated by the prospect of profiting from insurance proceeds.

Insurance underwriters recognise that analysis of an insured risk involves a kind of two-stage evaluation: determine the existing nature of the risk, and determine how the issuance of the policy affects that risk. The premium ultimately is based on some judgement of both elements.

The discussion of moral hazard could carry far beyond the subject of insurance. Virtually any risk management measure can produce a moral hazard effect. For example, requiring refuse collectors to wear lumbar support belts (to support lower back muscles while lifting) might encourage the wearers to lift more weight than they otherwise would. Some have argued that the mandating of seat belt usage, or the wearing of hard hats, or the use of other safety equipment might encourage users to act less safely than they should. Clearly, moral hazard (and the related phenomenon 'risk shifting') is a general feature of risk management, not just of insurance.

## The insurance contract

Insurance contracts share many common features with other contracts. By law they must serve a legal purpose, the parties must be competent to enter into the agreement, there must be offer and acceptance, and consideration must be given by the parties to the contract.

Despite core similarities, common law has recognised that insurance contracts have many features that are unique. As a result, the legal system has evolved a distinct area of contract law specific to insurance. These distinctions are discussed below, but one overarching characteristic of insurance contract law warrants mention here. Whereas contract law in the UK rests largely on a philosophy of *caveat emptor* (let the buyer beware), the special nature of insurance has influenced the law in such a way that buyers of insurance and sellers of insurance enjoy certain protections and privileges that commonly do not exist in other areas of contract law.

An area of particular development in recent years has been the growth in statutorily backed protection for personal and individual policyholders. The insurance industry in the UK has had a long history of self-regulation. However, the collapse of the Vehicle and General Insurance company in the late 1960s prompted Parliament to pass legislation requiring the Department of Trade and Industry to monitor the financial health of insurance companies. In addition, the Policyholders Protection Act (1975) reimburses and/or indemnifies personal policyholders up to 90 per cent of property loss and 100 per cent of injury/death loss in the event of insurance company failure. However, this protection is not available to corporate buyers of insurance.

## Legal characteristics of insurance

Insurance contracts are contracts of indemnity, conditional contracts, aleatory contracts, contracts negotiated in 'utmost good faith', and contracts of adhesion.

### Contracts of indemnity

A contract of indemnity restores a loss. In principle, an insured is returned to the tangible economic position that existed prior to the loss. As a practical matter, violations or exceptions to the concept of indemnity abound. For instance, the loss may exceed the policy limits, there may be a cost-sharing provision within the contract, the cause of loss may not be covered or is only partially covered, or it may simply not be possible to actually restore an object to its pre-loss value (e.g., a priceless work of art).

Broadly, insurance contracts handle the restoration of loss in two ways. The most common is to define the obligation on a 'replacement cost' basis. That is, the insurer promises to commit resources to replace the lost object with a new and similar object, often termed as 'reinstatement'. Some coverages modify that promise to an 'actual cash value' basis or 'average' basis, meaning that the proceeds paid to the insured are reduced by some amount to reflect the wear, tear, physical depreciation and obsolescence of the lost object. The second method is the 'valued or agreed amount' basis, which is a value determined in advance by the insured and insurer.

### Conditional contracts

Some contracts, when agreed to, are fulfilled automatically and with certainty. Others, like insurance, perform based on condition that some additional event occurs. In the case of insurance, of course, that additional event is a covered loss.

## Aleatory contracts

The notion that insurance is a conditional contract is extended by the fact that the conditional event is probabilistic. Some conditional contracts are based on additional events that are certain to occur, but aleatory contracts are arrangements where the conditional event is a chance event – like a fortuitous loss. Taken in combination, the aleatory and conditional features of insurance distinguish it from most contracts, which are commutative. Commutative arrangements are characterised by exchanges of equal value, but aleatory and conditional contracts are rarely, if ever, exchanges of equal economic value.

## Contracts of utmost good faith

The standard of utmost good faith implies a somewhat higher expectation for forthrightness and honesty in the insurance transaction. The courts have deemed this to be so because there is ample opportunity for fraud to occur in the buying and selling of insurance. Buyers may withhold information known only to them, which would be relevant to the insurer's decision to underwrite (e.g., a health condition). Equally, the insurer's consideration is merely a promise to perform at some future date, conditional on the occurrence of certain events. And, of course, the insured's ability to ascertain the insurer's future ability to perform is limited.

## Contracts of adhesion

This feature has become less and less relevant as risk management has developed and risk managers have become more sophisticated consumers. A contract of adhesion is one that is offered on a take-it-or-leave it basis.

Ordinarily, two parties will jointly draft a document and sign it when they are in agreement as to its wording. However, in insurance this historically has not been true, as the insurer has had sole control over the drafting of the contract language. Because this is so, the courts have tended to side with the insured when disputes arise over contract language and meaning. While this still is broadly true today, many risk managers (especially in large organisations) are able to exert considerable influence in contract formation. The result of such situations is a unique contract that – in the parlance of the industry – has been 'manuscripted'.

## *Contract structure*

A certain degree of contract standardisation has occurred in the insurance industry, despite trends towards customisation. However, it is not easy to summarise the format because insurance contracts address such a wide range of risks. For example, a life insurance policy must address a set of underwriting issues quite different from a police authority's liability policy. Further, some policies apply to groups (employee benefit coverages), while others apply to individuals.

Nevertheless, it is useful to have some sense of contract structure. One approach to the subject is to note that contracts generally contain four parts: the declarations or schedule, the insuring agreement, the conditions and the exclusions.

## The declarations or schedule

This often is the only unique part of a coverage document. It contains information on the insured, the properties or assets involved, the coverage amount and the premiums, as well as other matters that are specific to the particular contract. In some types of policies the term 'jacket' or 'schedule' is used, since the declarations wrap around a collection of coverages (e.g., property and liability coverages) and co-ordinate the protection provided.

## The insuring agreement

The insuring agreement is the meat of the contract. It describes the coverage provided, the perils protected against, the definitions of coverage terminology and in general terms the objects covered.

## The conditions section

Part of the consideration given by both parties is compliance with conditions that are part of the contract. The conditions will vary, but include such things as instructions on how and when losses are reported, what the insured and insurer must do after the loss, and so on. Importantly, a loss could be denied – though fully and completely covered in all other respects – if there is a failure to comply with the conditions section of the policy.

## The exclusions section

It might be assumed that if a contract is silent on a matter, that matter cannot be construed as being part of the contract. However, due to years of litigation over contract terminology, most insurance contracts now include a section that affirmatively asserts that certain things are excluded from coverage. As just one example, acts of war commonly are excluded as a covered cause of loss.

## The pricing of insurance

Insurance premiums are set to achieve two objectives: to assure that sufficient funds exist to cover the cost of losses and costs directly associated with losses, and to cover the insurer's overhead costs and profits. Commonly, the loss portion is referred to as the 'loss ratio', while the overhead/profits portion is the 'expense ratio'. The expense ratio consists of fixed and variable cost units, and is loaded into each premium after the loss ratio (sometimes called the 'pure premium') has been set.

The loss ratio is determined in a number of different ways, but all are based in part on an estimate of the average expected losses the insured is likely to incur. For smaller organisations and for individuals, the standard approach is classification rating. Under this scheme, risks are pooled together into groupings that have common attributes. The loss ratio is determined by computing the average losses of risks in a particular grouping. While certain credits or premium breaks may be added, readers should note that the individual insured's own actual loss experience does not factor into the initial computation.

Organisations that are larger may be eligible for experience rating. Under this approach, the insured is rated first on a classification basis, then the premium is adjusted to reflect the insured's own past loss experience. The degree to which the insured's own experience influences the ultimate premium is dictated by the statistical credibility of its loss experience. Experience rating is used extensively in liability-related coverages. A key attribute is that future premiums can be directly influenced by efforts to control and reduce risks.

For large organisations whose loss experience has a high degree of statistical credibility, retrospective rating may be employed. Under this arrangement, the ultimate premium is almost completely predicated on that insured's current loss experience. Thus, after making an initial premium payment to cover basic costs, the premium is determined at the end of the coverage period based on the actual losses that occur during that period. Retro plans also provide a loss-capping feature, which means that if losses exceed some predetermined level, the insurer will assume responsibility for excess claims. While retro-rating is used mainly for large insureds, it also might be used by an insurer when a prospective client represents unknown risk. Under a retro plan, the insurer is able to moderate its risk by requiring the insured to bear the cost of its losses up to some point.

A fourth method of pricing is judgement rating. Though not seen widely, this approach is used when statistical information is limited or poor in quality. In such cases, an underwriter may offer coverage at a price based on an educated judgement of the likelihood of loss.

While premiums do represent expected losses and expenses, they may or may not reflect investment income/time value of money. For instance, under many liability coverages, the premiums paid in a particular year may not be paid out in claims for several years, giving rise to an investment income opportunity. For the insurer, this represents a revenue opportunity and a sort of hedge against unexpected results in underwriting performance. For the insured, it represents a significant opportunity cost. Thus, risk managers are interested in either negotiating into the coverage recognition of the investment return or they may be tempted to retain the risk and capture the investment income directly.

Readers should note that insurance is priced on the assumption that, over time, an insured will pay in sufficient resources to cover or more than cover losses. The degree to which this happens is related in part to the size of the risk insured. For an individual buying private motor insurance, the typical result is a lifetime of premiums paid with few or no claims. Less commonly, an insured may have a claim that dwarfs the amount of premium paid in. In other words, only rarely do premiums even roughly correspond with claims proceeds. Insurance experts would note that uncertainty reduction also is being purchased and has economic value, but this is an argument that wins few supporters among consumers.

As Chapter 7 indicates, when organisations grow larger and larger, the preceding argument does take hold, however, and it becomes more apparent that over time the loss ratio roughly corresponds with the actual loss proceeds that are paid under a policy. This phenomenon suggests a key risk-financing insight. If the loss ratio and the claims paid are generally consistent with one another, then the decision to self-finance is based on the economics of the expense ratio (i.e., does that portion of the premium corresponding to the insurer's expenses and profits more than exceed the resources necessary to manage the related costs of retaining the risk, such as claims management costs?).

## A word on reinsurance

Reinsurance is insurance for insurance companies. Commonly, an insurance company will not wish to bear all the risk it has accumulated through the issuance of policies, and it will be particularly keen to protect itself against the possibility of large losses (either from a single event or an accumulation of small events). Reinsurance companies offer the chance to transfer away the catastrophic portion of the risk portfolio and thus stabilise financial performance.

Reinsurance is important for two reasons. First, a risk manager would not necessarily be aware of the reinsurance arrangements that an insurer has made, as the insured legally is not a party to the reinsurance transaction. But, the identity and financial solidity of the reinsurer is material to the risk manager's concern about the security of the risk-financing arrangement. A risk manager must make appropriate inquiries into the insurer's own financial management programmes.

Second, as the insurance industry has evolved, reinsurers have begun to deal directly with risk managers and other end users of their products. In part this is due to the reinsurer's quest to diversify its products and services, and in part it is due to the opportunities to do so. Regardless of the cause, reinsurance companies now deal directly with pools and other alternative risk-financing schemes and also directly with larger public bodies. While, in many respects, they are providing exactly the same service they provide to insurers (protection against large losses), their developing direct relationship with risk managers is spawning many new innovations drawn from the reinsurance industry. Loss portfolio transfers are just one such example, being arrangements where a public body can transfer a collection of past losses (yet to be settled or paid out) to the reinsurer as a means of removing loss reserves from financial statements or realising early releases of surplus.

## Institutional aspects of insurance

The insurance industry is widely varied and rapidly changing, and any effort at description runs some risk of becoming out of date in short order. For instance, although it is not addressed here except indirectly, the insurance industry rapidly is being subsumed by an emerging global financial services industry. In this new industry, banks, capital markets, and insurance and other financial institutions are competing in a single, though differentiated, marketplace. Regulation is evolving rapidly to keep pace, and it seems probable that risk managers will soon be able easily to access risk-financing products from investment banks, commercial banks and directly from capital markets, as well as from insurance companies.

The principal purposes of this section of Chapter 8 are to describe the structure of the insurance industry, to identify basic issues related to regulation of the industry and to comment on financial management issues relevant in evaluating the performance and security of an insurance company.

## Industry structure

In general, the insurance industry today can be divided into two segments – life and non-life. The life segment includes individual life, health, disability and annuity products. It also includes a subsegment known as group life, which includes life products commonly seen in employee benefit programmes. Non-life includes individual and commercial property and liability coverages, as well as a range of specialised coverages like motor vehicle, household, boiler and machinery, marine and aviation coverages.

While there have been significant mergers and acquisitions activities in the insurance sector in recent years, the Association of British Insurers represents over 400 insurance companies who, between them, account for around 90 per cent of the insurance business transacted in the UK. Insurance companies are legally organised as either proprietaries (for-profit corporations) or co-operatives (sometimes called 'mutuals', which are not-for-profit corporations). Proprietary and mutual companies are found in all areas of insurance, and the debate over which form is most advantageous has never been satisfactorily resolved. However, the ability of proprietary companies to access capital markets has led to something of a trend in recent years known as demutualisation, where co-operative insurers have converted to a stock-ownership form of organisation. This trend is explored in more detail in Chapter 9.

As a consequence of the UK's membership of the EU, insurance companies that are licensed to transact business in the UK are allowed to transact the same classes of insurance in all the other member countries. Conversely, insurance companies that are licensed to transact business in a member country are allowed to transact the same classes of insurance in the UK.

As mentioned previously, the reinsurance industry provides large loss protection for the direct or primary insurance industry. Reinsurance tends to be regulated more lightly, and the financial characteristics of this industry segment have led to significant consolidation and globalisation in recent years. The leading reinsurers are international firms that have grown to be very large.

One reinsurer of particular note is Lloyd's of London (now just 'Lloyd's'), which is influential beyond its actual size. Lloyd's has been in the insurance business for more than 300 years and its experience and reputation make it an 'opinion leader' in the world of insurance. Much of the industry takes its cue from Lloyd's underwriters. Lloyd's has emerged recently from a period of financial difficulty that nearly destroyed the organisation. As Lloyd's is not an insurer *per se*, but a marketplace for the buying and selling of reinsurance (and direct insurance too, such as marine and aviation coverage), its reorganisation has included allowing other insurance companies into the Lloyd's market. Historically, Lloyd's only permitted individuals to invest in the insurance business (an investment with unlimited liability), but the arrival of corporate investors and participants is changing the picture at Lloyd's.

## Distribution systems

In general, insurance companies have three ways to sell insurance: directly, through independent agents or through the brokerage system.

Direct writing involves a paid sales force, direct phone sales or the Internet. Independent agents are business owners who represent one or more insurance companies, are paid a commission by the insurer, but are not construed to be employees of that insurer. Brokers are independent business owners who represent the buyers of insurance and approach the insurers on behalf of the buyer. Confusingly, they are often paid commissions by the insurer, although they are legal representatives of the buyer. Many risk managers, in an effort to control the possible conflict of interest that could arise in such situations, negotiate fee-for-service arrangements with brokers. Chapter 10 discusses this issue in some detail.

Reinsurance companies tend to be direct writers, although brokers are present in the reinsurance industry as well.

## Regulation of the industry

In the UK the insurance industry has a history of self-regulation. Only in the last thirty years or so has the degree of statutory regulation increased, following the spectacular collapse of companies such as Vehicle and General. The government's principal vehicle for regulation is the Department of Trade and Industry.

### Principal regulatory statutes

The principal regulatory statutes governing the insurance industry are as follows.

### Insurance Companies Act 1982

Under this legislation and subsequent amendments under the Insurance (Third Insurance Directive) Act 1994 the Department of

Trade and Industry (DTI) is responsible for the regulation of insurance companies in the UK. The DTI's powers include the ability to authorise companies to write insurance, and the requirement to monitor and impose solvency margins and accounting requirements to ensure that an insurance company has sufficient assets available to meet its liabilities at all times. The DTI is empowered to petition the courts to wind up a company if it fails to comply with the requirements of the Insurance Companies Act. The effect of the Insurance (Third Insurance Directive) Act 1994 was to allow a company authorised in one country of the EU to transact insurance in any other.

## Policyholders Protection Act 1975

The Policyholders Protection Board, which was established by this legislation, imposes a levy on insurance companies. The fund thus established is used to meet an individual policyholder's claim if their insurance company has either become insolvent or is unable to meet its obligations to its policyholders. Under the legislation claims under compulsory coverages such as motor insurance and employers' liability insurance are met in full whereas only 90 per cent of other claims are met. The benefits available under and the protection provided by the Policyholders Protection Act 1975 are only available to private individuals and not to corporations or public bodies. The onus, therefore, for ensuring the financial solvency of actual or prospective insurance carriers rests with the organisation's own risk manager and/or intermediaries.

## Financial Services Act 1986

This regulates the sale of investment products such as long-term insurances, stocks, shares, debentures, loan stocks, bonds and unit trusts and its powers have been further enhanced by the Financial Services Act 1998. Parties engaged in the sale of investment products must be authorised or exempt and authorisation is provided either by the Financial Services Agency or by a recognised professional body such as the Insurance Brokers' Registration Council, the Institute of Chartered Accountants and the Institute of Actuaries or one of the following self-regulating organisations:

- the Personal Investment Authority regulating independent financial advisers, company representatives and tied agents
- the Investment Management Regulatory Organization regulating the management of investments
- the Securities and Futures Association regulating futures and options dealers, stockbrokers, securities dealers and the like.

## Codes of practice

The Association of British Insurers (ABI) was founded in 1985 with the express objectives of protecting and promoting the interests of its members (the insurance carriers), to represent its members' interests to central government and other agencies and to co-operate with other such associations. Its work is divided between the General Insurance Council and the Life Assurance Council. Particularly relevant to our consideration of regulation of the insurance industry, the ABI has developed two codes of practice – the Statement of General Insurance Practice and the Statement of Long-Term Insurance Practice – which lay down guidelines for the conduct of business between insurers, intermediaries and policyholders. They only apply, however, in respect of policies purchased by individuals, not corporations or public bodies. The General Insurance Standards Council (GISC) recently has been established to provide a single, independent regulatory regime on a non-statutory basis. For the time being, the ABI codes of practice operate alongside those of the GISC.

## Central government intervention

There are circumstances when central government has directly intervened to develop markets for insurance when public policy considerations are present. Some examples include the creation of Pool Re to provide policyholders with protection against terrorism following the exclusion of this peril by insurance companies from their policies in the wake of the increase in terrorism on mainland Britain. Similarly, the Motor Insurers' Bureau was created to provide protection for individuals injured by uninsured motorists. Specifically for public bodies, the Bellwin Scheme was established to defray some of the uninsured costs incurred by local authorities in dealing with the immediate aftermath of natural events. (See 'Read More About It' for further details about the Bellwin Scheme).

## *Financial assessment of insurers*

In view of the fact that corporations and public bodies receive less statutory protection than do individual policyholders, it is useful to examine the key financial aspects of insurance companies that influence performance and solidity.

Although a financial performance ratio, standing in isolation, provides little insight into any organisation, a reasonable starting point for thinking about insurer performance and solidity is consideration of a few key ratios.

The 'loss ratio' is central to a basic understanding of financial performance. It is commonly determined by relating losses incurred (losses an insurer becomes obligated to pay, plus expenses associated with settling the claims – in that context it is not surprising to recall that an individual premium contains a loss ratio as well) in some period of time to premiums earned (which, typically is something less than the premiums received due to accounting rules) in that same period of time.

While the loss ratio often is expressed as a percentage of the premium that is paid by the insured, it is more useful here to understand that the loss ratio represents the insurer's estimate of certain expenses – or almost literally of the 'cost of goods sold' – allowing for some degree of variability. Other things held constant, a high loss ratio implies that a significant portion of a premium will be returned to the insured as benefits and loss-related service, which might be a positive indication. If, for instance, a £10 000 premium were found to have a 90 per cent loss ratio, it could mean that the insurer is very efficient, with only £1000 being retained to cover overhead, such as taxes, commissions, profits and salaries. However, if the insurer had planned for a 60 per cent loss ratio, the same result would suggest a serious problem. Because the loss ratio could suggest positive or negative performance, it rarely is worth considering on its own.

The 'expense ratio' is another important ratio. In general, expenses would include claims-related costs (costs associated with handling/ investigating claims and engaging experts such as loss adjusters, engineers and legal representation). Custom and practice varies as to how these expenses are incurred. Where insurers outsource the claims-handling function these expenses typically are included in the loss ratio as they are somewhat variable and related to loss costs. Where insurers manage claims in-house the direct costs associated with this process, other than the costs of engaging experts such as loss adjusters, engineers and legal representation, are included within the expense ratio. The expense ratio also relates to underwriting and other non-claims expenses. These 'expenses incurred' are related to the 'premiums written' (this refers to premiums received during a period of time, and is commonly a larger value than 'premiums earned') and tend to relate to the portion of premium that is consumed in paying for overhead and other expenses. Other factors held constant, a low expense ratio suggests the insurer performs in a low-cost environment. Of course, low cost could mean cheap as well as efficient so the ratio can be misleading. Alternatively, a high expense ratio might suggest inefficiency, but could also reveal a higher level of investment in underwriting and loss control. As an extreme example of this point, boiler and machinery insurance (insurance protecting against explosion of boilers, large manufacturing equipment, refrigeration systems and the like) has extremely high expense ratios, but these expenses are incurred in providing inspections and loss control services that have the net effect of reducing the likelihood of losses.

The combined ratio is the sum of the loss ratio and expense ratio. The combined ratio, when adjusted for dividends, often is reported as an indicator of an insurance company's performance. For example, a loss ratio of .65 when added to an expense ratio of .30 yields a combined ratio of .95, which is not quite correctly interpreted as the percentage of premium pounds paid in losses and expenses. In this instance, the insurer collected £1 in premiums and paid 95 pence in losses and overhead expenses, producing an 'underwriting profit' of 5 pence. Logically, a 100 per cent combined ratio represents a breakeven underwriting performance, while 100+ per cent ratios signal problems in underwriting.

The combined ratio omits an important source of revenue for the insurer – investment income. While the insurer holds the premiums, it is able to invest those funds. In certain lines of insurance, that income can be significant because the holding period can last for years (e.g., public and employer's liability insurance). Since this is so, the combined ratio often is adjusted by subtracting the net investment income ratio (net investment income divided by premiums written). A 12 per cent net investment ratio would change the above combined ratio as follows:

Loss ratio + Expense ratio – Net investment ratio = Operating ratio
.65     +     .30     –         .12         =        .83

Or, put a different way, when investment income is considered, the insurer paid out 83 pence for every premium pound taken in.

A second basis for considering financial performance is the premium-to-surplus ratio, the ratio of net premiums written related to the policyholders' surplus (which is the difference between an insurer's assets and its liabilities). The policyholders' surplus represents, in a sense, the cushion an insurer has to protect itself against unexpected loss costs. In general, a high premium-to-surplus ratio implies that the insurer is vulnerable to adverse events. Put simply, such an insurer would have relatively fewer resources to draw on should losses end up being higher than expected. Typically, premium-to-surplus ratios range from 100 per cent to 300 per cent, and analysts advise that companies offering riskier and uncertain insurance coverages should have lower ratios than companies offering traditional and stable coverages.

Readers are reminded that reinsurance is important in judging insurer financial performance. Reinsurance can protect the primary insurer from adverse shocks, but the presence of the reinsurer raises monitoring issues for the risk manager. In insurance company accounts the amount of reinsurance purchased by an insurance company is identified separately as a line item, at least in monetary values and as a percentage of gross written premium. However, the identity of the reinsurers is rarely, if ever, disclosed. The financial solidity of the reinsurer becomes an additional subject of inquiry.

The typical public sector manager has limited time to conduct financial security analyses of insurance companies (although regulatory trends are tending to put more of a burden on organisations to evaluate insurer financial solidity). Fortunately, this type of expertise is one of the central reasons brokers are used. Brokerage houses commonly have resources to monitor insurer financial performance, and risk managers rely on brokers to steer them clear of troublesome or suspect insurance companies.

Publicly available ratings of insurance companies can also assist a risk manager. Moody's, Standard and Poors, and Best's all provide rating systems for financial security and performance. Best's, perhaps the most widely used rating agency, produces a system that grades insurers (A+, A, B+, etc.). A general rule of thumb is that risk managers should use insurance companies with an A or higher rating only. Of course, like all rules of thumb, blind adherence to the rule can be as problematic as using no evaluation system at all.

## APPLICATIONS

## A public body's typical insurance portfolio

While this chapter's discussion of insurance is wide-ranging, readers still might not have much of a feel for the types of insurance contracts that public bodies purchase. The purpose of this section is to outline and describe briefly the insurance coverages most likely to be seen in a local government's insurance portfolio.

### The insurance portfolio

The word 'portfolio' is important to understand because it suggests that the purchase of insurance coverage is driven by an overarching goal of achieving some level of coverage completeness. In other words, while some local authorities purchase a wide range of coverages without any thought of their relationships to one another, the concept of the insurance portfolio symbolises an integrated approach to insurance buying.

For newcomers to the subject of insurance, a couple of matters related to insurance buying are useful to highlight here. First, although it is unlikely that a single insurance company will offer all the coverages a local government might need, it is likely that a single agent or broker can facilitate the development of an insurance portfolio by accessing coverages from several insurers. Second, only rarely is the insurance coverage the only element of the financing programme. As Chapter 7 shows, organisations retain or self-finance many risks by design or oversight. The necessary limits of coverage may not be available in the marketplace, so the local authority may have to retain losses *above* the overall limits of the policy.

Conversely, by choice a local authority may retain lower levels of a risk. In its simplest form this may occur through the use of deductibles. Deductibles are a feature of insurance contracts where the policyholder agrees to pay the first part of some or all losses (e.g., the first £100, £200 or £500 of each loss). A more aggressive and conscious retention effort would be the establishment of a self-insured retention (SIR), which is an arrangement to retain all losses up to some level, £500 000 for example. Then the insurance programme begins to pay losses above that level. Usually, SIRs are only feasible for larger local authorities that have the financial capacity to retain large amounts of risk.

## Standard coverage types

An average insurance portfolio is likely to contain at least the following standard coverages.

### Property insurance

Property insurance covers all real and personal property the public body owns, or for which the body may be legally liable, against the risk of direct physical loss or damage.

Property and, normally, the contents therein are insured against damage occasioned by fire, lightning and explosion at a minimum. Public bodies will often insure against additional perils such as storm damage, flooding, damage occasioned by burst pipes, malicious damage and the like. Some contents, particularly those that are expensive or hard to replace, are insured on an 'all risks' basis. Cover ordinarily encompasses all forms of accidental damage but excludes loss occasioned by wear and tear, deterioration and maintenance type issues.

Often, because of the size and diversity of functions of local authorities in the UK, the amount of property they own is such that it is administratively unwieldy to specify and value each item of property individually. A more usual approach is to insure the property on what is known as a 'blanket' basis, where property is grouped by type (for example, housing, education properties, general properties) with one cumulative value per property type. The implicit understanding is that the value insured represents the total value of properties insured. The responsibility for maintaining schedules and valuations of properties insured is usually delegated to the policyholder. Losses are normally settled on a reinstatement basis, that is, the cost of replacing as new.

Smaller public bodies may have each property identified separately on a schedule. Difficult to duplicate or expensive items, such as works of art, jewellery, civic regalia and the like, are normally specified and valued individually.

## Boiler and machinery insurance

This coverage provides protection for sudden and accidental breakdown of insured boilers, machinery, air conditioning/refrigeration equipment and the like. Commonly, physical damage to the equipment must occur.

Large equipment usually is excluded from standard property coverages because damage to such equipment often results in collateral damage to other property, and thus insurers like to treat the risk separately. Because of the catastrophic potential, this coverage also provides business interruption and extra expenses coverage, and also extensive inspection services to ensure compliance with statutory requirements.

## Interruption and extra expense insurance

These coverages are only activated by the presence of a direct physical loss that is covered under the standard property policy, meaning that this coverage cannot technically be purchased alone. The coverage provides protection against loss of income or profit, and from extra expenses incurred during the time that the insured property cannot be used. Normally, the policy will put a time limit to the period during which benefits are payable following a direct physical loss.

## General liability insurance

Although many public bodies buy liability policies tailored for the needs of the sector, they all are more or less related to the commercial general liability (CGL) policy, which is the standard liability coverage available in the market. It provides coverage mainly for bodily injury and property damage to third parties caused by, or arising out of, a public body's operations or the use of its facilities.

More generally, the coverage provides protection for all sums the public body is legally obligated to pay, including legal expenses associated with the occurrence in question. It also covers for losses arising from personal injuries, which can include false arrest, defamation, invasion of privacy, wrongful eviction, discrimination and human rights violations, and other intentional torts.

This coverage extends beyond the body itself and covers employees as individuals while acting within the scope of their authority and responsibility.

## Officials indemnity insurance

This coverage is sometimes known as errors and omissions coverage in that it provides protection for any errors or omissions committed by an employee or official. This includes breaches of statutory duty arising from negligent action or inaction, mistake, misstatement, error, neglect, inadvertence or omission in the discharge of duties (and in some policies, also misfeasance, malfeasance, or nonfeasance). This cover is often extended to include liabilities arising out of the performance of the land search and conveyancing function by an authority for a prospective purchaser of land or property. Alternatively, this cover is provided as a stand-alone coverage.

## Motor vehicle insurance

Coverage provided under motor policies is dictated in part by the Motor (Compulsory Insurance) Act 1988. While public bodies are exempted from the terms of the act, by custom they tend to buy the coverage. In general, coverage is provided in two areas: third-party liability arising out of the operation of vehicles, and physical damage to the vehicles themselves.

## Environmental impairment liability insurance

Cover in respect of legal liabilities for injury and property damage arising out of sudden and accidental pollution and associated clean up costs is ordinarily provided as an extension to the general liability insurance coverage. Prior to the early 1990s most public bodies enjoyed protection in respect of legal liabilities for injury and property damage arising out of gradually occurring pollution, but by market agreement this wider cover was withdrawn. Today, some markets are beginning to offer gradual pollution cover in respect of specific sites, but usually only after a detailed site survey. This specific EIL coverage, as it is called, is usually very expensive but is an emerging form of coverage such as to warrant inclusion in this listing.

## Special events liability insurance

Parades, county fairs, conventions and other special events present a number of coverage problems that are not addressed by standard coverages. Special events coverages tend to be similar to general liability policies, except that they are limited to concentrated periods of time and may have particular features to respond to unique circumstances (large crowds, foods being served, fireworks, wild animals, and so on).

## Professional liability insurance

As a direct consequence of the budgetary pressures imposed upon local authorities by central government, many authorities have encouraged their professional service departments such as architects, accountants, information technology, engineers and lawyers, to generate additional revenue by selling their services to other public bodies. This raises an exposure that is not ordinarily covered by either the general liability or officials' indemnity coverages, namely the tort liability arising out of the negligent rendering of professional services. Most local authorities in the UK buy some form of professional negligence cover to protect against claims arising from the provision of services for which they receive some form of remuneration and which they are not statutorily obliged to provide.

## Employers' liability insurance

Employers' Liability insurance provides protection against legal liabilities arising out of death, disease or bodily injury sustained by an employee as a consequence of their employment. The Employers' Liability (Compulsory Insurance) Act 1989 makes this a mandatory coverage for all organisations employing workers. Although public bodies are exempt from this legislation, most public bodies buy Employers' Liability insurance. Originally this cover was available without a specific limit any one occurrence but after a succession of major disasters in the 1980s and the early 1990s, of which Piper Alpha was one of the last, the market imposed a limit of liability per occurrence. Recent changes in legislation now require employers to buy a minimum cover of £5 million any one occurrence, instead of the original £2 million imposed after the Piper Alpha tragedy.

Unlike workers' compensation systems which are prevalent in other parts of the EU, Employers' Liability cover operates on a negligence basis rather than under a no-fault regime. In other words, in order to succeed in their claim an employee has to demonstrate that the employer was negligent in some way, for example, by failing to provide safe working conditions or a safe system of work, rather than just demonstrating that they had been injured at work. While the Pearson Commission recommended a move to a no-fault compensation system in 1978, the proposal has not been acted upon and there seems no reason to anticipate that it will be. There has developed a specific set of case law relating to Employers' Liability.

## Fidelity guarantee insurance

Although public bodies are exempt from the statutory requirement to buy motor and employers' liability insurance, they are required to buy fidelity guarantee insurance. Essentially, this provides protection against fraud carried out by one or more employees against their employer. While the public body may buy coverage to protect against the actions of all employees, it is normal for them to buy higher limits in respect of specific employees in key positions where significant amounts of money are handled or who hold significant cheque signing responsibilities.

## Personal accident insurance

This coverage provides automatic compensation to employees who meet with an accident without the necessity of proving any negligence on the part of their employer. Protection can be bought which operates purely in the event of the employee being assaulted in the course of their employment or in the event of their meeting with an accident at work. Sometimes as an employee benefit public bodies purchase twenty-four hour coverage which operates irrespective of whether the accident occurred during the course of the employee's employment. Personal accident coverage normally provides compensation in the event of an employee's death, provided that the circumstances of death meet the scope of the coverage, for example, as a result of assault. Compensation under a personal accident scheme neither precludes an employee from making an Employers' Liability claim nor does it weaken an employer's ability to resist successfully a claim under the Employers' Liability policy. Benefits are payable either in the form of a set amount per type of injury or disability or on what is termed as the 'continental scale' which is a percentage of a figure payable in the event of death or total disablement.

# TOOLS YOU CAN USE

## How to analyse an insurance contract

Practising risk managers are required to have a high degree of knowledge regarding insurance and insurance contracts. Indeed, insurance expertise is a core competency since no one else in the organisation is likely to have that knowledge, and even when insurance is not present, the risk manager often employs concepts and practices that have been developed by insurance companies (claims management practices, actuarial analysis, underwriting).

Certainly, risk managers know how to analyse insurance contracts. Insurance contracts generally are readable and understandable, but there is a great deal of complexity behind them. Contracts can differ widely, so the commonalities are not always seen easily. Contract analysis is a skill that requires a great deal of experience and practice.

Since the purpose of this book is not to create instant risk managers, but rather to help foster a better understanding of risk management, this section offers a simplified version of a contract analysis method, a method that will not turn readers into expert analysts, but will allow those with a more general interest to navigate their way around most conventional insurance contracts.

### *The Williams method*

A well-known insurance scholar, C. Arthur Williams, Jr, proposed a simplified method of contract analysis that still stands as a useful approach to understanding insurance. His method is developed around three key questions:

1   What events are covered?
2   What must we do after a loss?
3   How much will the insurer pay?

The questions clearly align with the main interests a policyholder will have but, more importantly, they direct analysts to specific parts of the insurance contract. Recall that insurance contracts contain four general sections: the declarations pages, the insuring agreement, the exclusions and the conditions. The answers to each of the three questions will be found in the four sections of the standard contract, as will be seen below.

## What events are covered?

The first question really prompts several supporting questions, which allow the analyst to tease out the specific information necessary to understand what is covered. Those supporting questions are:

1   *What perils are covered?* Perils are causes of loss, so the key concern here is to identify what the organisation's exposures are protected against. In broad terms, contracts will either list the perils (a named perils contract) or will state that the contract covers all perils except for the listed perils it excludes (an all risk contract). This information is available in the insuring agreement section.

2   *What losses are covered?* A clause in the insuring agreement commonly will indicate whether direct, indirect, net income or consequential losses are covered. Normally, it should be assumed that only direct losses are covered in standard contracts.

3   *What property, sources of liability, and people are covered?* Normally the insuring agreement will contain clauses that identify in general terms the types of property, legal interests and individuals covered under the policy, but ordinarily the declarations section will provide specific information (individuals by name, specifically covered acts, itemised lists of covered property).

4   *What is the time frame covered?* The declarations section will indicate when coverage is in force. However, some additional information may be relevant in the insuring agreement (especially when, in the case of some liability coverages, residual coverage may extend beyond the actual contract period).

5   *What are the locations covered?* In general, the insuring agreement contains clauses that clarify where coverage applies and where it does not. For instance, property that is in transit may not be covered under standard property policies, unless endorsements or additional coverage is added. Specific addresses and locations (if necessary) will be itemised in the declarations section.

6   *Do any special conditions apply?* The conditions section of the policy may contain certain clauses about events covered, and any contract analysis should include a look at the conditions section to determine whether any conditions alter coverage described elsewhere in the contract.

## What must we do after a loss?

Most contracts contain provisions that describe what a policyholder must do after a loss; failure to do so can negate otherwise legitimate claims. Most information on post-loss provisions can be found in the conditions section of the insurance policy. Typical provisions include notification requirements after a loss, co-operation (with the insurer) requirements, requirements that reasonable steps be taken to minimise losses, and disclosure or proof of loss requirements.

## How much will the insurer pay?

Broadly speaking, four provisions in an insurance contract will determine the amount paid out. Those provisions are:

1   *Indemnity provisions.* Provisions usually contained in the declarations, but perhaps also in the insuring agreement, will define and explain the terms of indemnification (indemnification means the value of the loss is restored). Analysts should look for:
    (a)   a measure of loss provision which indicates the basis for reimbursement (actual cash value, replacement cost)
    (b)   an insurable interest clause, which indicates who may recover for a loss
    (c)   the duplicate coverage clause, which prevents claimants from collecting for one loss under multiple policies
    (d)   the subrogation provision, which indicates whether rights of recovery from a negligent third party are retained or transferred to the insurance company.
2   *The coinsurance clause.* A provision that is seen somewhat infrequently, it would be found in the insuring agreement and is simply a means by which the insurer encourages the policyholder to insure property at or near the full value of the property. A penalty may be invoked if property is significantly underinsured. Alternatively, a co-insurance clause may be present in a coverage where there is a high moral hazard element – e.g. libel and slander.
3   *The deductible provisions.* The declarations section commonly will identify whether there is a loss-sharing provision (a deductible) that applies to losses. Naturally this will influence how much the policyholder will receive.
4   *The contract limits.* Also found in the declarations section, the overall limits of the policy will govern the outer parameters of any indemnification payment. Sometimes property and liability policies have internal limits (i.e., although a policy will have an overall amount that can be paid out, certain items may have specific limits).

# READ MORE ABOUT IT

## The Bellwin Scheme

Under Section 155 of the Local Government and Housing Act 1989 the Department of Environment, Transport and the Regions (DETR) has the power to make discretionary payments to English local authorities and police authorities in certain circumstances under a scheme known as the Bellwin Scheme. Similar schemes are operated by the Scottish and Welsh Offices for authorities in their areas. The description of the scheme that follows is that operating in England.

To qualify for consideration under the Bellwin Scheme there has to be an emergency or disaster involving danger to life or property and expenditures qualifying for reimbursement can only relate to immediate action to safeguard life or property or to prevent inconvenience.

In the UK local authorities have statutory powers to deal with emergencies and are expected to plan accordingly. There is no automatic entitlement to special assistance under the Bellwin Scheme – consequently the scheme is entirely discretionary. Any incident for which assistance is sought must involve conditions that clearly are exceptional by local standards. Moreover, the damage to local authority infrastructure or communities must be exceptional in relation to normal experience. Typically, the scheme has been invoked in response to severe flooding and storms and then only in respect of the non-insurable elements thereof. Any application for assistance under the Bellwin Scheme must demonstrate that an undue financial burden would otherwise fall on the authority. Clearly, the purpose of the scheme is to provide emergency relief, not to put right all the ill effects of an incident.

For the scheme to be activated the local authority or authorities must notify the DETR within one month of the incident occurring and then submit full details of the incident. If the DETR decide that the incident is of sufficient gravity for the Bellwin Scheme to be invoked, the decision will be announced in Parliament.

The authority's chief finance officer or someone of similar standing will be required to sign any claim form to the effect that the claim complies in all respect with the terms of the scheme. Moreover, the claim will need to be signed by an auditor appointed by the Audit Commission. The DETR will set a deadline for the receipt of an audited form. In exceptional circumstances the DETR will make a payment on account to a local authority based on its estimate of the authority's entitlement to grant and subject to adjustment after audit. However, it is normal for a payment to be made once the local authority has completed its expenditure and is in a position to provide detailed and audited accounts.

Under the rules of the Bellwin Scheme for financial year 1999/2000 a local authority making a successful application for assistance will receive 85 per cent of qualifying expenditure above the authority's threshold. The threshold amount varies by local authority and for any given authority from year to year. The DETR calculates and publishes the threshold for each authority ahead of the financial year in which it applies. The amount of the threshold is based on 0.2 per cent of the local authority's SSA. There is no maximum limit to the amount a local authority may recover under the Bellwin Scheme in any one financial year, although as the qualifying expenditure is that which relates to immediate action it is, therefore, self-limiting to an extent.

The DETR make no specific budget provision for payments under the Bellwin Scheme, although they are reported as a line item in the departmental report and accounts. Theoretically, the DETR can make recoveries from the Treasury reserves but in practice meet the costs from savings from other local government schemes.

In the event that the Bellwin Scheme is invoked in respect of a particular incident, the local authority may recover 85 per cent of any amount in excess of the threshold of expenditure incurred

- by the local authority on or in connection with the taking of immediate action to safeguard life or property or to prevent suffering or inconvenience in its area or among its inhabitants
- as a result of the incidents specified in the scheme
- on works completed before a specified deadline (usually two months from the incident)

and which is

- not in respect of costs which are *normally* insurable either by the authority or any other party, for example, by householders under household insurance. (Non-ranking excesses are recoverable under the scheme but any additional deductible or self-insured retention are not.)
- net of any receipts
- not of a capital nature or capitalised.

## Qualifying and non-qualifying expenditures

Under the current rules of the Bellwin Scheme, Table 8.1 identifies what is normally deemed to be qualifying and non-qualifying expenditure. However, in all cases it must be borne in mind that the scheme is discretionary in nature and the intention is to provide emergency relief.

**Table 8.1**

| Qualifying expenditure | Non-qualifying expenditure |
|---|---|
| In relation to non administration purposes, the cost of setting up temporary premises, costs of removal, increased costs due to rent, rates, taxes, lighting, cleaning and insurance | Loss of income |
| Hire of additional vehicles, plant and machinery and incidental expenses | Normal wages and salaries of the authority's regular employees, whether diverted from their normal work or not, and the standing costs of the authority's plant and equipment |
| Removal of all trees and timber which is or may be dangerous to the public, irrespective of ownership | Longer-term works of repair or restoration e.g., tree planting, repair and refurbishment of damaged but not dangerous structures |
| Costs of initial repairs to highways, pavements and footpaths, where a tree, item of street furniture or debris from a damaged building has fallen and the surface of the road must be replaced at the time or temporarily patched | Payments to householders and others under Section 138 of the Local Government Act 1972 which do not meet the qualifying criteria, e.g., payments in respect of insurable items |
| The costs of initial land drainage works, clearing debris and unblocking water courses, which are or may be the cause of danger to the public | Any element of betterment |
| The costs of other work to clear debris causing obstruction or damage to highways, pavements and footpaths | Expenditure eligible for any other specific grant, e.g., police grant |
| Additional temporary employees or contractors to work on the emergency or replace permanent employees diverted from normal work | Any amounts in respect of specific works on coast protection or flood defence which had already been allocated within budgeted expenditure to these works before the incident occurred |

**Table 8.1**  continued

| Qualifying expenditure | Non-qualifying expenditure |
| --- | --- |
| Special overtime for employees either during the emergency or afterwards to catch up on work from which they were diverted by the incident | Any expenditure on flood defence or coast protection which will be compensated by the Ministry of Agriculture Fisheries and Food by means of grant or credit approvals |
| Emergency works required to safeguard dangerous structures, including making them secure, where not insurable | Any expenditure which is of a capital nature or capitalised |
| Costs of evacuating people from dangerous structures and temporary rehousing | |
| Costs of temporary mortuaries | |
| Costs of providing emergency supplies of food and other emergency provisions and key services to affected communities during the period of the emergency | |
| Costs of maintaining key communications, in particular clearing roads or providing emergency information to affected communities | |
| Costs incurred under the Military Assistance to the Civil Community Scheme | |
| Where repair is insufficient, the removal and replacement of street lighting, street signs, bus shelters and other street furniture, fences, railings and uninsured buildings damaged by the incident, where in its damaged state it presents a danger to public safety or security | |
| Legal clerical and other charges incurred on the above work | |
| Payments made under Section 138 of the Local Government Act 1972 where they meet the qualifying expenditure criteria | |
| Non-ranking insurance excesses | |

# 9

# Member-owned organisations and intergovernmental pooling

## EXECUTIVE SUMMARY

Member-owned organisations are defined as organisations owned by the members enjoying their services. By pooling and sharing resources the membership can achieve more collectively than they could individually and can help reduce their risks and uncertainties.

The worldwide intergovernmental pooling movement uses the member-owned organisational model to help its constituent members manage, control and finance their risks and exposures more effectively. The accepted view of public bodies is that they are hardly ever innovative or entrepreneurial. However, their response to the withdrawal of or their dissatisfaction with the commercial insurance market – the establishment of intergovernmental pools – gives the lie to this assertion.

Ten key factors crucial for the establishment of a successful pool are identified and discussed – finding and maintaining a sense of urgency, homogeneity of interest, organisational support and long-term commitment, quality underwriting, risk sharing and pricing, prudent funding, equitable profit and loss distribution, risk management and cost-effective programme administration.

However, the inherent weakness of the member-owned organisation, unavailability of external capital, the growing demutualisation movement and the re-emergence of a vibrant, competitive commercial insurance market all pose significant threats to the long-term viability of the movement. At the very least, these external threats are causing the intergovernmental pooling movement to question its *raison d'être*, to sharpen its focus and to accentuate the benefits of membership to its members.

# PRINCIPLES AND CONCEPTS

Around the world public bodies have used the member-owned organisational model in an innovative and entrepreneurial way to create intergovernmental pools in response to the absence of or their dissatisfaction with the commercial insurance market.

This chapter discusses the principles behind the member-owned organisational model and the forms in which it is normally found in the UK. The genesis of the intergovernmental pooling movement is then traced in five countries – the UK, the Netherlands, Japan, the USA and Australia. Ten key factors for the creation of a successful member-owned organisation are then identified and discussed. The chapter concludes with an examination of the future of member-owned organisations in general and intergovernmental pools in particular.

## The concept behind member-owned organisations

Member-owned organisations differ from shareholder-owned organisations by virtue of their being owned by the organisations and individuals enjoying their services. The principle behind member-owned organisations is both simple and complex. It is simple in the sense that the sharing or pooling of the resources purely for the benefit of the members is a means of protection; if a group of individuals pool their time and effort they can provide for a common defence that is more effective than could be provided through individual initiative. This is an example of resource pooling, which commonly has the goal of extending capabilities.

It is complex in the sense that the sharing or pooling of resources focuses more on the matter of risk or uncertainty reduction. The sharing or pooling of resources can improve predictability, stabilise budgeting and forecasting, and reduce fear and worry. As was discussed in Chapter 8, it is not the risks and exposures themselves that are being pooled but the resources required to deal with those risks and exposures.

For the purposes of this book, readers should recognise that two distinct things can result from the sharing of resources: participants are able to achieve more than they can as individuals, and uncertainty and risk can be reduced.

# Forms of member-owned organisations

The most common forms of member-owned organisations to be found in the UK are as follows.

## Guaranteed indemnity mutuals

In a UK insurance context this form of mutual provides a guaranteed indemnity to its members that is enforceable under contract law. These mutuals will comply with the Insurance Act 1982 to the extent that they have capitalised to at least the minimum requirement level and maintain at least the minimum surplus margin of assets over liabilities. Examples of guaranteed indemnity mutuals in the UK would include Municipal Mutual Insurance, Ecclesiastical Insurance and the many life insurance mutuals.

## Discretionary mutuals

These mutuals provide an indemnity to their members that is not enforceable under contract law. The managers or directors of the mutual may exercise their discretion in determining whether indemnity will be provided in any case. Following the landmark case of *Medical Defence Union* v. *Department of Trade and Industry* (1979), provided the discretionary mutual can show that it exercises its discretion impartially, then it can be held not to be transacting insurance. The benefits of this are that the discretionary mutual can avoid the necessity of complying with the Insurance Act 1982, particularly with regard to the level of initial capitalisation and maintenance of solvency margins. Examples of discretionary mutuals in the UK are the Medical Defence Union, the Solicitors' Indemnity Fund and the many marine Protection & Indemnity clubs.

Mutuals, whether offering guaranteed or discretionary indemnities, may have some form of assessibility provision within their articles of association because they cannot access external capital and are reliant upon their members' resources. Some mutuals have a limited ability to assess their members and this maximum amount they can levy is usually defined as a fixed sum (£10 per member in the case of Municipal Mutual Insurance, for example) or a percentage of contributions or loss costs. Other mutuals do not put a cap on the amount they can call from their members and, therefore, each member, theoretically at least, has an unlimited liability in the event that the mutual runs into difficulties. Some mutuals dispense with assessibility provisions entirely.

## Risk-purchasing groups

These would not exist to finance or retain risk in the way that guaranteed and discretionary mutuals do but, rather, to pool their resources collectively in order to obtain risk protection collectively at rates more advantageous than they would obtain individually. A risk-purchasing consortium exists for police authority property risks in the UK.

## Risk management pools

These exist to pool resources to manage risks as opposed to financing risks more effectively than would be possible by a member individually. For example, a public body may not be able to finance from its budget the salary and on-costs of a risk manager. However, by combining resources with other public bodies of a similar size, they may be able to employ such an individual collectively and each enjoy a share of their time. Interestingly, in the USA there is evidence that some pools that started out life as risk-financing pools are transmuting into risk management pools, partly as a way to withstand competition from the commercial insurance industry (see 'Read More About It' section).

# The intergovernmental pooling movement

Examples of member-owned organisations created by public bodies to manage and finance risk can be found throughout the world. Unbeknown to him, a councillor from St Pancras in London, the playwright George Bernard Shaw, was at the forefront of this movement. Their existence provides a powerful counter-argument to the view that public bodies are not innovative. With the possible exception of Australia, each country seems to have developed its pools in isolation and there is little evidence of any serious or sustained attempt to share experiences, successes and failures across countries. Intergovernmental pools are clearly a twentieth-century phenomenon with the real growth in pool population taking place in the last twenty-five years. Nonetheless, Municipal Mutual was formed in the UK in 1903 and three of the Japanese *kyousai* were created in the 1940s.

Pools have taken different forms and structures and have occasionally metamorphosed during the course of their existence into something else. So form and structure are not of themselves defining characteristics which immediately mark out an organisation as being an intergovernmental pool. What more precisely defines an inter-governmental pool?

Membership is the first defining characteristic. To be categorised as an intergovernmental pool an organisation has to serve public entities. This in turn requires definition. By public entity we mean a governmental or local agency, municipality or local authority which has elected members and which is charged with performing one or more services for the benefit of the local population. Public entities may be single-purpose specific such as school boards or fire services or may be complex multi-service providing bodies such as municipalities. But their overriding purpose, indeed their sole *raison d'être*, has to be the provision of or the facilitation of services which assist with the functioning of a community or are for the public good.

Membership of a pool must consist of more than one such public entity. While it can be argued that the individual functions of a complex multi-service providing organisation could be regarded as having the financial resources to be regarded as separate and distinct parts within an overall umbrella, only organisations with two or more separate and independent public entities in membership are regarded as intergovernmental pools. Moreover, entry and exit from membership must be regulated. Unlike a corporation, the domain in which a pool can operate and the membership it can attract are clearly prescribed in its rules and constitution. Membership of a pool is a commitment and, therefore, exit from membership must be carefully controlled to ensure the well-being of the pool and the remaining members.

The second defining characteristic is ownership. To be regarded as an intergovernmental pool the organisation has to be owned by its members. There are no shareholders external to the member entities. Mutual insurance companies and building societies are typical examples of organisations owned by their members. But only where the members are public entities could such a company be regarded as being an intergovernmental pool.

As a consequence of the way an intergovernmental pool is owned, financing is a third defining characteristic. Because the pool is the membership and vice versa, and there are no external shareholders, the only source of revenue for the pool is from the membership itself. The pools' operations are funded from contributions levied from the members. There is no access to external capital. Consequently, if the contributions levied from the members are not sufficient to meet its expenses then the only redress the pool has to obtain additional money is to make an additional call from its members. Although pools use different methods to assess the level of contribution to be paid by any one member, they usually have the facility within their powers to return to their membership for additional funds.

The fourth defining characteristic is focus. An intergovernmental pool's focus and *raison d'être* is to provide a service or services to its member public entities. Unlike a corporation which is created by its stockholders to provide services to clients external to the corporation, a pool is created to satisfy the needs of its membership, its stockholders. However, as a by-product, it may offer services to non-members because the service is unique or superior to that which is commercially available or simply as a function of oversupply. Pools are inward looking, not outward looking in terms of focus and service provision.

The fifth defining characteristic is that the mission of a pool is either to reduce uncertainty among its members or to extend resources through collective action.

More as a result of coincidence rather than a defining characteristic is the observation that pools frequently enjoy significant regulatory and tax advantages over commercial providers i.e., corporate providers of the self-same services. While this has clearly been of enormous benefit to pools and has helped many pools to survive and prosper, the absence of such advantages would not impact on our ability to recognise an organisation to be an intergovernmental pool.

In summary, what characterises an intergovernmental pool above all and without any of which the authors would debate long and hard that an organisation could not be regarded as being an intergovernmental pool are:

- membership consisting of two or more public entities and consisting exclusively of public entities
- owned exclusively by its members
- financed entirely by its members
- focused solely on the provision of services to its members
- mandated to reduce members' uncertainty and/or to extend their resources.

## Reasons for formation

### The UK

Mutualisation was a well-developed concept in nineteenth-century Britain. As Britain enjoyed the fruits of being at the forefront of the Industrial Revolution and a major manufacturing and trading power, civic pride came to the fore. Local communities, either through their own resources or through the patronage of local worthies, sought to broadcast to the world their affluence and growing self-confidence through municipal building programmes. Magnificent town halls, schools and other public buildings were built throughout the land. As prudent holders of the public purse, the proud municipalities insured the buildings in the established commercial insurance market, another area in which Victorian Britain was pre-eminent.

However, as the nineteenth century drew to a close, a number of municipalities began to question whether the commercial insurance market was providing them with value for money. In comparison with many buildings erected commercially in the period, municipal buildings were sturdier, of sounder construction and represented less of a fire risk to insurers. A survey commissioned by the County Treasurer of Northumberland County Council in the late 1890s showed that the fire premiums paid by county and non-county borough and county councils over the preceding twenty years exceeded the total sum received by way of claim payments by a factor of 300 per cent.

Prior to the formation of Municipal Mutual in 1903 there was evidence that the idea of creating a mutual insurance company for municipal authorities was finding favour:

1   Some county councils and the County Councils' Association had been actively considering the subject since at least 1898, and probably before.
2   The Urban District Councils' Association had debated the idea in 1899.
3   Municipal authorities of all kinds were on record as being in favour of the idea.
4   Three conferences had been formed – in the north, London and Eastbourne – to explore the viability of the concept.
5   The London County Council had included a clause, subsequently withdrawn, in their General Powers Act 1902 enabling them to set up a mutual insurance facility.

Municipalities in the UK were, and still are, creatures of statute, meaning that they have no powers and rights outside those prescribed by legislation. There was a concern as to whether municipalities were empowered to establish their own mutual insurance company, in other words 'was it *intra vires*?' Comfort was obtained from Alexander Macmorran QC, a leading specialist in local government law, who opined in June 1900 that:

it may be assumed that every municipal body may lawfully insure against fire. And it may further be assumed that they have a wide discretion as to the manner in which they will insure . . . there seems no good reason why they should not hand over their insurance premiums to Trustees constituted for the purpose of receiving, managing and applying them . . . they would insure with the Trustees as if the Trustees were a company and I cannot see anything ultra vires in their so doing . . . after the first year or two it would be manifestly to the advantage of every authority to insure through the Trustees and so share in the benefit of the Scheme.

George Bernard Shaw, in his capacity as representative of St Pancras Borough Council, read out a statement of support for the proposition that a mutual insurance company be formed in January 1903. On 20 January 1903 the Memorandum and Articles of Association were approved. On 13 March 1903 Municipal Mutual Insurance Limited was registered with a mission to enable metropolitan borough councils, boards of guardians, municipal corporations, county councils, local authorities, school boards, public commissioners, charity trustees and charitable institutions and other public bodies and authorities by co-operation to insure against fire and other risks on the most favourable terms. By 1974 Municipal Mutual was the predominant provider of all classes of insurance to the public sector in the UK, to the extent that hardly any commercial insurer bothered with the sector. The authors are indebted to *Covering 75 Years* by A.E. MacDonald, published by Municipal Mutual Insurance Ltd, 1978, for this section.

## The Netherlands

An intergovernmental pool called FOG was created in 1940 in rather unusual circumstances. FOG provides fidelity and money coverages and, latterly, has extended its brief to include computer related risks. Up until 1940 Dutch municipalities bought these coverages from Lloyd's of London. However, following the German occupation of the Netherlands early in the Second World War, commerce with England was no longer possible and so the councils were forced to create their own risk-financing vehicle to provide the coverages. In the mid-1990s some Dutch municipalities, frustrated by the cost and breadth of cover available in the commercial insurance market, created another intergovernmental pool, AOG, to manage their liability exposures.

## Japan

The beginning of the intergovernmental *kyousai* (roughly, 'pool') movement can be traced to 1924 when legislation was unsuccessfully put forward to create a mutual financial aid programme for

towns and villages in Japan. Although the objective of this legislation was not realised until 1948, the effort reflected early concerns
among local authority leaders that towns and villages did not have
the financial means to withstand property losses due to fortuitous
events. It also directly influenced measures that were taken between
1924 and 1948; measures that played a role in setting the stage for
the passage of enabling legislation.

Interestingly, the specific impetus for the 1924 legislation was
concern about the affordability and availability of commercial insurance coverage. Although evidence is sketchy, it appears that the cost
of commercial property coverage was viewed as 'excessively high'
during this period, and there is some suggestion from the documents
of this period (the 1920s) that terms and conditions of coverage were
dictated by the insurance industry to local authorities, with little
sensitivity to issues relevant to public sector institutions.

As a result of this reality (or perception of reality), the national
association representing towns and villages initiated a lobbying effort
directed at the national government to permit creation of a *kyousai*,
and the 1924 legislation was the result. Unfortunately for the towns
and villages, their lobbying efforts were countered – according to
reports from that time – by fierce insurance industry lobbying, and the
legislation did not pass. Between 1924 and 1940, lesser efforts were
periodically undertaken to press for the *kyousai* concept. Although
none were directly successful, the cumulative effect of these recurring
efforts was an initiative undertaken in 1941 by the Ministry of
Commerce and Industry to broker an agreement between the towns
and villages association and the insurance industry. This process produced a group insurance purchasing arrangement, which provided the
basis for group purchase of fire insurance at a negotiated discounted
rate. It also included some provision for association involvement in
loss control and claims administration. This arrangement lasted until
1945; not coincidentally, the year the Second World War concluded.

After 1945, and concurrent with US directed efforts to reform
national and local government in Japan, the towns and villages association sought to renegotiate the group purchasing arrangement with
the insurance industry. However ,the economically uncertain post-
war period prevented a satisfactory resolution to this problem and,
in 1947–8, the association once again sought national legislation to
permit formation of a *kyousai*, which finally occurred in 1948.

The passage of legislation in 1948 is a rather interesting story in
its own right. In 1946 the National Towns and Villages Association
started renegotiating a new contract to continue the group
purchasing programme that had been in place since 1941. Due to
numerous economic and social factors (including, importantly,

extremely high inflation), the insurance industry offered a minimal discount. The association reluctantly accepted this arrangement but then began a lobbying effort with the national Diet to reform local government legislation to permit a full pooling arrangement to exist.

The Diet and the Ministry of Finance did not take strong positions on this idea, and intense lobbying by the insurance industry at least partly explains this reticence. However, other factors were at work. At the time Japan was under allied forces' administration, and thus it was impossible to legislate without the approval of the General Headquarters (GHQ). The towns and villages association petitioned GHQ, which responded with the following concerns:

1   How could towns and villages implement the technically difficult insurance administration?
2   How could towns and villages finance the reserve for the huge amount covered, which might be incurred at the beginning of the *kyousai's* life?

In order to ease those concerns, the association undertook an intensive lobbying and educational effort directed at GHQ, and eventually GHQ came to embrace enthusiastically the idea. It was due to this support that Article 263-2 of the Local Autonomy Law was passed into law in early 1948. By April of that year the National Towns and Villages Association had cancelled its commercial insurance and the *kyousai* programme had taken effect.

The early success of this *kyousai* prompted the formation of the other *kyousai* within a period of four years.

Although the *kyousai* programmes were intended to cover property losses, three of them (all but the public-housing kyousai) added automobile property coverage in the 1950s. The reasons for this addition were:

1   Local governments began to have a much greater exposure in this area.
2   Covering automobile damage became a more visible burden to public finances.
3   Since commercial automobile insurance rates were high, purchasing commercial automobile insurance imposed an additional burden on public resources.
4   In 1955, the Automobile Compensation Security Law created a strict liability (no fault) environment for accidents.

In 1970 the prefectures *kyousai* started covering machine damage at hydroelectric plants. This initiative was prompted by significant damages to several plants in 1965 and 1967 arising from torrential rainfall in those years. Despite the fact that commercial property coverage was in place, claims were uniformly denied due to the fact that the losses were flood related. Frustration among the prefectures led to a special programme for these plants.

## The USA

State and local governments have experienced two insurance crises, the first occurring in the mid- to late 1970s and the second in the mid-1980s. These downturns in the insurance market were the result of cyclical market problems, the state of the economy preceding each episode, insurance industry management practices, and inherent insurance pricing problems. The basic riskiness (or perceived riskiness) of the insured – state and local governments – probably was a factor as well. Regardless of the causes, the result has been a twenty-year period in which state and local governments have been able to afford insurance (particularly liability insurance) only intermittently – if insurance has been available at all.

In response to this problem, local governments, government associations and, even, state governments acted to create alternative risk-financing mechanisms to provide coverage for local governments. These mechanisms, commonly referred to as self-insurance pools, enabled local governments within a state to pool together risks and resources to finance the costs of fortuitous losses. Initially, the pools provided mainly liability and workers' compensation coverage for members. However, pools today provide a wide range of coverages, ranging from property coverage to employee benefits.

A 1988 study of pools found that approximately 200 public risk-financing pools operated in the USA. Those pools, with an estimated aggregate membership of between 15 000 and 20 000 entities, were found in almost all regions of the country (although more than half of the pools were located in California). Almost all pools were homogeneous as to membership; that is, school districts pooled with school districts, counties with counties, and so on. The pools tended to be homogeneous as to member population/size as well. Almost all pool participants could be characterised as small local governments. The pools themselves, however, varied widely in terms of size; the smallest pools reported three to five participating governments and the largest reported 1100 to 1300 members.

In 1994, a follow-up study was conducted to find out the degree to which the pooling environment had changed. It had changed, dramatically. The findings indicated that there were at least 400 pools in operation, and that these pools had an aggregate membership of 30 000 to 35 000 local entities. Pools still remained the preserve of small local governments, with membership consisting largely of entities in communities with populations under 25 000.

By 1994, pooling had spread throughout the USA, and California no longer dominated the pooling world. Over half the pools were sponsored by associations (leagues of cities, counties, school board associations, etc.) and the estimated aggregate contributions were thought to be about $5.5 billion.

Since 1994, evidence suggests that pool growth has moderated. No updating studies have been undertaken as of 2000, but experienced observers suggest that the number of pools has plateaued at somewhere between 425 and 450. The reasons for the slowdown in expansion will be identified later, but certainly the re-emergence of a vigorous and competitive commercial insurance marketplace has been a key factor.

## Australia

Municipal Mutual Australia, a subsidiary of the UK's Municipal Mutual, established operations in the late 1980s and wrote municipal business very aggressively, establishing significant market presence in a very short period of time. However, the problems besetting the UK mutual forced Municipal Mutual Australia to stop writing business. Rather like their US counterparts, the Australian local authorities had no insurance market to meet their risk-financing needs. As in the USA, a number of Australian councils took matters into their own hands and established intergovernmental pools in the early 1990s. It has to be said, however, that the level of commitment to pools shown by the councils and the level of success has been more questionable than in other parts of the world.

## Conclusion

The brief review of the genesis of intergovernmental pooling across four continents has a common thread – either the complete absence of a commercial insurance market (the USA, the Netherlands and Australia) or frustration at the pricing and breadth of cover offered to municipalities by the commercial insurance industry (the UK and Japan).

# Key factors for success

Hugh Rosenbaum of Tillinghast–Towers Perrin, a promoter of captive insurance companies in the private sector, developed ten key factors for success. These factors are equally as relevant to any form of member-owned organisation.

## Finding and maintaining a sense of urgency

As we have seen earlier, many public sector member-owned organisations around the world were established in response to either the non-availability or unaffordability of insurance in the conventional insurance market. The strong sense of dissatisfaction and, in some cases, crisis drove many public bodies to take very innovative actions. However, the return of commercially available insurance has challenged the very *raison d'être* of the intergovernmental pooling movement, which in the USA is the common term given to member-owned organisations formed by public entities. The 'Read More About It' section explores the challenges facing many pools in the USA but, clearly, these organisations need to find ways of demonstrating their value to their members. The demutualisation movement is symptomatic of members losing faith in the advantages of member-owned organisations.

## Homogeneity of interest

This helps to provide focus and enables the member-owned organisation to become the pre-eminent expert in managing its members' risks and exposures.

## Organisational support

Commitment to the member-owned organisation by the senior managers and elected members or stakeholders of the constituent members strengthens its ability to meet its long-term objectives without overly concerning itself about the stability of membership numbers. The recent 'carpetbagging' movement threatening many member-owned organisations shows the inherent instability of member-owned organisations that lack member commitment. Corporate members have probably got a greater degree of in-built inertia than do organisations whose membership comprises of individuals.

## Long-term commitment

Of course, there are many ways in which member-owned organisations can create organisational support by introducing some form of impediment to easy exit. Common devices include 'handcuffs' such as exit fees where a member has to pay an additional sum to leave, an initial capital investment over and above any premium requirement or the commitment to pay a small amount of capital over a period of time. Devices such as these provide the member-owned organisation with the stability required to keep going, particularly at the outset.

## Quality underwriting

Member-owned organisations which are risk-taking and risk-financing vehicles can only survive in the long term by virtue of the quality of their underwriting. While price is clearly a determinant (and many member-owned organisations have tax advantages over their commercial insurance competitors), their focus and restricted membership enables them to be more innovative, particularly in respect of programme structure and breadth of coverage.

## Risk sharing and pricing

Demonstrable equity of pricing is a key success factor. A key question member-owned organisations have to ask themselves is to what extent they want a members' own loss experience to determine their risk-financing costs. Particularly for public bodies, whose own budgetary processes cannot afford the peaks and troughs of the commercial insurance market, predictability and stability of costs are very important, probably more so to smaller members than equity of costs relative to loss experience.

## Prudent funding

Member-owned organisations that do not have to comply legally with any minimum solvency margins (the amount by which assets exceed liabilities) have the choice of funding losses on a pay-as-you-go basis or on a pre-funded basis. Superficially, the pay-as-you-go approach has attractions because it means that a loss has only to be specifically funded for when it is being settled. Particularly with long-tail risks such as general and employers' liability where the time span between incident occurrence, claim notification and claim settlement is often measured in years, a pay-as-you-go approach can result in relatively little having to be found in the early years to pay losses but in accelerating funding requirements as the account matures. A pre-funded loss approach means that on day one an amount is set aside which is commensurate with the anticipated cost of losses for that year. A pay-as-you-go approach means a lower entry price initially into the member-owned organisation but a pre-funded approach means, all things being equal, a more consistent cost year on year.

Whichever approach is used, prudence in establishing funds should be exercised and assistance in achieving this at the outset and in monitoring its continuing adequacy can be obtained from consulting actuaries. As predictability and stability of costs is of key concern to many public bodies, this argues strongly for the pre-funded approach.

## Equitable profit and loss distribution

Critics of member-owned organisations point out that an inherent weakness is that they have no access to external capital and have to rely on the assets of their membership. It is vitally important, therefore, on creation of a member-owned organisation that the issue of member assessment has been considered. How are assessments to be made if the organisation needs more money? Assessibility provisions should be promoted. They are not an admission of weakness but rather a sign of prudence so that all members know what their obligations are. Clearly the organisation should operate and fund in a way that the assessibility provision is unlikely to be invoked but, nonetheless, the provision, if required, contains no surprises for the membership. Equally, member-owned organisations must consider ahead of time how to handle surpluses either when they wind up operations or when they have more money than they need. They need to consider whether surplus is to be redistributed and, if so, whether the formula for redistribution is to be based on contributions or loss experience, or whether the surplus is to be used to provide more cover or services. Either way, the key to a contented membership is a clearly laid out strategy so that there are no surprises.

## Risk control and claims management

The real opportunity for member-owned organisations to make a difference is not in funding losses properly but in promoting sufficient risk management initiatives to change the risk profile so that real losses come down and members save money and receive returns by way of surplus distribution. The key to this is focused and effective risk control and claims management programmes.

## Cost-effectiveness

A key challenge for member-owned organisations is to demonstrate that they are providing their services more cost-effectively than the shareholder-owned organisations. However, it is important to recognise with what expenses are being compared. If the organisation is so successful that it eliminates all losses, then its expense ratio will be 100 per cent. In the USA many pools have invested in proactive risk and loss control such that they have reduced the overall loss profile but, because expenses now represent a larger proportion of the overall cost of risk, their expense ratio is being compared adversely with those of insurance companies. If, however, they were to reduce their expense ratio they run the risk of losses rising again. It is important, therefore, to put the expense ratio into perspective and to understand the base against which it is being measured. (See Chapter 8 for a fuller discussion on the ratios used to assess the performance of insurance companies.)

## The future for member-owned organisations

The demise of Municipal Mutual, the pre-eminent public sector risk-financing mutual in the UK, in 1992 suggests *prima facie* that the future for such organisations may not be too bright. The 'Read More About It' section to this chapter gives an analysis of the collapse of Municipal Mutual and the implications this may have in general for the public sector pooling movement. Some of the reasons for Municipal Mutual's demise highlight the inherent weaknesses of member-owned organisations – their inability to access external capital and to withstand a sustained price war in a soft and vibrant insurance market. As purely risk-financing vehicles, they are in their element when the insurance market is either hard or nonexistent. Nowadays, with soft insurance market conditions, excess capacity and aggressive competition their reason for existence is more questionable.

As well as sustained and aggressive competition, the current trend of 'carpetbagging' poses enormous threats to member-owned organisations. Members are no longer content to be a member of a mutual. They realise that if their share of the mutual was translated into equity value in a shareholder-owned organisation, they would obtain significantly more, in the short term at least, than they do by way of dividends or subsidised premiums or rates. Many mutual building societies and mutual insurance companies are fighting rearguard battles to prevent their members from voting to transfer the status of their organisation from member owned to shareholder owned. Some already have lost the battle and others have given up without a fight. 'Carpetbagging' or the demand by its members for an organisation to demutualise casts a significant shadow over the future of member-owned organisations.

However, the future is not all doom and gloom. 'Carpetbagging' has been prevalent among member-owned organisations where the membership comprises of individuals rather than organisations. Member-owned organisations comprising of organisations are less volatile. The temptation to make a 'fast buck' is less attractive to an organisation than to an individual. While 'carpetbagging' may prove an insurmountable problem for the long-term viability of member-owned organisations comprising of individuals, the same may not be true where the membership comprises of organisations.

Second, the current Labour government has assisted the member-owned organisation movement in the public sector by effectively forcing National Health Trusts, at least for their liability and property risks, out of the commercial insurance sector and back into a mutual risk-financing arrangement. While the economic rationale for this move in the Health Minister's statement showed a degree of financial naivety, it could suggest that the Labour government sees the natural home for the financing of public sector risks as the pooled resources of the organisations creating the risk in the first place. Central government's imprimatur cannot but help the prospects of the member-owned organisation movement in the public sector.

---

# APPLICATIONS

## Pool formation challenges

A well-known academic article, Barry D. Smith's 'A model for workers' compensation group self insurance: the Delaware Valley School Districts plan' (*Journal of Risk and Insurance*, September 1983) presents a 'present at the creation' story regarding the formation of an early pool. A brief retelling of parts of the story serves to flesh out the abstract discussion of pools presented in the chapter.

The Delaware Valley School Districts' Self-Insured Workers' Compensation Association is an 'intermediate unit' of the school system in the state of Pennsylvania. It is located just west of Philadelphia, and in the early 1980s it developed the idea of forming a pool for financing the workers' compensation exposure of its nineteen member entities. Initial thinking was favourable to pooling because each member had annual payrolls of $3 million to $17 million; they were not inconsequential entities, but they were not capable of self-financing the risk on their own. The entities were relatively homogeneous (an important feature for pooling common risks), and their loss experiences were roughly similar. To add to the motivation, the commercial insurance industry seemed to be overcharging for insurance, since the average loss ratio for the members was about 30 per cent.

The association reasoned that the pooling of risks would not only produce lower year-in/year-out costs to members, but would also facilitate better and more focused loss control efforts to be undertaken by the pool.

In Smith's analysis of the pool, he observed that there were three key features of the plan:

- the use of a self-insured retention level for each individual school district
- the development of a jointly financed central fund to pay losses exceeding each school district's retention level
- the purchase of excess insurance for the catastrophic exposure.

Two criteria were determined to be important in setting proper retention levels. First, the level had to be high enough to relieve the central fund of the administrative burden of payments for most losses. Second, a level had to be set that would encourage loss prevention activities. The same line of reasoning was applied in thinking about the attachment point between the pool's retention and the excess insurance programme.

At the time the article was written, the author speculated whether other pools would follow suit and develop a structure that was organised along the lines described in his article. Sixteen years of subsequent experience have shown that this approach is about the most widely adopted methodology used in pooling.

---

# TOOLS YOU CAN USE

## Evaluating a pool

Although the growth of pools is not as dynamic as it was in the 1980s and early 1990s, local authorities may still find themselves in a position of looking at a pool as an option for their risk-financing. Or a local government may currently participate in a pool and be evaluating the wisdom of continued participation. In either circumstance, organising one's thinking about pools *as a financing option* is an important matter. The following discussion provides a general framework for evaluation.

### Step 1: Needs evaluation

Logically, a consideration of any risk-financing programme begins with a degree of self-awareness about the needs of the local authority. Broadly speaking, one could characterize the needs as being either control or financing focused, meaning that the public body needs to be clear whether its principal issues revolve around a need to better manage and control risks or around a narrower need to find a means of financing losses.

In a sense, all local authorities should assume that they have a broader need for effective risk control, unless they can demonstrate to themselves that they currently are meeting this need. It is important to adopt this frame of reference because risk management (control) more or less drives the cost of risk-financing. Or, to put it slightly differently, no financing solution will work if loss-generating activities are out of control.

This observation suggests an important comparative principle when a local authority considers its financing options. One way or another, a degree of risk control will need to accompany any financing option, and this means that a public body needs to be mindful that it is comparing 'apples with apples' when comparing pools and commercial insurance. A full-service risk management pool may be providing a wide range of services, including risk control, while an insurance-only arrangement with a commercial insurer will only offer a financing arrangement.

Readers should be careful in overgeneralising the preceding paragraph. There are pools that only offer financing, and there are commercial insurance companies that offer a rather wide range of technical services, so one might find a situation where a commercial insurer actually has a competitive advantage in delivering risk management services.

## *Step 2: Pool evaluation*

Since the pooling world is fairly well established, there is little likelihood that a local authority will encounter a pool where limited information on performance is available. Most pools have been in operation for a number of years, and general information is available in annual reports, marketing pieces and interviews with current members. Financial reporting standards have begun to regularise reporting practices (at least since about 1993), so comparisons between pools should be more easily made. However, a local authority is not likely to find itself choosing between pools since only rarely are there two pools competing for the same local authority's business. Nevertheless, evaluation of a particular pool might be enhanced by understanding how it compares with other pools elsewhere.

What does a public body want to know about a pool? It seems that a pool should satisfy the entity's concerns about the following general areas.

## Financial performance

In general, the most critical issue surrounding financial performance is the pool's ability to pay claims. This is not a simple matter since the pool is pledging to respond to an event that is highly probabilistic as to time, location, amount and detail. How does the pool assure members that it can meet this obligation?

Broadly speaking, a pool's ability to pay claims is predicated on:

*   the amount of contributions it collects from members
*   how it manages and invests those contributions
*   how it manages claims and settles losses
*   its ability to absorb unexpected losses.

These factors must be considered together. For example, a pool might charge very low initial contributions, but rely on an unlimited assessment capability to go back to members for additional funds if losses are unexpectedly high. Alternatively, initial contributions might include a charge for surplus or contingency funds which will build over time and diminish the need to assess members. Or reinsurance/excess loss insurance might be purchased to cap the maximum amount a pool would pay. In order to understand financial performance, a local authority should want to know answers to the following questions:

1   What is the method by which initial contributions are set?
2   How does the pool finance for contingencies beyond the expected losses? Does it assess, build a surplus fund, purchase reinsurance, or have some other arrangement?
3   How does the pool manage and invest contributions while in its possession?
4   Does the pool pay dividends back to members for good performance? If not, are there other means by which good loss performance is recognised?
5   How does the pool set aside (reserve) for losses? How accurately has the pool been in determining reserve levels?
6   Has the pool been subjected to an outside actuarial audit; if so, what has the audit found? (Be sure to ask for the notes that any audit report may include, as notes may reveal future financing issues that are not yet reportable but are potentially material.)

Notably, A. M. Best, the insurance industry rating organisation, now can provide rating grades for pools in the same way that insurance companies are graded. However, this is not widely adopted yet, so a local authority should not expect to see a pool with a Best rating. Nevertheless, competitive pressures may quickly force pools to submit to a Best rating evaluation.

## Coverage evaluation and performance

Although it is tempting to think that insurance and pool coverage contracts are interchangeable (some would say, a commodity), pools have been departing from insurance industry formats, and this means that the coverage provided by a pool may be quite different from that offered by a commercial insurer. A public body should make sure it is conscious that differences may be present and to subject competing coverages to some type of analysis. Commonly, an entity's legal counsel may provide contract evaluation assistance, but a capable broker or agent should be able to offer the same kind of technical help.

## Claims process evaluation

The method by which a pool investigates and settles claims may seem to be of limited consequence in the decision-making process, but this is an incorrect perception. For most of the general public, the claims management process is the pool's sole interface with citizens and constituents. Thus the manner in which a claim is managed can reflect back on the local authority, and that reflection can be very good or very bad. At a minimum, a local authority should want to know:

1   What is the claims philosophy of the pool? (Are claims managers 'scrapyard dogs' or 'Father Christmas'?)
2   What expertise do claims managers have? Are they in-house employees of the pool or contracted third-party providers? If they are third-party providers, what is the turnover rate of claims managers?
3   What role can the local authority play in the adjudication and settlement of its claims?
4   Can the pool demonstrate the performance of claims services either through benchmarking comparisons with insurance companies or other pools, or through expense ratio comparisons?

## Risk management services evaluation

If a pool only provides financing, this area of evaluation is not appropriate, although in such cases a local authority might still want to understand how (if at all) a pool rewards the risk management practices of a member.

For a pool that provides broader risk management services, a public body naturally should understand what those services are, but additionally should understand:

- how those services are made available to members
- how those services are financed
- how adoption of those services relates to the cost of financing
- the demonstrated effectiveness of those services.

## Governance and management evaluation

The pooling movement has been in existence long enough that there are now individuals with experience as pooling administrators. However, local authorities should realise that pools still are a relatively young phenomenon, and pools have many unique attributes. This means that very few people have the necessary blend of insurance company, public sector and executive management experience to be successful. As a result, most effective pool administrators today are successful because they grew up with the pooling movement. The sources of new outside management talent are a bit more problematic to find, and this means that good pool administrators are a real find because there are not thousands of possible candidates.

It is important to emphasise the qualifications of the pool administrator because most pools are relatively small operations, so the personal capabilities of the administrator are essential to pool performance. Therefore any evaluation of a pool should include some consideration of pool management experience and performance.

Governance of pools usually involves a board of directors to oversee the pool's operations. An evaluation of a pool should include discovery of the means by which a board is selected, what its duties and obligations are and, where appropriate, the pooling experience of board members. Additionally, when a pool is sponsored by an association, the board's relationship to that parent organisation should be examined.

Related to governance, pool charter and by-laws should be considered, as they will touch upon numerous critical issues: a member's right of appeal, how members are accepted or rejected, voting rights, matters related to pool dissolution, and so on. Since in most pools the members are pooling risks, it is important for a potential member to understand what each member's ultimate obligation is to other members and their losses. A moment's thought will reveal that a small pool with one bad member could potentially wreak havoc on the other member's budgets if proper care is not taken.

Of course, where appropriate, other staff members may be subject to some inquiry.

---

## READ MORE ABOUT IT

## The future of pooling

*Peter C. Young and Martin Fone[1]*

### Introduction

The United States pooling movement is well into its third decade of existence and though pools face some significant challenges at present, there is no indication that the movement is nearing an end. So, whereas in the past it might have been possible to dismiss pools as a short-lived response to transitory market conditions (and, therefore, unworthy of critical analysis), we can no longer make such an assertion. Pooling deserves serious attention as a public sector phenomenon.

Public risk financing pools have proliferated in the United States. Today, most experts reckon that about 430 pools operate throughout the nation, providing coverage for somewhere between 30–35,000 public entities (about 40 percent of all such entities). These pools mainly were formed to respond to two hard markets for government liability insurance: One occurring in the mid-1970s, the second and more serious of the two occurring in the mid-1980s. The reasons for insurance unavailability/unaffordability have been discussed widely and can be summarised as arising from unusually precipitate underwriting cycles, general economic conditions, overall insurance industry financial performance, and the then widely-held opinion that public entities were poor risks.

Pools provide a wide variety of coverages and risk management services for members. However, it is relatively safe to say that pools most commonly provide liability and workers' compensation coverage with broader risk management services being provided to a much lesser degree. This emphasis is changing, and product/service diversification is an important current trend.

Due to the nature of government in the United States, pools almost invariably are confined to a single state. Due to custom, operating realities, and some legal factors, pools tend to be homogeneous as to member type. Thus, an outsider observing pools in America will find generally that towns from one state (or region of a state) will participate in one pool while counties or school districts from that same state or area will participate in a separate pool. However, having noted the state-based, homogeneous nature of pooling, readers should realise that one of the bigger current trends in pooling is consideration of the formation of regional or national excess or reinsurance pools (the National League of Cities already sponsors one such pool). Exploration of interstate primary-level pools also has occurred to some degree. Further, some pools are looking to diversify by underwriting different types of local entities, so a move towards 'heterogeneity' also might be called something of a trend.

Although virtually no pools have ceased operation, the survival of pools is a topic of considerable debate in the United States. Most pools have begun to experience competition from commercial insurers and some competition from each other. The reason for the return of commercial insurers is interesting as it involves a basic economic explanation.

Despite the fact that there is some dispute over whether pools will be successful over the long haul, there is little doubt that pools have served an important market-organizing function. One characteristic of the pre-pooling government insurance market was the virtual absence of information on governmental entity risk characteristics and loss experience (most of which was never disaggregated from insurers' commercial claims data). The presence of pools has reduced a great deal of uncertainty about public entities, and this has made the public sector a more attractive market. Other peripheral factors have drawn commercial insurers back to the public sector market, but it is difficult to deny the important uncertainty-reducing role of pools.

The emergence of competition has raised a number of issues for pools. If a competitive private market for some good exists, does the public sector have an active role to play? If so, can essentially public organisations compete effectively with commercial insurers and service providers? Does pooling represent some form of public-private collaboration that can be emulated elsewhere in the public sector? These questions have no answer presently, but will be the subject of serious inquiry over the coming years. Regardless of how these more profound questions are answered, pools today face an interesting practical problem in that they are part of a market that has numerous well-financed, competitively-attuned, niche marketing new entrants. From a purely objective perspective, the strategic and tactical challenges for pools and their responses to those challenges will be interesting to observe. Of course, for the pools themselves these issues might become a matter of life or death.

Given this new world, it is important for pools to begin considering their future from a competitive strategy perspective. While pools may retain some advantages over insurance companies (see Sidebar 9.1), the presence of competition will require pools to reformulate or establish their strategy in accordance with the new 'rules'. As a general proposition, managing strategically will pose a real challenge for the majority of pools inasmuch as they have not had to think strategically in the past – and also – they have come from the public sector where competitive strategy is not a central activity of organisational management (at least not until very recently).

Our purpose in this article is to identify seven propositions that we believe will profoundly affect the strategies that pools can/ will/must pursue. It is *not* our intention here to present a discussion of the strategies themselves, since strategy derives from the specific circumstances of any particular pool. Having noted that, we believe our discussion will suggest consideration of certain strategic choices while discouraging – implicitly – consideration of others.

## Seven strategic propositions about the future of pooling

*Proposition One: Pools are in the risk management business, not solely in the risk-financing business.* This may be the most pivotal of the propositions because it addresses a 'vision' or 'mission' issue.

Most pools were formed in response to a specific crisis – lack of insurance – and thus the mission of pooling has tended to focus on risk financing. This focus on risk financing may be understandable, but is does rather misspecify the 'problem'. To put it plainly, the historic orientation of pools is based upon the proposition that the fundamental problem is *insurance availability*, and that unavailability is due largely to a commercial insurer reluctance to underwrite governments. But, reluctance to underwrite is not a cause, it is a response to a set of conditions. Admittedly, some of these conditions are the result of insurer and insurance market behaviour, but some have more to do with the 'risks themselves;' for example, there is no denying that governments are relatively risky organisations. Thus, while providing risk financing may be important, the more fundamental problem is/was a lack of risk management, not a lack of insurance.

## Sidebar 9.1 Why pools have 'succeeded'

Can we say that pools have succeeded? It depends; that is, it depends on how we define the standard for success. If we say that success is defined as an ability to provide coverage for local governments between 1975 and 1995, the answer is a resounding 'yes'. If, we broaden our measure to include the next 10 years (1996–2006), things become a bit more equivocal. Since pools mainly are involved in long-tail liability and since more than half of all pools are less than 10 years old, we must conclude that the jury is still out.

In any event, it is difficult to generalise about pools, let alone their success, however defined. Pools are quite different in form, function, and purpose, so while – hypothetically – some pools might be facing dire futures, others may face brighter prospects. And yet, we are compelled to generalise if only to attempt to make sense of this complex phenomenon. Generalising can be useful, for it provides a point of reference and helps direct questions regarding the unique or divergent characteristics of individual pools.

Let us define success, for the time being, as the 'apparent ability to provide relatively low cost coverage at relatively stable rates for members'. This somewhat imprecise definition does suggest a couple of useful things. First, it implies continuity and stability; at least until the present, pools have provided coverage for members year in and year out. It also implies cost-effectiveness; that is, members have, via pooling, been managing the cost of risk through the pricing mechanism and through risk control practices.

In the absence of financial data, and recognising that the next 10 years will 'tell the story', we believe there are six factors that have contributed to the success of pooling thus far:

1   *The windfall factor.* Most pools have enjoyed a 'windfall' advantage. Since they are not insurance companies, legally they avoid many of the costs of doing business that insurers must bear; compliance costs necessary for admission into a state, contributions to joint underwriting associations and high risk pools, state guaranty fund assessments, premium taxes and income taxes, and they commonly are not subject to other regulatory influences (state approval of contract language, pricing restrictions, report filings with the state, and so on).

2    *A lack of competitive pressure.* Most pools had no competi-
     tion from anyone until the early 1990s, giving them a
     monopolist's advantage. Interestingly, the result of this factor
     was not excess profits (profit was explicitly not the purpose
     of pools, but even if it were, overall pool rates have not been
     subjected to any kind of pricing analysis so we could not
     prove the point either way). Rather, the absence of compe-
     tition allowed pools to focus attention and resources inwardly
     to maximum effect. The lack of alternatives provided pools
     a breathing space to learn how to pool, to experiment and
     make mistakes without suffering the harsh consequences
     that certainly would occur in a competitive market.

3    *The market for risk management services.* Commercial
     insurers, brokers, and agents have contributed to the
     continued existence of pools. The burgeoning market for risk
     management services (claims management, actuarial consul-
     tation, investment management, loss control services, etc.)
     allowed the public sector to rent technical insurance/risk
     management expertise it did not possess initially. In some
     respects this reason was not so much a reason for success
     as it was a 'reason for lack of failure;' meaning that while
     these third-party providers are not necessarily superior to
     insurance company technical/managerial experts – indeed,
     they are often the same individuals – they permitted the
     public sector to negate one possible disadvantage they other-
     wise might have held: a lack of technical insurance expertise.

     We confess that there is something of a chicken-and-egg
     aspect to this factor. Risk management services enabled pools
     to form, but the presence of the pools also motivated the
     development of the risk management services market.
     Further, for reasons mentioned subsequently, pools 'organ-
     ised the market', that is, their efforts served to attract
     providers into the market. However, the general public sector
     and private sector trend towards self-insurance – which influ-
     enced the formation of risk management services – predates
     pooling. Thus, while acknowledging the circularity of this
     factor, we think the presence of this market has positively
     influenced pools, at least it did during the crucial formative
     years of the pooling movement.

4    *Pooling's focus.* Since many pools were formed to do one
     thing, make risk-financing (and later, risk management)
     available and affordable to government entities, pools have
     tended to have a niche approach to their business. This

succeeds as a strategy when the market or the product/service is clearly defined and understood, as it was for pools by circumstance. Sticking with a focus can be a successful strategy, as long as no competitors adopt the same strategy and do it better.

5   *Knowledge of the public sector.* Due to the complexity of the public sector, insurers saw little reward in fully understanding that market, at least prior to the advent of pooling. Pools come from the public sector and their knowledge of government is a classic 'core competency'.

6   *The motivation to practice risk management.* We have a strong hunch that pools have the same effect on members that self-insuring has on a single organisation. That is, the cause–effect relationship between losses and the cost of risk is made plain and this typically spurs action in the loss control/loss prevention area. Put another way, pooling reduces moral hazard.

Factor 2 really does not exist today and Factor 1 is in some jeopardy. The changing nature of these factors will force pools to articulate their uniqueness. In all honesty, many pools are indistinguishable from commercial insurance companies and as insurers continue to re-enter the market it will become more important for pools to be able to justify their special treatment by regulators and the state. If they cannot, we think they ultimately will be treated like insurance companies.

That is not to say that the treatment of all pools as insurance companies is inevitable. It is to say that the continued special regulatory treatment of pools and the continued existence of these public players in a competitive market will require pools to recalibrate their explanation for what they are and why they exist. Factors 4, 5, and 6 may serve as bases for developing that explanation.

It is axiomatic in risk management that risk financing is guided by overall risk management strategy, and so it is true for pools that, while risk financing may be something that is done for members, the broader mission is to serve as a provider of risk management. This idea has profound implications for the remainder of our propositions, for though one might make an argument that government does not belong in a market that has fully functioning private participants, one is hard-pressed to make the argument that public organisations have no business managing their risks. Indeed, risk management is a core government activity, since one of government's basic roles is risk-bearing. If a single entity is unable to effectively manage its risks alone (as many small governments are not), pooling the management of risk with other entities becomes a rational extension of this logical argument.

Interestingly, by adopting the risk management mission, most pools can put themselves both ahead and outside of the competitive fray. They are ahead of the competition in that there is virtually no competition for 'being the risk manager' for public entities – though some brokers have made a valiant try. They are outside of the competition in that a risk management pool can take advantage of competitive markets. If a pool is truly the risk manager of its members and the commercial market is considered to be favourable, the pool would sell its risk to the commercial insurers and pass the savings back to the members (or use the savings for other purposes). If the commercial market is unfavourable, the pool retains the risk. The subtle change that is occurring in this scenario is that the pool is unequivocally 'of the members' and not just another provider of services to the members It bears mentioning that some pools are sponsored by associations or by brokers, and they might bridle at this notion since such an approach would affect revenue flows to the sponsor. This is true, and we would simply add that if supporting a sponsoring organisation financially is a strategic role of the pool, then everyone concerned should explicitly say so and the pool's strategy should be built to accommodate this different mission or purpose.

*Proposition Two: Windfall advantages can only disappear over time.* Pools have reaped the benefits of certain windfalls. Unlike insurance companies, pools – typically – do not pay premium taxes, pay taxes of any kind, participate in state guarantee funds or high-risk pools, submit themselves to regulatory oversight, nor comply with the myriad rules and procedures imposed on insurance companies.

Windfall benefits are unremarkable when competition is not present, but economists would quickly note that the presence of windfalls in a competitive market has a distorting effect on market efficiency. We even might make a more general comment, 'windfalls are not fair, except when other compelling factors override considerations of fairness'.

We both have heard arguments justifying the continuation of windfall benefits ('these are public dollars, and citizens should not be expected to incur these frictional costs'). There may be something to this observation, but we hope readers will concede that this argument becomes harder to make in the face of private-sector competition (e.g., are the premium dollars paid by a municipality to an insurance company any less deserving of favourable treatment than those same dollars paid to a pool?)

It is true that local authorities may enjoy certain political advantages in lobbying state legislature and this may slow the erosion of windfall benefits, but a fundamental effect of true competitive markets is the elimination of windfall advantages (what economists call 'excess profits').

We might also note in passing that state legislatures are looking high and low for alternative sources of revenue, and this fact will have some bearing on the future of windfalls, as will the general public concern for greater accountability in government.

*Proposition Three: In the absence of windfall advantages or high barriers to entry, market dominant status can only be sustained over the long run at extraordinary cost.* This proposition is a companion to Proposition Two. Many pools hold a market dominant status. However, sustainable market dominance requires certain things like maintaining high barriers to entry. Other factors like control of technical expertise or information also might sustain market-dominant status. In our opinion, one cannot make the case that there are natural features of the public entity risk financing market that support the inevitability of market dominance. Granted, one might argue that local governments may be reluctant to leave a market-dominant pool for a commercial insurer (either because of hostility to the insurance industry or out of inertia); but we think it is a little unnerving to hitch a pool's future prospects to the hope that members remain angry and inert.

*Proposition Four: Cost leadership (competing on the basis of lowest cost) will become an increasingly difficult strategy to pursue.* Market dominance may be maintained in one way; through cost leadership. And, pools do possess a distinct advantage in that they do not have to factor regulatory and compliance costs into pricing. We have been told by some pool administrators that this gives their pools a 10–20 percent pricing advantage right out of the box. Fair enough, but if we are to be consistent with our previous comments, we would point out that this pricing advantage will likely deteriorate over time. Further, even if advantages remain cost leadership is difficult long-term strategy unless sufficient resources are available to compete on 'volume', and unless pool overhead is razor-thin. Unfortunately for pools, they are dwarfed financially by any reasonably sized commercial insurer, which means that a commercial insurer could sustain a low-price competitive strategy longer than most pools could countenance; and this observation is especially true if the commercial insurer's strategy is based upon a targeted, rather than a general, market focus.

*Proposition Five: For most pools, a well-articulated client focus, deriving from a product/service differentiation strategy, is the direction most likely to prove fruitful.* If cost-leadership is not a viable long term strategy, what is? Earlier we noted that strategy will be specific to each pool, but plainly, pools have only two or three general strategic options – they can focus, they can redefine the 'market' they serve, or they can collaborate.

The 'focus' strategy has certain appeal since pools are focused by definition (see Sidebar 9.1). Indeed, good pools possess a significant core competency knowledge of the public sector in their state – that most commercial insurers can never own. However, having that knowledge and using it are two different things, and competition will require pools to more clearly articulate the value-added nature of this knowledge. Or, to state it more plainly, this expertise must be valued by the members and the only way it will be valued by them is:

1   If this expertise translates into services and products not otherwise obtainable, and
2   Customers can differentiate between the quality provided by pools and by commercial insurers.

While many pool administrators would say that this is already true of their pool today, we would remind them that competition will continually pressure them to understand their members needs as well as their own competitive advantages. This will require strategic thinking, of course, but it will also require pools to practice some pretty sophisticated marketing.

The second possible strategy is to redefine the market. In the case of pools this might mean redefining themselves as 'risk managers' rather than as 'risk financers' (see above discussion under Proposition One). This reduces some of the competitive pressure, since the pool 'owns' this market, but it does not lessen the pressure to understand public risk management and risk financing in a competitive market context.

The third possible strategy is collaboration. Although the circumstances would have to be right, one might imagine a pool developing relationships with commercial insurers or vendors to provide a variety of services that would present members with unique set of products and services not available elsewhere.

*Proposition Six: Innovation is necessary; diversification is tricky.* Sidebar 9.2 provides a reminder that diversification is a difficult thing. As with almost anything, there are benefits to specialisation and focus. Benefits can include reduced uncertainty, fewer surprises, lower deadweight costs, and fewer unexpected interactions between factors that influence the organisation. Thus, it is virtually axiomatic that while it is important to maintain value and the perception of value through innovation, it is very difficult to be all things to all people (just consider the fortunes of private companies that pursued the 'conglomerate' or 'one-stop-shopping' strategy in the 1970s and 1980s). Readers might be interested to learn that a number of pools in the United States are considering diversification as their next major move, including extending into financial services, life insurance, investment management, and a host of other activities. This is a trend worth watching.

*Proposition Seven: The biggest internal strategic challenge facing pools is leadership.* Most of the propositions are outwardly focused in that they address factors that pools encounter. However, there are very important internal issues as well. Emblematic of these internal issues (and probably the most important of all internal concerns) is the question of leadership.

Most pool administrators come from a public-sector background and their lack of private-sector/insurance management experience was of little consequence when there were no alternatives to pools. Of course, the key question is, are pool managers equipped presently to manage in a world of competition? We do not know the answer at present, but if the answer is 'no ' then we have to ask ourselves from where the pool administrators of the future will come. Adoption of the risk *management* mission changes the leadership question somewhat, but even then pools will have to understand themselves more in a competitive market context.

There is a second leadership issue present. Even if the external factors influencing pools were not present, question about future leadership would exist. It generally is recognised in the study of organisational leadership that organisations need different types of leaders at different points in the organisation's life cycle. Dynamic, visionary, true-believer leadership may be essential in formative phases of the cycle, but as an organisation matures its needs evolve. We might refer to this matter as a 'succession' issue, and note that while it naturally will overlap with the other leadership issue mentioned above it would exist as an issue even in the absence of external change. Readers might be interested to note that pooling appears to be entering such a transition point at present, and therefore leadership is a central issue for most pools.

## Sidebar 9.2 The demise of Municipal Mutual

Municipal Mutual was formed in 1903 by a group of UK local authorities in response to a hardening insurance market where coverage was limited and perceived to be expensive. Following local government reorganisation in 1974, over 90 percent of the UK public entities had placed some form of insurance with the mutual and a majority had placed all their cover with it. However, on September 30, 1992, the mutual went into runoff and sought buyers to take over its goodwill, staff, and transferable assets. What factors led to its demise?

1  *Predominant market position*
   Given its predominant market position, the mutual's strategy in the late 1970s and 1980s essentially was defensive. Its principal concern was preservation of market share, which meant that it was poorly positioned to impose premiums commensurate with changes in underlying exposure, particularly if the response from the public entities was to seek alternative quotations from the insurance market.

2  *Provision of 'ground up' insurance*
   The mutual, as a direct writer, refused to deal with brokers and consultants, even in an advisory capacity, rather than a placing role and – as a consequence – was often the only source of advice on insurance matters for public entities. Its standard product offering was ground up insurance, particularly for casualty risks – arguably an inefficient use of an authority's resources, given their unique accounting conventions and tax status.

3  *Impact on risk management*
   As the preferred provider of services to public entities and as a predominantly ground up insurer, the mutual's position had the unfortunate side effect of diminishing the role of the insurance buyer with a local authority and of removing the incentive to improve risk profiles which a degree of risk retention encourages. It is interesting to observe that when the mutual's difficulties were more widely known and after its collapse, risk management gained a much higher profile within the entities.

4  *Diversification*
   Like many organisations in the 1980s, the mutual's holding company embarked upon an ambitious diversification programme, although the genesis of this strategy could be

observed in the late 1970s. Municipal General provided personal lines and, later, commercial lines coverages through the broker market. Municipal Life (later relaunched as Prosperity) provided life and financial products. A private health company was bought and in the late 1980s the group became a provider of Electronic Data Processing and other related services to the public sector. Companies were bought in Spain and Greece, among others, and the group wrote public sector business aggressively in Australia. All these new ventures cost money, and Municipal Mutual was destined to generate the revenue to fund these new developments. This, in turn, created more pressure on the mutual to maintain market share and premium income at all costs.

5    *External factors*

(a)   *Financial Pressures on Local Government.* In the 1980s, local government came under significant attack from central government. The municipalities' ability to generate revenue was substantially limited. Local authorities' resources were capped. This meant that the public entities were faced with having to provide the same range of services with reduced financial resources. This meant, logically, that the quality of service was likely to be reduced and that the potential for accusations of negligent service provision was likely to increase.

(b)   *Unpopularity of Local Government.* In 1988 the old system of local taxation based on the ratable value of properties was replaced by the Community Charge (Poll Tax) whereby a standard was levied per adult living in a property. The Poll Tax invoked waves of popular indignation against both central and local government and people were more ready to 'get one back' on local government by making a claim against them.

The consequence to the mutual of the change in social attitudes and in the financial position of local government was an increase in the frequency of claims of which Municipal Mutual, as a ground up insurer, bore the full brunt.

(c)   *Loss of Focus.* The Local Government and Housing Act, promulgated in 1989, was designed to restrict the ability of local authorities to own or have a substantial stake in a company, a mechanism which was beginning to be employed to circumvent the resource capping. Up until

1988, each member of Municipal Mutual had one vote for every 100 British pounds sterling (about $160 U.S.) of premium spent, which meant that the bulk of the voting power was with the local authorities. In an effort to avoid the potential implications of the 1989 act, a resolution was passed at an extraordinary general meeting to change the voting rights to one member/one vote, thus increasing the personal lines policyholder's rights at the expense of the local authorities. But, to some observers, this was the point – in conjunction with the diversification programme – that the mutual passed fully from servicing the local government community which created it in the first place.

6   *Absence of access to external sources of capital*
The mutual's ability to make calls from its members had not kept pace with the progress of time. Even in 1992, each member's maximum liability was 10 British pounds sterling ($16 U.S.) in the event of assets not being sufficient to meet its liabilities. Unlike some of the major UK composites, who in the late 1980s had launched rights issues, Municipal Mutual had limited access to external capital.

7   *Investment strategy*
A significant proportion of the mutual's investment portfolio was in commercial real estate and at the turn of the decade (1990) the bottom fell out of this market causing its asset base to decline at the same time as its liabilities (arising from the increase in frequency of claims and the poor performance of the other parts of the group) were increasing.

Although the mutual took steps in the early 1990s to ameliorate its position through the imposition of large premium increases on its casualty portfolio and, later, through the imposition of large deductibles and adopting a risk management stance, these actions were insufficient to offset the fatal combination of a declining asset base and increasing liabilities. The mutual's demise became inevitable.

## *Summary*

We are reminded that market leadership cannot be taken for granted, that focus requires effort, that temptations to diversify must be considered with care, that the fundamental strategic orientation is 'focus' and 'risk management', and that serving/working in the public sector does require certain expertise and a great understanding of the differences that exist between the public and private sectors. For pools, these 'propositions' serve as a useful reminder that success requires effort, energy and vigilance. Change is a constant in our lives and complacency, or worse, a yearning for the old days are inappropriate responses for pool managers and leaders.

## Note

1   Reprinted with the permission of PRIMA from *Public Risk*, October 1996.

# 10

# Risk management programme administration

## EXECUTIVE SUMMARY

The ORM idea envisages an organisation-wide approach to risk management. This requires executive level commitment and assumes that senior managers and elected members set the overall objectives and purposes of risk management. Through a co-ordinated system of management, all managers and employees assume certain risk management responsibilities for risks within their functional purview.

In the ORM concept, executive level co-ordination and control is assumed, and the notion of a chief risk officer is used to convey the scope and sweep of ORM's objectives.

Since a chief risk officer is more manager than technician, key responsibilities for this risk manager are communication, co-ordination, motivation, team-building and process management. Though technical expertise, such as insurance, is very important as well, the evolving world of the risk management services marketplace now allows risk managers to access a wide range of technical capabilities previously unavailable. Thus, management expertise is growing in importance as the hallmark of a successful risk manager.

## PRINCIPLES AND CONCEPTS

The preceding nine chapters have focused on the risk side of risk management. This chapter discusses the management side. The imbalance in emphasis should not mislead readers, however. The main distinguishing difference between effective and ineffective risk managers is an (in)ability to manage. Indeed, in today's environment almost any technical aspect of risk management can be bought, rented or borrowed – from claims management services, to actuarial consultation, to legal services, to risk audit services, to financing and investment management. It is the management of these technical elements that cannot be outsourced. Only an effective manager understands the organisation, its politics and culture, the appropriate means of communications, and how to get things done. Management competence matters – it matters a lot.

The focus of this chapter is on the effective design and implementation of risk management practices within public bodies. The chapter begins with a discussion of risk management mission statements, goals and objectives. It then turns to programme design and implementation. Finally, the chapter deals with several key management challenges: risk communications, contract management, procurement of broker and insurer services, and programme audit tactics.

# The risk management mission

What is the purpose of risk management in a public body? The question is more difficult to answer than it might be thought at first glance. Historically, the field of risk management has been dominated by the notion of risk reduction or elimination. Indeed, this book carries a considerable amount of evidence as to the influence of this view. Many of the tools and techniques discussed here address the challenge of preventing, avoiding, controlling or eliminating risks. Readers might be tempted to conclude that this book, too, views the perfect world as one without risk.

Setting aside for the moment the impossibility of a risk-free world, there are other reasons to doubt the wisdom of risk elimination as the singular mission of risk management. The world simply is too complicated and the typical organisation's resources too limited for anything but the most modest risk reduction to occur. Further, managers – being human – can only know, manage and do so much. Not only is risk elimination a metaphysical impossibility, it would be far beyond the capability of individuals and organisations to even eliminate a meaningful slice of the risk they encounter.

But, beyond these constraints, it is reasonable to wonder whether the reduction of risk (even in a narrow sense) is sensible. For example, as this book argues, the portfolio of risks that constitute an organisation's risk profile is interdependent, includes the pure and speculative, includes the objective and subjective, and is related to the overall purposes of the organisation. Thus, virtually every negative risk is related to or influenced by positive attributes. A simple example is the hiring of an employee. That person's risks of loss are not separable from the productivity and other positive attributes he or she brings to the organisation. That imagery can be expanded to the organisation. It is a complete thing in and of itself, and consideration of hazards and perils cannot really be done without a recognition of the related risk factors and opportunities.

Additionally, singular risks have both upside and downside potential, and the elimination of downside risk may simply eliminate the risk, period. Humans are motivated by the presence of risk, sometimes to run away but often to run towards it. It probably is not putting too fine a point on it to say that the elimination of risk would make for a pretty dull and unproductive existence.

Finally, on the point of risk management mission, remember that the act of managing risks alters the risks and creates new ones. Recall the discussion of moral hazard in Chapter 8, and the notion that the presence of insurance can alter the underlying risk – elevating, for example, the possibility of fire (arson) losses. Moral hazard is a general problem of risk management; requiring drivers to be trained may encourage more aggressive driving as the trained individuals may have more confidence than they should. Safer roads can encourage faster and less responsible driving, lumbar support belts can encourage workers to lift more weight than is proper, information on a work-related hazard might produce too much caution. In other words, risk management might actually make some situations worse, or at least might shift a risk from one exposure to another.

So, then, what is the purpose of risk management? Earlier, risk management was identified as serving the overall purposes of the organisation, and that seems as good a place to start as any.

In public bodies, the overall purposes are mixed. Certainly, they aspire to manage public affairs competently. They also have 'process' objectives, which means that democratic institutions must extend the notion of competence beyond management science or economic tests to include political considerations (representation, justice, fairness, equity, and so on). To emphasise this point in the extreme, it could be observed that outcomes sometimes play second-fiddle to process, and an utter failure from a management science or economics perspective may be a political triumph.

Thus, the mission of risk management in public institutions must in some fundamental way contribute to both competence and process. But, how does this occur?

Start with the competence side of things. Political scientists could wrangle over this issue for ages, but in a book like this we can leap past a vast array of points and counterpoints and arrive at a generally accepted proposition, which is that local public bodies exist mainly to deliver services. Those services include police and fire protection, social services, road construction and maintenance, schools, recreational facilities, and so on. Competence in each of these areas is a technical matter (sometimes hotly contested) that must be judged on the merits of the situation – test scores, arrest and incarceration rates, vehicle accident rates. Risk management techniques can be employed to address specific aspects of the service, but the overall purpose of risk management is to assure that service is not negatively affected by extraneous factors, and indeed may be positively influenced by extraneous factors.

Detection of extraneous factors is a key purpose of risk assessment, the objective of which is to address those that detract from competence and those that might enhance it. For example, the promise of a competent fire protection service to a community is a promise that may be unfulfilled for a number of reasons. Improperly maintained equipment, inadequately trained fire fighters, insufficient resources to acquire fire-fighting assets – all these things are the subject of risk management concern. Objectively, risk management entails the efforts necessary to minimise the impact of such risks. In this sense, risk management can be said to be in the 'elimination or minimisation' business. Losses due to these types of risks are effectively dead-weight losses and the fewer of them, the better.

However, the promise to provide fire protection also presents circumstances that may enhance the ability to deliver. Investment in innovative training, opportunities for public/private partnerships, community-based solutions are all things that are enhancing upside potential and examples of conscious risk taking – which this book has argued is a form of risk management as well. In this sense, risk management can be said to be in the 'maximisation' business.

So, which is it? Maximisation or minimisation of risk? Well, it is both, although an explanation of this point requires some care. The preceding paragraphs can be said to describe a hedging arrangement where risk is being neutralised through offsetting risks. But this is not right, because organisational risks are not precisely hedgeable. More convincingly, it may be said that the goal is stability, meaning that there always are just the right number and quality of resources to deliver on the promise (never too few, never too many).

Stability is a risk management objective in the sense that most public managers value predictability in their environment. Indeed, the public budgeting cycle reveals the practical illustration of this point – managers have almost as much difficulty managing too much money as managing too little. If this were not true, there would be fewer unsightly end of the fiscal year spending sprees.

But stability may not be the only thing going on here. Risk management can directly affect the seeking out of new risks, the decisions to take those risks and the measures that enhance the prospects of success. So, arguing that the competence-based risk management goals are driven by stability considerations ignores the important upside potential that risk management provides. Thus, competence-maximisation can be a risk management objective too.

What about process? In this role, risk management is focused on the assurance of process, meaning that risks that affect the political process are risks of concern. What are the risks that impinge on fairness, on representation and voice, on political equity? Often it is not a risk manager *per se* who addresses these concerns but the courts; however, that does not make process risk management any less of a public sector risk management concern. Equally, risk-taking guided by political values can be construed as upside risk management, and perhaps the most definitive thing that can be said at the present time is that this probably is the risk management domain of the elected member.

Where does this leave the discussion of mission? Broadly speaking, the purpose of public sector risk management is to enable institutions to achieve their overall mission as effectively as possible. More technically, the purpose of risk management in public bodies is to assure resource stability in the service of competence, seek risk in the service of competence enhancement, and support the essential nature of process in democratic institutions.

# Risk management programme design and implementation

The traditional venue of risk management is either the finance/accounting or purchasing department within a public body (See Chapter 2, 'Read More About It' section, for further details). In an important sense, neither choice is illogical, as insurance-buying and risk-financing clearly can be viewed as purchasing or financial management concerns. The implications of the Turnbull Report with its emphasis on risk management as part of the panoply of an organisation's internal controls may further accelerate the positioning of the risk management function in the financial management department, at least in the private sector.

However, the broader view of risk management introduced in this book suggests that problems might arise from defining risk management as a subfunction of finance or purchasing. The organisation-wide stance presented in this book offers many circumstances in which finance/purchasing managers are unqualified to act – political risks, human resource concerns, information technology issues, training matters. Financial issues are critical concerns for risk managers, but risk management is far more than financial management.

Further, risk management has at least four levels of existence within an organisation: political, strategic, tactical/managerial and operational/functional (see Chapter 2, 'Applications' section). The political and strategic levels of risk management concern themselves with the purview of elected members and senior managers. It is focused on political risks ranging from process assurance (see above), to maintaining constitutionality, to getting re-elected.

The tactical/managerial level of risk management is defined as the provenance of department heads and concerns itself with risk as it affects budgets and interacts with broader goals of the entity.

The operational/functional level of risk management is the ground level and concerns itself with the implementation of specific risk management tools and techniques – safety training courses, accident investigation, enforcement of loss control techniques.

When looked at in this light, it is easy to see an explanation for the principal frustration voiced by traditional risk managers, which is the inability to get support from the elected members and the difficulty in persuading department heads and colleagues to take risk management seriously. Conventionally, risk managers sit somewhere between the tactical and operational level – and this is a difficult position from which to effect organisation-wide change.

There are two important insights that arise from understanding the 'levels of risk management' idea. First, the design of a risk management function must take into consideration the impact of organisation design on the management of risk. Second, it strongly suggests that political/strategic support (and, probably, organisational proximity to that level) is essential to effective risk management practice. We discuss these points in reverse order.

## *Political and strategic levels of support*

In both a real and conceptual sense, the chief executive in a public body is the chief risk officer of the organisation. It is essential that this dimension of their positions be more explicitly known.

Commonly, such a revelation will not require, say, the chief executive to serve all the functional aspects of risk management, but it does mean that the chief executive (and, ultimately, the council including the elected members) must establish a clear position on risk management and delegate responsibility. Equally important, this political level must become more self-conscious of the risk management elements of their actions and decisions. At a minimum, the risk management mission statement must emanate from the political/strategic level of the organisation.

Although this need not occur, at least not literally, an individual with organisation-wide responsibilities should assume the chief risk officer mantle. For example, a senior manager might assume responsibility for risk management at the strategic level, the added dimension here being that this person could oversee the implementation of risk management within the organisation and assure that risk management is practised in accordance with overall political and strategic objectives. The key, however, is that risk management policy is being set at the executive level of the organisation.

The tactical level of responsibility is practised in this model at the department level of the organisation. Thus, the departmental managers take effective responsibility for risks within their purview – while practically, they are likely to delegate the actual practice to their own deputies. Likewise, operational risk management responsibilities are delegated to work unit/individual employee levels.

This organisation-wide approach can be defined as one where there is a top-down approach with respect to strategy, but where the actual practice of risk management is organic, with every employee being the 'risk manager' of risks within his or her area of responsibility. Of course, in such an environment, risk management expectations become part of the job description and performance is evaluated with some recognition of this expectation.

## The impact of organisation design

The fact that most organisations do not practise risk management in the manner described above is a concern but not a fatal flaw. Clearly, the model suggested in the previous paragraphs is a benchmark – attainable to be sure, but nevertheless at least a way of thinking about actual practices. Deviation is possible, and even desirable in some circumstances, but the model forces us to consider why the deviation exists and whether it is helpful or harmful to the risk management cause. Consideration of deviations may also provide insight into obstacles or barriers to effective risk management.

The scope of organisation-wide risk management is sufficiently broad to suggest that the risk management function within an organisation is probably not best suited to a 'command and control' form of structure. Certainly, overall direction comes from the executive level, but the diverse range of risks and management needs suggests that more flexible matrix or team-based approaches to risk management are a more suitable functional design.

The matrix/team-based approach to risk management could range from a free-form structure with groups and individuals organised on an as-needed basis to solve risk management problems, to a more organised approach with permanent teams co-ordinating overall risk management implementation. Temporary teams or assignments would still exist in the more structured form of this approach.

The logic for a team-based approach lies not only with the diverse challenge of managing organisational risks, but also with the organisational design and process issues common with most public-sector organisations. That is, most local governments operate with a great deal of functional separation and democratically derived decision processes are essential (see Exhibit 10.1).

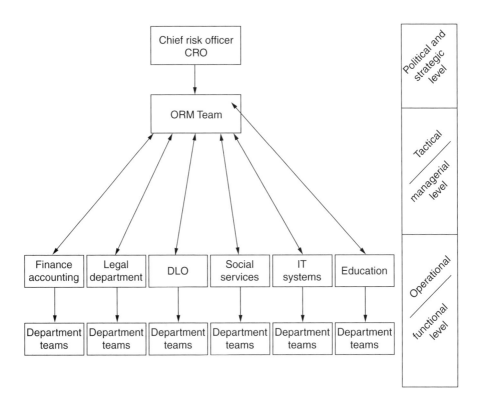

**Exhibit 10.1** Example of an organisation risk management function chart

# Risk communications

Risk communications corresponds roughly to the idea of organisational behaviour – at least as it relates to matters of organisation
design. In other words, while the previous discussion focused on the
structure of risk management within a public body, this section
trains the reader's attention on the 'dynamics' of risk management
programmes.

Broadly, the premise behind risk communications is that risk
management must be effectively communicated within and outwith
the organisation. Equally important, communications – at least as
it is defined here – is central to effective management as well.

The subject of risk communications is a growing field of academic
study, although for a number of reasons the work in this area tends
to focus on risk and public policy (inoculations against infectious
diseases, earthquake preparedness, road safety) rather than on
communications within an organisational setting. However, some of
the key products and insights that arise from the research can be
applied – or at least summarised – here:

> Organisational communication should be understood as a system,
> meaning any effort to communicate information occurs in an envi-
> ronment where there is a communicator, a communicatee, a message
> and a medium of communication. Each element of this system can
> contribute to the effectiveness/ineffectiveness of the communication
> effort.

> Risk presents a number of substantive challenges when communi-
> cating information to an audience, including:
>
> - Audiences, typically, are not knowledgeable about risk manage-
>   ment concepts and principles.
> - Technical aspects of risk management are difficult to understand,
>   even when communicated.
> - Key risk management issues often require very specific technical
>   knowledge (engineering, medical, legal, etc.).
> - Attitudes towards risk are subjective and difficult to measure and
>   compare.
> - Audiences often underestimate the value of risk management.

> Cultural filters affect people's understanding of risk, and can produce
> unexpected (although not unpredictable) responses.

> Communication can occur through various media, but in organisations
> the use of incentive and disincentive tools (implied or explicit) can
> assist in the effectiveness of the effort.

On the final point, it is worth mentioning that executive-level support
is the critical incentive in effective risk communications, but often
communication efforts rely on other tools to provide incentives, such

as rewards, cost allocation systems, penalties, audit evaluations, and the like. The key point here is that motivation must be understood and incorporated into any effort to communicate.

## Information management

Conventional use of the term 'information management' focuses on the use of risk management information systems (RMIS) as a tool towards effective risk management. Risk management information systems can range from simple spreadsheet-based software to very complicated programmes designed to organise, analyse and manage large amounts of data on risks, insurance programmes, claims, forecasting and budgeting.

However, in this book the term includes all systems and efforts used in an organisation to gather and communicate information regarding risks. In this light, information includes decidedly low-tech approaches like having managers report incidents that might produce claims, or to have organisational expectations in place that encourage employees to keep risk managers 'in the loop' when new or evolving risks appear on the horizon. Equally, information management can include very advanced approaches to automated data management.

Perhaps the simplest way to reinforce the broader concept of risk communication is to say that the approach should enable an organisation to answer at least the following questions:

1   What risk information is it necessary for us to have?
2   Whence may this information/data be retrieved?
3   What are the relevant timing issues? When must we have this information?
4   How is this relevant information most effectively and efficiently transmitted?
5   What will be done with the information?
6   Who needs to receive the information captured in this system, when do they need it, and in what form is it best received?
7   What are the impediments and filters to the flow of information or data and how can they be managed?
8   What are the cultural and political implications of information management within and outwith the organisation?

## Cost allocation systems

Cost allocation systems have an explicit and implicit purpose. Obviously, they represent a type of cost accounting mechanism that allows an organisation to identify and track costs associated with specific risk-related activities and objects. Less obviously, perhaps, such systems represent an important means of communicating information and providing incentives to managers and employees. To put it simply, managers tend to pay attention when budgets are at stake.

Although a wide variety of approaches might be taken in designing a cost allocation system, they all seem to strike a balance between risk distributing and risk pooling. Imagine the spectrum of systems to be anchored at one end by a model where all costs are allocated back to the source (a department generating 45 per cent of a local authority's overall employers' liability costs is allocated 45 per cent of that total cost), while at the other end a system might retain all costs at central administration.

By considering the two extremes of cost allocation, it is possible to see the potential benefits and problems of these systems. A fully dispersed cost of risk model does effectively tell managers where losses are being produced and it does provide a powerful motivation to practise risk management. However, many losses are not within the control of unit managers so there is a question about whether it is fair to assess their budgets when they were simply the victims of dumb luck. Additionally, from a 'good government' perspective, it is hard to argue that a single bad year of losses should wipe out a unit's budget since – after all – it is the people who obtain services from that unit that suffer ultimately. Thus, there seem to be some problems in a system that fully allocates loss costs back to the source.

A fully pooled environment does insulate the various divisions and departments from the vicissitudes of fortune (thus offering a degree of budget stability), but the cost of this approach is that it removes an important incentive for managers to practise risk management.

Consequently, a cost allocation system should strike some balance between distribution and pooling of costs. How that balance is effected will depend on circumstances and preferences, but the following matters should be kept in mind when designing a cost allocation system:

1    Care should be taken to recognize that systems have a tendency to reward good risk management practices in the long run, while penalising or creating inconvenience in the short run. Good risk management practice has the effect of smoothing out experience over multiple budget periods, while some of the costs of undertaking such efforts are borne immediately. Additionally, conventional budgeting creates a strong disincentive to risk management in one important sense – that is, if a unit manager reduces losses and saves money, there is a reasonable chance

those funds will not be allocated to the unit in future budget years. Good risk management could result in budget shrinkage over time, which might be good news for taxpayers, but which creates all sorts of disincentives for managers in public bodies.

2   Loss experience is likely to be erratic for most divisions or units, so it may take many years before an organisation has an accurate sense as to what is going on within that unit and how much of that activity is within the unit's control.

3   Identifying the cost to be allocated is difficult. Is it only the direct cost or the indirect or consequential costs as well?

4   Where is the motivational effect of cost allocation being felt? Many programmes founder on the difficulty in matching cost allocation precisely with the risk source. For example, risk of worker injury may be influenced by cost allocation, but the impact is likely to be borne by the manager and not the workers themselves. In some circumstances, it is the workers' behaviour (and not the manager's inattentiveness) that is the critical loss-producing factor, so cost allocation may be ineffective.

5   Timing of allocation can become an issue. Budget setting and planning occurs at fixed or regular intervals, while the timing of losses mainly is random. Are loss costs assessed at the beginning of a budget year or at the end? In and of itself, the timing of assessments can play a major role in the effectiveness of such a system.

6   Simplicity and equity are the guiding stars of cost allocation system design. They should be easy to understand, they should be fair and they should be perceived to be fair.

## Contract management

The phenomenon of outsourcing is of such importance in the public sector that it warrants comment here because outsourcing is a risk-generating activity and a fair amount of the outsourcing may be occurring in the risk management area.

The concept of organisations as collections of COCAs is addressed elsewhere in the book, but it is worth a reminder that contract management is a broad and general risk management concern for a public body. Many of the issues raised in this section are relevant to all contracts and formal arrangements.

However, the main purpose of this discussion is to focus on the risk-management specific contracts that may be entered into by a public sector risk manager. And, in principle, these contracts might be numerous. The evolution of the risk management services industry is such that a risk manager today can rent or hire virtually any kind of technical risk management service imaginable. Indeed, except for the risk manager, an entire risk management function could be outsourced, and a current scan of the market would find numerous examples of this practice.

In an effort to give some substance to the notion of the risk manager as a manager of contracted relationships, the following discussion focuses on three issues: the management of insurance broker/agent relationships, bidding processes for third-party services and financially securing risk management arrangements. Although each of these points is specific, it is generally applicable to virtually any aspect of contract management a risk manager might encounter.

## Managing brokers/agents

Agents and brokers each have a different legal status, although the terms often are used interchangeably. A broker is a representative of a buyer in an insurance transaction, while an agent is a representative of the seller. This distinction is confused by the fact that both broker and agent services, historically, are paid for by the insurance company through a commission.

Following the introduction of the Insurance Brokers (Registration) Act 1977 only intermediaries who are registered with the Insurance Brokers Registration Council (IRBC) can use the term insurance broker. The IRBC takes responsibility for the registration and regulation of brokers, has developed a code of conduct for brokers and has the power to discipline and even disqualify brokers found to be in breach of the code. These responsibilities for regulating the broker industry are being taken by the General Insurance Standards Council (GISC) whose regulations currently co-exist with those of the IRBC.

While, typically, agents and brokers are viewed as being intermediaries in the risk financing marketplace, it would be misleading to conclude that broking is the only service provided. Due to broad competitive and market forces, most agents and brokers offer a wide range of services, including:

- underwriting and claims management services
- actuarial services
- training, research and education services
- captive and pool management
- risk management information services
- access to capital markets and alternative risk-financing solutions
- risk management audits and consulting
- loss control services.

For public bodies that are too small to develop sophisticated risk management programmes, a broker/agent can provide much needed professional assistance in the creation of an effective risk management strategy. Certainly, an agent/broker can provide knowledge of the insurance market, which will enable the client entity to obtain the best insurance arrangements possible. Thus, obtaining the services of a qualified and capable broker/agent becomes key to the creation of effective risk management practices. Even for larger bodies with significant in-house capabilities, broker/agents can bring great expertise in solving complicated risk management issues.

Selection of a broker/agent should be based on at least four criteria: marketing competence, consultation expertise, administrative competence and basis of remuneration.

Marketing competence refers to the broker/agent's knowledge of insurance markets and relationships with insurers. Consultation expertise means the capacity of that broker/agent to provide a wide range of consultative services – and the ability to understand the specific needs of public sector clients. Administrative competence refers to the broker/agent's ability to manage the account and the specific services or needs of the client. The remuneration issue relates to the methods of compensation. Previously, it was mentioned that broker/agents are paid a commission by the insurance company, but recent developments in the insurance industry have resulted in the emergence of fee-for-service compensation arrangements. Under the fee-for-service approach, the risk manager negotiates a flat fee for the broker's services, and the broker then finds insurance that is quoted 'net of commissions'. The cost of either approach may be roughly equivalent, but many risk managers argue that fee-for-service contracts help avoid conflicts of interest and enable them to see more clearly what they are paying for the services they receive.

## Bidding for third-party services

The way in which public bodies within the EU purchase third-party services changed fundamentally following the implementation of the Council Directive 92/50/EEC of 18 June 1992 relating to the co-ordination of procedures for the award of public service contracts. This was incorporated in the UK by way of the Public Service Contracts Regulations 1993. Prior to the advent of these regulations, most local authorities in the UK regularly tendered their purchase of insurance and related third-party services in accordance with their standing orders. Others tendered for third-party services on an *ad hoc* basis. However, following the introduction of the regulations, where the value of the services to be supplied exceeds the threshold level, the organization must follow a set procedure in order to comply with its purchasing obligations.

The theory behind the regulations was laudable. The European Commission was seeking to reduce trade barriers such that any service provider within the European Community was free to compete for the provision of services to any public body within the EU. Whether this objective has been met fully yet is still questionable and some critics of the regulations would argue that they have increased the transactional costs associated with the purchasing of services.

The thresholds currently are 200 000 ECU (approximately £150 000) in respect of an individual contract for a service (inclusive of premiums, fees and commission) and 750 000 ECU (£562 500) in respect of all qualifying premiums, fees and commissions for the year. It is possible within the regulations to treat as one contract for services a contract with options to renew provided that the options to renew are transparent in advance and that there is no renegotiation of terms. In the event that services do not exceed the thresholds then there is no requirement to comply with the purchasing regulations.

Assuming thresholds are breached the following procedures and timetable must be followed:

1    Publication of Prior Information Notice (PIN) – this is published in the *Official Journal of the European Community*. There is an obligation to publish a PIN when a public body anticipates that within the next twelve months it will award a contract for the provision of services in excess of either the individual or aggregate thresholds. The PIN must state the services to be awarded, will state how the contracts are to be awarded and may be the only call for competition for those services in that year. The PIN will also request written expressions of interest from potential service providers. Publication of a PIN reduces the minimum time periods required to complete the tender process.

2    Develop, review or amend selection criteria for potential service providers – this gives the public body the opportunity to identify minimum standards of, for example, financial security and sector expertise they would expect of a potential service provider.

3    Develop, review or amend the most economically advantageous terms (MEAT) criteria – public bodies can identify MEAT criteria ahead of time by which they propose to judge the respective merits of each tender response. If they fail to specify MEAT criteria they will be required to accept the lowest price offered.

4    Prepare contract information – this is the information upon which the potential service providers will base their tender responses.

5    Select one of three tender procedures:
   (a) Open –all interested parties may respond to an invitation to tender published in the *OJEC* and all respondents have an equal chance in the selection process. The last date for receipt of tenders is fifty-two days following submission of notice to *OJEC* unless a PIN was published, in which case it is thirty-six days.
   (b) Restricted – only potential service providers invited or selected by the tenderer may respond, in other words, they have met the selection criteria. The restricted procedure is one where negotiations with potential suppliers is not allowed although alternative proposals may be entertained if the *OJEC* notice specifically so states. The final date for receipt of tenders is no less than forty days after the invitations to tender were issued, although if a PIN is published this time period reduces to twenty-six days and, in urgent situations, to ten days.
   (c) Negotiated – only those service providers specifically invited by the tenderer participate and the procedure allows for negotiations to be entered into by both parties. If there are a number of suitable tenderers, a minimum of three must be selected.

6    Evaluate the tenders and award contract – this must be done either by using the pre-published MEAT criteria or, where MEAT criteria have not been specified, by awarding to the lowest price provider. The successful tenderer must be informed but there is no requirement to advise unsuccessful tenderers.

7    Maintain records – awarding bodies are required by the regulations to keep a record of all award procedures.

8    Publish contract award notice – within forty-eight days of the award the contract award notice must be sent to the *OJEC*.

## Security for risk management programmes

Increasingly public bodies are relying on alternative financing arrangements that require the risk manager takes additional steps to assure that the programme is financially secure.

Commercial banks offer a variety of collection systems and credit-based products to assist the risk manager in meeting the security objective. Collection systems allow a bank to facilitate transactions through document processing (bills of lading, invoices, certificates of origination, etc.). Additionally, these services can include enforcement and legal services, foreign exchange management services and myriad related financial risk services.

Credit-based products tend to be related to letters and lines of credit. The letter of credit is a banking mechanism that secures payment of an obligation. It is, effectively, a promise made by a bank to provide financing should it become necessary, and there are many different letter of credit models (e.g., revocable or irrevocable, straight or negotiable, confirmed or unconfirmed). Lines of credit are more narrowly defined and typically act to secure a fairly confined situation like a retrospectively rated insurance policy.

## Programme audit and review

Risk management programmes should be audited and reviewed periodically, from both an inside and an outside perspective. Indeed, the Audit Commission, the major external auditors of local authorities, now views the risk management function as being an area for specific comment. Risk management must also deal with the challenges posed by best value, that is, demonstrate that it represents the best use of the organisation's resources. Conventionally, a risk manager should have in place a process whereby the entire programme is subject to an ongoing and thorough audit process (this includes not just a financial audit and an actuarial audit – when necessary – but also a performance audit). Less frequently, risk management programmes would be advised to submit to an external audit. Although outside evaluation comes with some risk, external validation can become an important tool in promoting the risk management function within the entity.

One review function that warrants further discussion is the risk manager's role in claims adjudication and resolution. Regardless of whether the public body self-insures or insures its risks, the risk manager has a supervisory role in the claims management process. Claims management requires technical knowledge and, because of this, few risk managers retain complete responsibility for the claims process. If the risk is not insured, the risk manager is likely to have one or more third-party administrators involved in the claim management process. However, whether insured or self-insured with third-party administrator services, the risk manager has a general responsibility for setting claims policy, monitoring and advising the administrator, participating in litigation management and providing decision-making guidance.

# APPLICATIONS

## Corporate governance, best value and their organisational risk management implications

In the UK in the 1990s much attention has been focused in the private sector on the issue of corporate governance. Broadly put, corporate governance encompasses the responsibilities and standards of duty and care expected of directors, both executive and non-executive. The then Conservative government initiated the first major review and the findings, in the form of the Cadbury Report, were published in 1992.

Of particular interest to students and practitioners of risk management was the view propounded in sections 4.23 and 2.2.4 of the report that 'the Board should make a collective decision on risk management policies'. Moreover, section 4.5 states that 'directors should report on the effectiveness of the company's system of internal control' and Appendix 3, section 2b states that a 'director's responsibilities include safeguarding the assets of the company and preventing and detecting fraud and other irregularities'.

Clearly the Cadbury Report developed an important linkage between the management of an organisation's risks, exposures and uncertainties and its systems of internal control. As a method of internal control, risk management requires board endorsement and attention. The subsequent Rutteman Report and the Combined Code on Corporate Governance developed by the Hampel Committee and published in June 1998 went on to develop further the internal control aspects of the Cadbury Report.

The Turnbull Committee, which reported under the auspices of the Institute of Chartered Accountants, issued its draft guidance in April 1999 and its final report in late September of that year. One of its key findings was that risk management should be integrated with a company's internal controls. Internal controls were defined as 'all those policies and procedures that, taken together, support a company's effective and efficient operation and enable it to respond to significant business, operational, financial, compliance and other risks'. Some current risk management practitioners have reacted somewhat adversely to the report's implication that risk management's place is within an organisation's financial management and reporting function, fearing that the over-concentration on the internal control aspects will impact adversely on an organisation's entrepreneurial spirit. To an extent, this may just be jockeying for positions between risk managers and accountants but, equally, it is true that the upside characteristics of organisational risk are hardly catered for. For the time being adherents of the form of organisational risk management this book espouses have to be content with the fact that risk management is squarely on the boardroom agenda. Many skirmishes will have to be fought before we can ascertain whether its impact is to curtail risk-taking activity or rather to allow corporations to take informed decisions on risk.

## Public sector implications

What implications does all this have on public bodies? The trite answer might be none at all. The Cadbury Committee reported on corporate governance within the private sector while the Turnbull Committee's focus was on companies publicly quoted on the Stock Exchange. But there are signs that the public sector is watching these private sector developments very carefully. The Audit Commission in a Technical Release published in July 1997 (TR 26/97) was of the view that there was no reason why the Cadbury Report should not apply equally to local authorities.

It has also gone on record to the effect that:

> it is important that authorities have arrangements in place for reviewing both the nature and severity of risks ... such a review should not be restricted to 'obvious tangible' risks such as arson, vandalism and other damage to property ... risk management should be an integral part of an authority's overall management arrangements. In order to be successful it is likely that the approach will be cross-departmental and inter-disciplinary and that senior management will demonstrate commitment.

Clearly the Audit Commission has begun to recognise that the management of risks and exposures is a key component to an authority's ability to deliver services effectively and efficiently.

Some parts of the public sector have already formalised their internal controls' procedures. The National Health Service has already in place a controls assurance regime and each Health Trust is required to report annually on its compliance with the defined internal controls and may be audited on its compliance. The Housing Corporation has established a similar regime with which its members must comply. The governments of Australia and New Zealand have published their own risk management standards, which are minimum standard for risk management practitioners in those countries.

The conclusion can only be that in the fullness of time, and probably sooner rather than later, risk management will be incorporated formally into the internal control processes of public bodies and that the UK will publish its own risk management standards. Whether with its enhanced status within the public body, risk management will be used merely to tighten controls or, rather, positively to assist the organisation meet its strategic goals and objectives will largely be down to the strength of commitment within the senior management team and the risk manager's character.

## Best value

While issues surrounding corporate governance have principally concerned the private sector, best value is very much a public sector issue. The current Labour government has replaced the previous compulsory competitive tendering regime with that of best value. Instead of requiring certain services to be put out to competitive tender periodically, local authorities are now required to demonstrate that whatever course they have adopted provides best value to the organisation. Best value has been succinctly described as the requirement to apply good management practices to local government services (see Sidebar 10.1).

The process of determining best value involves utilisation of the 4 Cs:

- challenge
- consult
- compare
- compete.

1   *Challenge* – an authority must in relation to each of its functions examine:
    (a)  its objectives in relation to that function
    (b)  what needs it meets and whether there are needs it does not meet
    (c)  whether the function is required at all, the level and way in which it should be exercising the function
    (d)  whether there are better ways in meeting the needs.
2   *Consult* – under this process the authority must identify the stakeholders for the particular service in question and test satisfaction levels and seek ideas for improvement. Community-wide consultation must also be undertaken.
3   *Compare* – the competitiveness of the service must be assessed by comparison with others across a range of relevant indicators, taking into account the views of service users and potential suppliers. Actual performance needs to be compared with the upper quartile in terms of performance indicators.

---

## Sidebar 10.1 Best value

*England and Wales*

The statutory requirement for local authorities in England and Wales to adopt a best value regime is enshrined in Section 3(1) of the Local Government Act 1999. Authorities are required to secure continuous improvement in their functions with regard to economy, efficiency and effectiveness. Best value started in England on 1 April 2000 and in Wales in June 2000.

The duty to consult stakeholders on how best to fulfil the best value duty came into force in England on 10 August 1999 and in Wales on 1 October 1999. The first best value performance plans were to be produced by 31 March 2000 and annually thereafter.

The key requirements of the initial performance plans were to:

- summarise the local authority's objectives and assess the discharge of their functions
- specify the statutory best value review period and the review timetable to which they are working
- specify applicable performance indicators, standards and targets appropriate to each function
- summarise the local authority's performance in the current financial year and to compare it with previous financial years.

The performance plans are subject to external inspection by inspectors from the Best Value Inspectorate Forum.

Audit reports are to be released to the local authority itself, the Audit Commission and, in cases where statutory action is recommended, to the Secretary of State.

At the end of each inspection the inspectors have to assess the local authority's performance on two criteria:

- how good the services are
- whether they will improve in the way best value requires.

In making their assessment the Best Value Inspectors will consider:

- whether the local authority's aims are clear and challenging
- whether the particular service under review meets its aims
- how its performance compares with the applicable performance indicators, standards and targets
- whether the best value review will drive improvement

- the quality of the local authority's improvement plan
- whether the local authority will actually deliver the improvements.

Where statutory action is recommended, the Secretary of State has an extensive array of powers available by virtue of Section 15 of the Local Government Act 1999. Powers include:

- requiring the Audit Commission to carry out a best value inspection
- requiring a local authority to amend its best value performance review
- transferring a local authority's responsibilities to another authority or third party
- directing a local authority to take any action the Secretary of State considers necessary to achieve best value.

Best value reviews of all functions are to be completed by 31 March 2005, although there is a graded timetable for fire authorities.

*Scotland*
A less stringent best value regime exists for the thirty-two Scottish unitary authorities. While the Scottish system shares many of the characteristics of the one operating in England and Wales – it is based on a five-year rolling programme reviews designed to generate continuous improvement – there are a number of significant differences:

1   Unlike in England and Wales there is no framework legislation. Legislation is anticipated but the detailed legislative approach adopted in England is not being considered.
2   In England some local authorities will have to measure their performance against nearly 200 nationally defined performance indicators as well as developing their own local indicators. In Scotland the Accounts Commission has developed some seventy-six nationally defined indicators.
3   Scottish authorities had to submit their Public Performance Reporting frameworks to the Scottish Executive in 1999. Within the document each authority states the timetable and the format for reporting on each of the services.
4   In Scotland the best value verification process is performed by the Accounts Commission, rather than a newly created body as in England, through the performance management and planning (PMP) system, introduced in 1999.

5    PMP requires each authority to answer four questions about the services under audit:
     (a)   How do we know we are doing the right thing?
     (b)   How do we know we are doing things right?
     (c)   How do we plan to improve?
     (d)   How do we account for our performance?
6    The Audit Commission is required under PMP to collect evidence of performance against ten criteria:
     (a)   We understand the needs, expectations and priorities of all our stakeholders – Q1.
     (b)   We have decided on the best ways to meet these needs, expectations and priorities – Q1.
     (c)   We have detailed plans for achieving our goals – Q1.
     (d)   Our plans are clearly based on the resources we have available – Q1.
     (e)   We make best use of our available resources – Q2.
     (f)   We make best use of our people – Q2.
     (g)   We monitor and control our overall performance – Q2.
     (h)   We have sound financial control and reporting – Q2.
     (i)   We actively support continuous improvement – Q3.
     (j)   We provide our stakeholders with the information they need about our services and performance and listen to their feedback – Q4.
7    Scottish authorities made submissions in 1999 for three of their services and in the following year on a further three together with a review of corporate arrangements.
8    Whereas in England each service audit will result in a visit by inspectors, the PMP audit adopts more of a sampling approach, drilling down into detail in one area within the targeted service area.

4    *Compete* – authorities are required to use competition extensively. Retaining work in-house should only be justified where the authority can demonstrate it is competitive with the best alternative.

Without question, the concept of best value can do nothing but enhance the status of public sector risk management. Can a public sector organisation be deemed to be delivering best value if it is not managing it risks and exposures effectively and reducing the costs of uncertainty within its operations?

The determination of whether best value is being achieved is not without its challenges, however. The process of determining best value will require public bodies to, first, define the components of total cost of risk and then to track these components in ways they have not had to do hitherto. Best value will also require the formulation and adoption of best practice and will accelerate the adoption of national benchmarks. Only once these are in place will authorities be able to demonstrate that best value is being achieved.

## Conclusions

Both the corporate governance and best value initiatives are likely to place risk management among the core control competencies within an organisation. They are also likely to accelerate the process towards the development of national risk management standards and benchmarks. This is to be warmly welcomed but organisational risk management must not allow itself to become a means whereby entrepreneurial spirit and informed risk-taking decisions are suppressed.

---

# TOOLS YOU CAN USE

## The manager's skill set

An important theme of this book has been the notion that risk management is moving towards a 'general management' orientation. As a result, specific technical knowledge of insurance, claims handling, safety and other traditional competencies are becoming *relatively* less important while general managerial skills like planning, communicating, motivating, delegating and co-ordinating, organising, budgeting and supervising are gaining in value. Of course, effective risk managers have long recognised the importance of being good managers–but what has changed is the scope of risk management. Put plainly, one person is unlikely to know everything necessary to run the entire risk management show for a local authority. The organisation has to be fully engaged in managing its risks and as a result the risk manager – while still needing to provide technical expertise – will find that more and more time is devoted to managing the efforts of others.

A second reason behind the changing emphasis on management is the emergence of what might be called a risk management services industry. It probably is no exaggeration to say that any risk management service can now be purchased or rented from service providers – from actuarial services, to claims handling, to risk communications services, to training, to management information systems, to audit services, and everything in between. As a result, a risk manager

need no longer be the sole repository of technical knowledge or expertise. Thus, managing relationships with service providers also places
pressure on the risk management field to 'generalise'.

Certainly, risk managers need to have technical competence. It
could hardly be expected that a risk manager would negotiate the
best terms and conditions for insurance coverage without a solid
working knowledge of insurance contracts and law. However, in the
subtle shift of emphasis that is occurring in the profession, it is not
so much a matter of the risk manager having all the answers as it
is a matter of knowing how to ask the right questions. 'Asking the
right questions' does require a certain degree of technical knowledge, but it also requires a strong knowledge of the public sector,
of one's own organisation, of the broad risk management perspective, as well as a sense of where to go to find the right answer. For
example, a broker – that is, a good broker – can ably assist a risk
manager in conducting technical analysis; but a broker cannot know
what is in the best interest of the local authority.

What makes an effective manager? Even academic proponents of
the management sciences concede that some of the characteristics
are not quantifiable or even qualitatively describable. Illustrative of
this difficulty is the elusive quality of 'leadership'. What makes an
individual an effective leader? Certainly, personality traits could be
identified that would seem to meet the broad test of leadership –
clarity of vision, judicious reliance on the advice of others, intelli-
gence and decisiveness, all could be associated with effective
leadership.

However, a more careful evaluation of the concept of leadership
would have to consider the organisation's culture, the nature of the
task or objective, the broader culture and belief systems, the political system, and so on. In other words, effective leadership is not
just a matter of personal qualities; it is a matter of matching certain
personal qualities with the appropriate context. A successful wartime
leader frequently is the product of particular skills and traits applied
in the specific context of battle. Those skills may be wholly inappropriate in, say, a public hospital.

A methodical exploration of management theory and practice would
take this book far beyond its intended purposes. Readers interested
in beginning an investigation of the broader subject of managerial
effectiveness in public institutions should review a widely recognised
textbook on the subject, *Public Administration: An Action Orientation*
(by Robert B. Denhardt, 2nd edn, Harcourt Brace and Company,
1995), which not only lays the foundations for an overall view of
public sector management but provides a wealth of references for
readers interested in exploring the subject in depth. For the present

text, let the following few paragraphs suffice in addressing the subject of general management.

In 1937, Luther Gulick and Lyndall Urwick published *Papers on the Science of Administration*, which arguably is one of the twentieth century's two or three most important treatments of the subject of public administration. Although management science has evolved since that time, Gulick and Urwick established seven principles of public sector administration that still define adequately the nature of the management challenge.

In their work, Gulick and Urwick develop the idea that effective management involves a somewhat fluid balance of competencies among the tasks of:

- planning
- organising
- staffing
- directing
- co-ordinating
- reporting
- budgeting.

It is not particularly necessary to develop the meaning that Gulick and Urwick ascribed to each of these terms. Indeed, given previous comments about managerial 'intangibles' it probably is accurate to say that the meanings will change from organisation to organisation. So, for example, in some organisations 'reporting' might be tightly defined as a matter of producing required documents and supporting information to explain risk management decisions, while in other organisations reporting might more loosely be defined as 'risk communications, however undertaken'.

Perhaps the point here is that risk managers need to recognise that effective managers explicitly or implicitly address each of these managerial principles within the context of their particular job. Thus, in thinking about developing managerial skilfulness, a risk manager should consider his or her own needs *vis-à-vis* each of these areas. For instance, a review of the seven principles could lead a new risk manager to develop the following response:

1  *Planning*. Planning in general requires an appreciation of the broad purposes of local authorities, politics and strategic planning principles and practices. I should look into getting a book or taking a course on public administration and/or strategic planning (the more ambitious might consider pursuing a masters degree in public administration).

2   *Organising.* Short of taking a management theory and science
    course, I may need to evaluate how I organise my own time
    and manage my workload. Perhaps a short course on time
    management may be a helpful starting point.

3   *Staffing.* I need to better understand human resource manage-
    ment issues, including behavioural psychology issues as well as
    legal foundations of human resource management.

4   *Directing.* I need to find mentors within my organisation that
    can help me better understand the local authority's manage-
    ment culture and to learn how leadership occurs within that
    culture.

5   *Co-ordinating.* I need to have opportunities to work in team
    environments so I better understand collaborative management
    techniques and practices.

6   *Reporting.* I have a strong interest in developing my writing,
    speaking and listening skills. Perhaps workshops are available
    for becoming a more effective communicator.

7   *Budgeting.* Financial management skills require specialised
    knowledge. I need to enrol in a course in public finance and
    budgeting, and perhaps get an exposure to the subject of public
    sector accounting.

---

## READ MORE ABOUT IT

## A short risk management case study

This section differs from others in this book as it offers an insight
into an actual risk management scenario. The case study intentionally does not offer answers to the dilemma faced by the risk
manager, but a series of questions at the end of the case can direct
the reader's attention to the critical issues raised by the story.

### Case study exercise: Risk management in Anywhere Council

Risk management is a managerial function that has a relatively
brief history, particularly so in the public sector. Until very recently,
risk management was viewed as 'insurance-buying', with perhaps
a little safety engineering thrown in for good measure. However,
recently the practice of risk management has begun to broaden
dramatically, and its meaning and practice have changed irrevocably.

Today, risk management is defined as an aspect of general management that focuses upon the control and financing of risk and

uncertainty. A brief conceptualisation of this definition may be useful. All management efforts in an organisation focus upon three core elements: strategic management, operations management and risk management. Strategic management entails all those management functions and activities that establish the mission or goals and objectives of the organisation, as well as those that involve planning and forecasting, and those that monitor progress towards goals and objectives. Operations management are those activities that actually move the organisation towards its objective; the making of the product or the providing of the service in accordance with overall goals and objectives. Finally, risk management involves all those activities that seek to enable the organisation to move towards its goals and objectives in the straightest possible trajectory.

This broader definition of risk management has important effects on the case study. First, it means that risk management is not merely an individual or department. Rather, risk management is a function that is carried out by everyone in an organisation. In other words, this definition of risk management does not lead to an image of a risk manager struggling to make her organisation 'act safely'. It does lead to an image of a risk manager co-ordinating and facilitating the internal and external resources that must be brought to bear in order to manage organisational risk. Every employee has a role in risk management.

Second, this broader view means that risk management is concerned with every type of risk and uncertainty an organisation encounters; whether that is the risk of a fire, the risk of an unexpected revenue shortfall, the risk of a private contractor creating a vicarious liability exposure or, even, the risk of currency exchange problems that may arise when employing a foreign contractor for a capital project. Risk management also means uncertainty management. Uncertainty exacts a cost on organisations, even if losses never occur. Resources are misallocated. Desirable but risky public projects are forgone because of a fear of unfavourable outcomes. Managers lose sleep!

Finally, risk management involves the management of perceptions of risk. Risk has intangible but profound effects on organisations that cannot be ignored. For instance, a local government may consider some solution for dealing with hazardous waste, and the elected members may come to believe that the solution is the best for the community because the level of risk is 'acceptable'. However, if constituents have a very different perception of the risks involved, problems can emerge. Managing or responding to those public perceptions is risk management too.

The case study is intended to broaden the reader's view of risk management, and to help develop some appreciation for the multi-disciplinary nature of the function. This case centres on a unitary authority that is encountering serious difficulties with employee injuries.

## Anywhere Council

Anywhere Council is a unitary authority created as a result of the latest round of local government reorganisation in the UK. Like many authorities of its type the council is under enormous financial pressure. Over the last three years each department head has had to find a minimum budget saving of 5 per cent per annum while maintaining the same level of service delivery. Predominantly these savings have been found by downsizing the workforce.

A small senior management team runs the council. Each of its five departments – Executive Services, Technical Services, Finance and Information Technology, Education, Social Services – has a high degree of operational autonomy. Decentralisation has resulted in each department operating its own human resources policy and procedures.

Politically, the ruling party has a one-seat majority but pundits anticipate that the balance of power will alter at the next round of elections. Since the closure of Superalloys plc, the area's largest employer, the council has run a high profile 'Anywhere is Best' campaign to attract new investment into the area.

Joe McDuff has recently been appointed risk manager at Anywhere Council, replacing Michael Staid who had been Insurance Officer for the authority and its predecessor for the last twenty years. Joe's appointment was intended to signal an effort by the authority to create a fully functioning risk management programme. As the first true risk manager, Joe must confront the fact that very little in the way of risk control has ever been done in Anywhere. One of his first activities was a risk audit. In addition to its basic research value, the audit was intended to identify any potential 'hot spots' or trouble areas that might warrant immediate attention. As he anticipated, trouble areas were found but none more troubling than the issue of employee safety and health.

## Key findings of the risk audit

1   Absenteeism was running at a level higher than the national average for the public sector and in the Technical Services Department it is twice the national average.

2    Anywhere was generating on average sixty Employer's Liability claims per annum. Networking through ALARM, Joe discovered that this figure was considerably higher than in authorities of a comparable size.

3    Analysis of the Employer's Liability claims produced the information shown in Table 10.1. Technical Services Department claims amount to 65 per cent of the total value of claims and just over 70 per cent by number. The claim relating to the Finance and Information Technology Department is one where the employee is alleging that the stressful working environment at the council has induced her illness.

4    Analysis of the Employer's Liability claims sustained by employees within the Technical Services Department revealed the results in Table 10.2.

5    Nineteen of the forty multiple injuries include some type of back injury.

6    Analysis of the loss data showed that of the twelve employees aged forty-five or over who had sustained back injuries, Technical Services had offered early retirement to eight.

7    There is a distinct pattern of back injuries being sustained between 8 a.m. and 10 a.m., and Monday is the highest claims reporting day of the week for all claims.

**Table 10.1**  Employer's Liability claims: past three years

| Department | Number of claims (3 years) | Value (£) | Average cost per claim (£) |
|---|---|---|---|
| Executive Services | 4 | 40 000 | 10 000 |
| Technical Services | 128 | 1 152 000 | 9 003 |
| Finance and Information Technology | 1 | 50 000 | 50 000 |
| Education | 10 | 67 500 | 6 750 |
| Social Services | 37 | 444 000 | 12 000 |
| Total | 180 | 1 753 500 | |

**Table 10.2**  Employer's liability claims, by type

| Cause | Number of claims |
|---|---|
| Back | 44 |
| Multiple | 40 |
| Hand/wrist | 17 |
| Leg/foot/ankle/knee | 20 |
| Eyes | 4 |
| Shoulder/neck | 3 |
| Total | 128 |

As might be expected, the budgetary pressures have had a significant impact on the workload of the authority in general and the Technical Services Department in particular. Interviews with employees suggest that stress and workload levels have risen markedly in the last two years.

Frontline managers and employees within the Technical Services Department voice an almost unanimous opinion that the senior managers at Anywhere Council do not appreciate their workload, do not support budgetary requests and are uninterested in the department's problems.

The *Anywhere Gazette* has recently run stories on high levels of absenteeism at the Civic Centre and on Technical Services employees using Council materials and tools for private cash jobs.

A review of the Technical Services Department personnel reveals that while the average age of the manual workers is twenty-eight, very few of the employees were aged between twenty-five and forty. In terms of raw numbers, the most represented age groups for manual workers was eighteen to twenty-five and forty to forty-five.

## The emergency

Upon arriving at work one morning, only shortly after reviewing his evaluation of the Technical Services Department, Joe is notified that a serious incident has occurred. Earlier that morning, a worker from the Technical Services Department had been killed. He was run over by a fellow employee who was operating a fork-lift truck. The facts of the incident are not yet known, but a witness on the scene suggested that the driver of the fork-lift truck probably had been drinking. Further, investigation revealed that the driver had had two previous drink-drive convictions and, indeed, was currently banned from driving. Although his fellow workers knew of this, none felt that it was appropriate to alert their management of this fact.

## Assignments

1   Assume you are Joe McDuff, and you are still on the phone with the Chief Executive discussing the emergency. The Chief Executive asks, in exasperation, 'What in the world is going on in that division? You've been looking at that division for a few days now, Joe. What is your read on the problem with employee accidents?' How would you respond?

2   Budgetary constraint is a governing factor of life for Anywhere Council officials. Identify risks associated with this state of affairs that could imperil:

(a)   the physical assets of the council

(b)   the employees of the council

(c)   the council, through legal liability exposures.

3   Back injuries and back-related injuries are the most troubling Employer's Liability claims. Why do you think that these injuries would be so common? Why do you think they would tend to be expensive? Why are they so difficult to manage and treat?

4   Carpal tunnel syndrome is the most well-known type of 'repetitive motion' injury and repetitive motion injuries are an identified problem in Anywhere Council. What is carpal tunnel syndrome? Why does it occur? What may be done to prevent or control it?

5   The alleged stress claim opens some interesting issues for Anywhere Council. Historically, Employer's Liability and tort law have been reluctant to address health problems that could be categorised as 'stress-based' events. As risk manager, how would you seek to assess the extent of work-related stress within the council and what strategies would you develop to manage this exposure?

6   One of the facts uncovered regarding the Technical Services Department is that claims are filed disproportionately in the early morning and on Mondays. What does this suggest to you? Is there more than one possible explanation?

7   Clearly, the Technical Services Department is a problem from a worker injury standpoint. As risk manager, what would you do to attack this problem? Specifically:

(a)   What are your specific goals and objectives for attacking this problem?

(b)   What loss prevention techniques might you consider employing?

(c)   What loss reduction techniques might you consider using?

(d)   What might you do to motivate division managers to actively work with you to attack this problem? Can you devise an incentive/disincentive system to do this?

8   Write a memo to the head of the Technical Services Department. In that memo, explain your research findings, explain your conclusions, and lay out your action plan for attacking this problem. Be mindful of the political, personal and organisational ramifications of such a communication.

9   The cost of Employer's Liability claims can be insured or at least partially self-insured by organisations of Anywhere Council's size. In general, what might be the advantages and disadvantages of transferring the risk to an insurer versus retaining that risk and paying for the losses directly?

10   A big part of the risk manager's job is 'information manage-
     ment'. As the risk manager of Anywhere Council, what would
     you do (in general terms) to assure that you were receiving
     timely and relevant information on worker injuries and illness,
     and that you were providing timely and relevant information
     to administrators and managers in the council?

11   Risk management can involve the management of perceptions
     of and attitudes towards risk. Indeed, we might refer to this
     as 'litigation management in the court of public opinion'. This
     case study presents us with two public relations/perceptions
     issues:

     (a)   What types of things might the risk manager do to commu-
           nicate (to the citizens) that the council is on top of the
           problem of worker safety, and that positive steps are forth-
           coming to rectify the problem?

     (b)   What would your strategy be to mitigate the public rela-
           tions problems that can arise from the emergency you
           are now facing as well as the more obvious costs of the
           event? In other words, the disaster has already happened.
           What do you do limit the tangible cost of the event (insur-
           ance claims, lost time and productivity, legal costs, etc.)
           and what do you do to limit the intangible cost of the
           event (loss of public support, employee morale, adverse
           publicity, etc.)?

# 11

# *Risk management decision analysis*

## EXECUTIVE SUMMARY

Risk management does involve the management of objective risk, and so risk managers are expected to have statistical knowledge and capabilities. However, many, if not most, risks do not offer much in the way of quantitative information, and even when they do there may be significant problems with data quality. Thus experts argue that the use of statistical or actuarial analysis tools are best used in the context of a broader approach to organising and analysing information and data.

The analysis challenge for risk managers is likened to that of the historian. An appreciation of present circumstances and future possibilities requires a keen understanding of the past, including an understanding of the differences between past, present and future. Critical to a broader analytical framework is the development of the narrative of a particular issue or problem. From that framework, the problem can be studied and the risk manager can even evaluate how his or her perceptions influence the analysis.

Of course, many risk management analyses are enhanced by statistical analysis, and standard cost-benefit approaches tend to fit neatly into the broader analytical framework. A risk manager can introduce a high level of sophistication into decision analysis by using quantitative techniques that support the cost-benefit process. Importantly today, new and increasingly powerful software can assist risk managers in their work.

# PRINCIPLES AND CONCEPTS

How do risk managers decide what to do? Chapters 1 to 10 discuss a wide range of tools, techniques, strategies and ideas that can help a public body more effectively manage risk. But, the book has remained largely silent on the issue of deciding which things to undertake.

Chapter 11 focuses on the challenge of organising data (whether quantitative or qualitative), submitting the data to some form of analysis and using the results of analysis for assisting in the decision-making process. In the course of discussing this challenge, several key matters are explained, for instance, the unique properties of decision analysis when the issues are risk related, the challenge of decision analysis when data are limited in amount or quality, the matter of subjective risk and its incorporation into the analysis, and the use of conventional tools like cost-benefit analysis.

To this end, Chapter 11 begins with a presentation of critical issues related to decision analysis, especially when applied to public sector risk management concerns. Then, the chapter develops a framework for analysis that can accommodate problems where statistical data are abundant or virtually nonexistent. Discussion of this framework leads to an exploration of the influence of subjective risk on decision analysis, and a simple model for considering attitudes towards risk is introduced. Then the discussion of subjective risk gives way to an explanation of conventional analytical tools. This final section includes examples of these tools in application.

## Framing risk management problems: common elements

The development of methods for decision analysis in the public sector is important, in that the purpose is to provide a systematised and justifiable process by which managers allocate and expend public resources. Citizens expect that there is some level of rationality in the decisions that guide public management, and that expectation is the driving force behind the following discussion. The move towards a best value approach will reinforce this expectation.

Managers invariably discover that decision-making in a public environment presents a number of challenges that largely are not found in the private sector. Key among these distinctions are

- decisions are subject to open public scrutiny – while they are being made

- authority, power and decision-making processes are dispersed and not necessarily co-ordinated
- public goals and objectives are not always amenable to measurement or quantification
- institutional and bureaucratic processes and procedures impose limitations and expectations.

Undoubtedly, these characteristics affect risk management decisions and problems too. The question of whether to outsource refuse collection services illustrates this point for while risk management considerations might be important, they easily could be overwhelmed by politics, competing decision processes (e.g., executive v. members), lack of clarity as to the measures of costs and benefits, and civil service/union considerations.

These factors are profoundly important in developing an appreciation of decision-making in a public setting, but there are additional factors that further characterise risk management decision-making in a public setting, including time horizons, externalities, data credibility, interdependencies, uncertainty recognition and measurement of cost-benefits (known generally by the acronym TEDIUM).

The TEDIUM concept serves as an important reminder of a particular set of problems and factors that challenge risk managers. The TEDIUM concept does not argue that only risk managers face these issues, but it does assert that – taken as a whole – risk management problems tend to be characterised to a large degree by the presence of each of these factors. Thus, each of these issues warrants some attention.

## Time horizons

Many, if not most, risk management projects are long-term investments – often requiring time horizons of ten to twenty years. For example, a commitment to a safety programme for employees is not likely to be fully realised for at least three to five years and then the positive effects can only be understood in the context of reduced claims/losses over an extended period of time. Many liability exposure areas, such as asbestos, environmental impairment, discrimination and fiduciary liability, have long tails (a term referring to the length of time between when an event occurs and when a claim is settled) in excess of ten years.

## Externalities

A vexing aspect of public sector risk management is that costs and benefits are not precisely captured by the parties involved. A common illustration of externalities is pollution, because the 'cost' of pollution is borne by the surrounding community and not necessarily by the producer of pollution or by the buyers of the producer's products. These spillover effects can be profound, and indeed, their presence is one important reason why government becomes involved in certain risks – either by assuming responsibility for the externality-producing activity or by regulating that activity. Readers should note that externalities can be positive, as when a public inoculation campaign reduces the likelihood of health problems for those who receive the inoculations and those who might become exposed to those individuals.

## Data credibility

Often, discussions of risk management problem solving are organised around a statistical analysis of some risk. A common methodology is to develop estimates of future loss experience based on the past experience of an organisation or a group of similar organisations. However, the use of such data may be limited due to an insufficient amount of data to provide any statistical credibility, out-of-date or irrelevant data (the underlying risk has changed) or concerns about validity or quality.

## Interdependencies

Most statistical techniques employ an assumption of independence, meaning that individual exposures to risk are not influenced by other exposures (e.g., a fire in one building does not increase the likelihood of a fire in another building). While independence may be more or less assumed by an insurance company underwriting thousands of motor vehicles, independence is not easily assumed in single organisations. For example, many buildings may be clustered together, or vehicles may be parked and stored in a common location.

Interdependency has an abstract context as well. Chapter 3 discusses the concept of organisations as collections of COCAs. By definition, these risk-generating arrangements are related to one another since they are assembled to serve broadly common purposes. They are interdependent.

## Uncertainty recognition

How is a value placed on a state of mind? Uncertainty is the doubt we have about our ability to know or understand a fact or circumstance. While economists struggle with measurement in the context of 'disutility', it is probably more appropriate to recognise that uncertainty has a value, although that value may not be economic.

## Measurement of costs and benefits

Although this chapter develops a cost-benefit framework in a later section, readers should recognise that the measurement of costs and benefits is never easy and may be sufficiently problematic as to destroy the value of cost-benefit analysis. Common problems here are:

- a failure to identify all costs and benefits
- an inability to convert costs and benefits to a common metric (usually economic)
- an inability to find any measurement values
- problems with spillover effects.

One particularly vexing feature of cost-benefit analysis in risk management is the difficulty in understanding the value of benefits. Many, if not most, risk management techniques are preventive or pre-emptive, meaning the initiative results in 'things not happening'. For example, installing non-skid surfaces on the town hall floors will result in 'falls that will not occur'. Thus, while the cost of the initiative is easily measured, the benefits are ephemeral at worst and difficult to measure at best.

## The analytical framework

The preceding discussion suggests that decision analysis will almost never be a straightforward plug-in-the-numbers process. There simply are too many qualifiers, contingencies and limitations to complete reliance on conventional statistical approaches.

To that end, the analytical framework presented here adopts an approach that is almost the exact opposite of those presented in typical risk management and insurance textbooks. Conventional discussions start with a presentation of a decision methodology (e.g., decision trees, net present value analysis, cost-benefit analysis) and conclude with a postscript comment on the practical limitations to its use. This chapter begins with a full recognition of the limitations of traditional decision methods, organises a framework around those limitations and then concludes with the insertion of a conventional decision analysis method into this broader framework. The result, it is hoped, is an approach to thinking about risk management implementation in a more intuitive and practically useful way.

## The Neustadt-May framework

In their book *Thinking in Time* (Free Press, 1986), authors Richard Neustadt and Ernest May present a series of essays on the uses of history and historical research in modern management (particularly public management). A central contention is that most problems and challenges faced by managers are similar in construct to those encountered by historians (i.e., data are limited and/or contradictory, information exists in many non-comparable forms, perspectives or points of view matter, and context is important to understand).

The perspective presented in the Neustadt and May book differs from typical management 'how to' books in that complexity, opacity, incomplete information and uncertainty are not viewed as nuisances to decision analysis but rather central characteristics of the decision challenge. Not surprisingly, this framework would seem to hold promise in the area of organisation risk.

The Neustadt-May model can be summarised as a three-stage process, involving:

- development of the narrative
- structuring the current context
- framing the decision.

### Development of the narrative

The critical first step of the Neustadt-May model is development of a history of the situation encountered by the manager, and seeks to answer the central question, how did we get here?

The creation of a narrative has two levels of logic. First, cause-and-effect relationships are important to understand when the end result is a practical risk management application. But second, and equally importantly, humans tend to better understand information in a story format. Significant research in the areas of risk communication and the psychology of learning have shown that humans comprehend and process information that is represented in a narrative format – perhaps not a surprising finding when we consider how complex legends and myths existed only in an oral form for hundreds of years.

The process of narrative development involves several steps and several questions. The first step is to decide where the narrative must begin. This is not always easy and, of course, it invariably must be somewhat arbitrary. It is tempting to adopt a metaphysical point of view and start every narrative with Genesis. So the key to establishing a narrative format is to arrive at some plausible and arguable starting point.

The second step is to establish the parameters or boundaries of the narrative. Again, this element of narrative formation has a degree of arbitrariness, but it nevertheless is necessary to set narrative boundaries.

The third step is to clarify and establish the sequence and timing of key events. This is done by first setting the key 'plot points' (i.e., the driving or catalytic points in the story). Plot points consist of one or more elements, of which there are four generic types: people, things, events and situations. The final part of the third step is to connect the plot points along a narrative line.

The final step of narrative development is narrative assessment. Neustadt and May argue for a journalistic approach to narrative assessment, meaning that the assembled narrative is subjected to a 'who, where, what, why and when' analysis as well as a self-critical exploration of the assessment (are we sure? what is the degree of confidence we have in this assessment? why might we be wrong?).

The result of this first stage is a story that can be accepted as the explanation for why current circumstances exist as they do.

## Structuring the current context

The second stage involves building the current context. Neustadt and May assert that the current context should be developed under three headings:

- What is known?
- What is unclear?
- What is presumed?

It is essential that the current situation be framed in that way to explicitly address the issues of uncertainty, information limitations, and assumptions.

When the current context has been described in the categories of what is known, unclear and presumed, the next step of stage two is to ask/answer:

- What is the problem?
- Whose problem is it?

The purpose of these two questions is obvious, but there is a subtext. A process of examining the background narrative and the current context leads to a more insightful framing of the problem in question (rather than allowing the problem to frame our understanding of past and present). Less evidently, focusing on the second

question allows a more explicit recognition of the politics of decision-making in the public sector. Perceptions of risk can be considered
here, as can the process issues related to politically based decision-
making.

The next step is an identification of the desired outcomes of the
defined problem. What result would satisfy the key stakeholders or
at least meet the minimum tests of acceptability? Obviously, this
step would include the development of relevant decision criteria.

Stage two also includes an assessment step. Is our description of
the current context accurate? It may also be relevant here to consider
what Neustadt and May call the 'analogous past'. Are there circumstances here or elsewhere that may provide us with guidance –
particularly with respect to how similar situations turned out.

## Framing the decision

The third stage of the Neustadt-May process involves organising the
decision into a rational form. The specifics of this stage largely are
predicated in the particular aspects of the issues in question.
However, Neustadt and May argue that the framing of a decision
should include:

- a listing of the options
- an assigning of odds associated with each option
- some recognition of the uncertainty associated with both the
  options and the process of framing the options.

Readers will find a remarkable convergence between the three points
above and the discussions in Chapters 1, 3 and 4 regarding the
measurement of risk. In this book the measurement of risk has
included an assessment of the range of alternatives that might occur,
the probabilities associated with the various outcomes, and a recognition of the subjective risk. Thus, it can be imagined that more
traditional decision frameworks might be employed at this point to
organise the analysis of options.

The applications section in this chapter includes an outline of the
Neustadt-May process.

# Incorporating subjectivity into the analysis

The Neustadt-May process identifies a number of points in the
analysis where assumptions are questioned and the process itself
is held up to critical review. This feature of the process is wholly

consonant with the philosophy of this book. Uncertainty, attitudes towards risk, subjective risk and cognitive risk matter.

But, arguing that such concerns matter does little to improve the reader's understanding of the way in which such considerations are included in decision analysis. This section intends to remedy that problem.

Economists tend to frame decision analysis in a manner that compels the elements of the problem to be translated into financial terms. Even preferences and attitudes are converted to monetary values or surrogate monetary measures are used. However, there are a number of fundamental and practical problems with this economics-based cost and benefit approach. Simply put, many costs and benefits cannot be quantified in monetary terms. Unfortunately, as this chapter suggests in an earlier section, the conventional use of cost-benefit analysis forces all possible elements of the decision into the model, and then deals with the messy leftovers as a nuisance. This, of course, is problematic for a public sector risk manager because the 'messy bits' may be the key elements of the risk or its solution.

The principal benefit of the Neustadt-May model is that it forces consideration of the non-economic factors to the front of the analysis. But, by doing so, the process forces serious consideration of the need to formalise or order thinking about the non-economic dimension of risk management decisions. Perhaps surprisingly, a possible solution can be found in the work of cultural anthropologists and behavioural psychologists.

Perception of risk is influenced by nearly infinite arrangements of factors. Recent genetic research shows that there may be gene-related predispositions to risk, while psychological study has found that environment (both immediate and general), information or its absence, proximity to risk, peer pressure and dynamics, and a host of other factors influence attitudes towards risk. Anthropologists have found that culture imposes 'filters' through which risks are perceived and addressed.

Which influence is paramount? This is an important question, but not a particularly pressing matter here. What is of concern is a way to recognise that these factors may be in play and to account for them when making risk management decisions. Fortunately, a fairly useful model exists for organising thinking about individual and collective attitudes towards risk – the subjective risk matrix.

## The subjective risk matrix

Readers interested in a fuller treatment of the subjective risk matrix are encouraged to read John Adams's *Risk* (UCL Press, 1998), a highly readable book that focuses on risk and broad public policy considerations. Relevant to this chapter is the specific application of Adams's arguments to the issue of subjective risk.

The subjective risk matrix (SRM) is based on the premise that attitudes towards risk are importantly (though not exclusively) influenced by culture and by an individual's psychological makeup (see Table 11.1). This premise then builds a set of psychological and cultural prototypes that provide a framework for thinking about subjective risk. Although scholars would rightly protest that these prototypes might become stereotypes, and indeed might make complex matters misleadingly simple, the practical manager could do a lot worse than attempting to organise an analysis of subjective risk around this approach.

Table 11.1 identifies psychological types as falling in four categories: egalitarian, fatalist, hierarchist and individualist. While not mutually exclusive categories (a person can fall into more than one category depending on the situation), the definitions do create clear distinctions.

1    *Egalitarians* are individuals with strong group loyalties but little regard for externally imposed rules – except those imposed by nature. Group decision-making tends to be democratic and leadership is effected by example and persuasion.
2    *Fatalists* are individuals who perceive that they have little control over their lives. They commonly do not participate in processes where decisions – which can affect their lives – are made.
3    *Hierarchists* are individuals who endorse groups with strong boundaries and rules. Group dynamics are seen to be naturally hierarchical, with individuals seeing and understanding their position within the group.

**Table 11.1**  Subjective risk matrix with illustrative stereotypes

|              | Egalitarian        | Fatalist          | Hierarchist            | Individualist                   |
| ------------ | ------------------ | ----------------- | ---------------------- | ------------------------------- |
| Ephemeral    | Environmentalist   | Hell's Angel      | Victorian gentleman    | Bankrupt venture capitalist     |
| Capricious   | Lottery winner     | Kosovar Albanian  | Local weather forecaster | Riverboat gambler             |
| Perverse/tolerant | Political adviser | James Dean      | Non-profit executive   | Venture capitalist              |
| Benign       | Utopian socialist  | Religious martyr  | Civil servant          | George Soros                    |

4   *Individualists* are individuals who see themselves as relatively free of control by others, and who exert effort to control their environment and the people in it. They tend not to be process-oriented in group decision-making situations.

The second dimension of the SRM relates to perceptions of the world, which might be derived from individual experience, but which also correspond with broad cultural constructs. These four world-views are described as:

1   *Ephemeral*. The world is viewed as fragile, precarious and unforgiving. It is viewed as being in constant danger of harm due to human carelessness.
2   *Capricious*. The world is viewed as unpredictable. It is impossible to predict what will happen, which tends to lead to a *laissez-faire* attitude towards the environment.
3   *Perverse/tolerant*. The world is viewed as a sort of combination of the first and last views. Within certain parameters, the environment is resilient, benign, and predictable. Outside those parameters, however, the environment is more fragile.
4   *Benign*. The world is viewed as predictable, resilient, and robust. Broadly speaking, the environment is able to absorb the harm humankind might inflict on it.

An analytical process can be imagined where, by using the SRM, a risk manager could begin to anticipate individual and group positions/responses with respect to certain risks. In the context of developing the narrative, for example, this line of thinking could be used to judge the relative influence of people in the overall plot.

One thing the SRM most assuredly does not do is explain why a group or an individual fits into a particular category, but presumably the initial analysis might prompt a further investigation into why.

A second moment in the Neustadt-May process where the SRM may be beneficial is the inquiry into whose problem the issue at hand is. The matrix allows a rudimentary line of thinking to emerge regarding the various positions of stakeholders and some level of appreciation as to their responses to possible risk management solutions. The matrix also may allow a more explicit consideration of attitudes towards risk to emerge. For example, the matrix could be used as a means of moving council members towards some common appreciation of their varying attitudes towards risk and towards some agreed upon method of incorporating differing attitudes into their decisions.

# Cost-benefit analysis

Some seemingly negative comments have been made regarding economics-based decision methodologies, but those methodologies have an important role within the larger framework of decision analysis. Obviously, many aspects of risk management are financial or quantitative, and the fact that quantifying risks can be difficult does not mean the effort should not be made.

Conventional cost-benefit analysis involves the following steps:

1   Forecasting the benefits and costs associated with a particular project.
2   Determining the appropriate time value/rate of return factor for discounting benefits and costs to a present value.
3   Applying the discount factor to each of the costs and benefits to determine a present value.
4   Subtracting the present value of costs from the present value of benefits to produce the net present value.
5   Adjusting the net present value for considerations not included in the first four steps.

Two specific issues are important for the public sector risk manager. First, determination of the appropriate discount rate is problematic. Theories abound on what the appropriate rate to be adopted should be (e.g., the risk-free interest rate, the weighted average of displaced returns of taxpayers). There is a degree of philosophy and practicality regardless of the discounting method used. Those who believe that public expenditures should be consciously aware of the private investment such expenditure displaces are likely to suggest a discount rate that reflects a market orientation. Those who believe that public investment inhabits a realm that is not precisely comparable with private sector investment will be inclined to seek something closer to the risk-free interest rate. A possible compromise is to conduct a sensitivity analysis, and use a range of discount rates to determine possible investment outcomes under varying conditions.

The second problem that confronts the risk manager is the failure of cost-benefit analysis to account for risk, an irony that should be difficult for risk managers to ignore. Analysts forecast costs and benefits, but these are uncertain variables; an investment in a safety training programme may or may not reduce accidents by 10 per cent a year. There are at least two ways this can be addressed. First, the costs and benefits (like the discount rate) could be subjected to a sensitivity analysis so that the value of the project can be compared across a range of possible scenarios. The second approach is to adjust the discount rate to reflect the riskiness of the cost and benefit flows. Publicly traded companies have some science to support their ability to rely on the second approach, since modern finance theory allows them to adjust discount rates to reflect the riskiness of cash flows (this adjustment is known as the corporation's beta). No such theory exists in the public sector, so such an adjustment must be done subjectively (larger adjustments for risky projects, smaller or no adjustments for low-risk projects).

For example, imagine that a local authority is considering the introduction of a major loss control programme, which is intended to reduce work-related injuries among employees. The particulars of this programme will require some training and education to be undertaken, some introduction of new processes and procedures, and the use of some new safety equipment. Naturally, costs would include a mechanism to monitor and measure the impact of the loss control programme. To illustrate this cost-benefit analysis (see Tables 11.2 and 11.3), a few assumptions are necessary:

1   The project has a ten-year life, and has no externality or indirect effects.
2   The risk-free rate of interest is 5 per cent.
3   The expected return on a market portfolio (a balanced investment portfolio representing the market's weighted average return on investment) is 16.5 per cent.
4   Loss control programme costs involve a first-year cost of £55 000, followed by annual costs of £5000.
5   Loss control programme benefits are projected to be £20 000 a year in reduced accident costs, beginning in year two.
6   The initial programme investment is assumed to be incurred immediately, while the future costs and benefits are assumed to be recognised at the same time each year, which is the end of the year.
7   The decision rule is to accept the project if it has a positive net present value.

For purposes of contrast, the computation is conducted assuming, first, a risk-free discount rate, and then using a market-based rate. Readers are reminded that matters related to risk, externalities, and the other non-quantitative issues discussed earlier in the chapter also must be considered.

The two analyses produce different conclusions. In the case of the market-based analysis, the project is rejected – it yields a negative cost-benefit value of £998. The risk-free analysis produces a different

**Table 11.2** Hypothetical risk management project cost-benefit analysis (risk-free rate of return, 5 per cent)

| End of year | Initial invest-ment (£) | Expected cost savings (£) | Operating expenses (£) | Annual net cost-benefits (£) | Discount factor | Present value (£) |
|---|---|---|---|---|---|---|
| 0 | 55 000 | – | – | (55 000) | 1.00 | (55 000) |
| 1 | – | – | £5 000 | (5 000) | 0.95 | (4 750) |
| 2 | – | 20 000 | £5 000 | 15 000 | 0.91 | 13 650 |
| 3 | – | 20 000 | 5 000 | 15 000 | 0.86 | 12 900 |
| 4 | – | 20 000 | 5 000 | 15 000 | 0.82 | 12 300 |
| 5 | – | 20 000 | 5 000 | 15 000 | 0.78 | 11 700 |
| 6 | – | 20 000 | 5 000 | 15 000 | 0.75 | 11 250 |
| 7 | – | 20 000 | 5 000 | 15 000 | 0.71 | 10 650 |
| 8 | – | 20 000 | 5 000 | 15 000 | 0.68 | 10 200 |
| 9 | – | 20 000 | 5 000 | 15 000 | 0.65 | 9 700 |
| 10 | – | 20 000 | 5 000 | 15 000 | 0.61 | 9 150 |
|  |  |  |  |  |  | 41 800 |

**Table 11.3** Hypothetical risk management project cost-benefit analysis (market rate of return, 16.5 per cent)

| End of year | Initial invest-ment (£) | Expected cost savings (£) | Operating expenses (£) | Annual net cost-benefits (£) | Discount factor | Present value (£) |
|---|---|---|---|---|---|---|
| 0 | 55 000 | – | – | (55 000) | 1.00 | (55 000) |
| 1 | – | – | 5 000 | (5 000) | 0.86 | (4 292) |
| 2 | – | 20 000 | 5 000 | 15 000 | 0.74 | 11 052 |
| 3 | – | 20 000 | 5 000 | 15 000 | 0.63 | 9 487 |
| 4 | – | 20 000 | 5 000 | 15 000 | 0.54 | 8 143 |
| 5 | – | 20 000 | 5 000 | 15 000 | 0.47 | 6 990 |
| 6 | – | 20 000 | 5 000 | 15 000 | 0.40 | 6 000 |
| 7 | – | 20 000 | 5 000 | 15 000 | 0.34 | 5 150 |
| 8 | – | 20 000 | 5 000 | 15 000 | 0.29 | 4 421 |
| 9 | – | 20 000 | 5 000 | 15 000 | 0.25 | 3 795 |
| 10 | – | 20 000 | 5 000 | 15 000 | 0.22 | 3 257 |
|  |  |  |  |  |  | (998) |

result – a cost-benefit value of £41 800. Readers with little financial management experience might well wonder what is happening.

The simple answer is that they are witness to the miracle of compound interest. An eleven and a half point swing in discount rates has an enormous effect on the results of the analysis. However, as impressive as compound interest may be, other observations should be drawn from the comparison.

First, longer-term projects have a difficult time passing muster in a discounting regimen. Even if lower interest rates apply, it can easily be deduced that – everything else being equal – cost-benefit analysis will favour projects that produce benefits sooner rather than later. Readers might ponder the implications in light of the earlier observation that risk management projects tend to have long time lines.

Second, higher discount rates can be associated with two phenomena: higher returns in the marketplace and riskiness of future cost and benefit flows. Regarding the higher returns issue, the analysis shows that higher expected returns or discount rates present greater hurdles to longer-term projects. Using higher rates implies a private sector standard is employed to judge public-sector projects. This might be reasonable – for instance, if the policy-makers are concerned with minimising government's role and preventing excessive displacement of private investment, or if higher interest/discount rates force risk managers to demonstrate a higher standard of performance. Of course, some might say it only provides an incentive to fiddle with the assumptions, but this could be a problem in any analytical framework.

Regarding the riskiness of future cost and benefit flows, intuitively it can be agreed that risk is related to returns (the riskier an investment, the higher its anticipated rate of return should be), so naturally risky endeavours should be subject to the same expectation. Thus, another way of thinking about the illustrations in this chapter is to say that the more uncertain the future benefits and costs, the higher the discount rate should be. And this seems to make basic sense, as the discount rate provides a layer of protection against high-risk projects. For instance, consideration of a highly experimental risk management measure with no track record probably should be evaluated using a higher standard (i.e., discount rate).

So what are we to conclude about this all? Probably first and foremost, cost-benefit analysis in risk management should be subject to sensitivity analysis (the analysis should be conducted several times, adjusting the variables each time) to provide decision-makers with a range of scenarios. By doing so, they can isolate the influence of cost-benefit flow timing, rates of return, riskiness of future benefits and costs and, even, the basic assumptions that underlie the framing of the analysis.

Secondly, however, the illustrations suggest that the output of the analysis is only as good as the setup. 'Garbage in, garbage out' is a central admonition of decision analysis, and it is relevant here. By looking at Tables 11.2 and 11.3, we can appreciate how sensitive the output can be to minor changes in the assumptions. And, in turn, this realisation may reinforce the necessity of developing a broad and systematic quantitative and qualitative method for investigating risk management challenges, a method that might not be too dissimilar from the one developed throughout this chapter.

## The matter of allocating cost burden

A final question is worth mentioning here – one that is not so prominent in the private sector: who pays for the initiative?

In principle there are two possible guiding rationales: the cost of the risk management programme is socialised, or the cost of the risk management programme is distributed to those who enjoy its benefit. Although this matter is philosophical as well as practical, the risk management response would tend to be a mix of the two. Where benefits are appropriable (i.e., we can identify precisely who is benefiting from the programme and can charge them accordingly), the tendency would be to distribute the cost burden to the beneficiary. In the case of the introduction of safety lighting in a public car park, financing might be borne through a user's fee.

In the case where the risk is non-appropriable or where the parties in question are incapable (economically or politically) to finance the cost, the burden is borne by the general taxpaying public.

Timing also can be a concern in answering the question of who pays, which is why debt financing may be considered (costs are borne partly by future taxpayers who enjoy the longer-term benefits of the risk management programme).

The example of a worker safety programme is one where the cost burden issue is not central. The programme is, in effect, freeing general funds for a wide range of uses and thus it is likely to be a general revenue matter.

---

# APPLICATIONS

## The Neustadt-May process

The Neustadt-May process discussed in the chapter can be reduced to an outline form, which should be useful to readers who want to apply this line of analysis to a problem of particular interest to them.

**Table 11.4**  The Neustadt-May process

| | |
|---|---|
| Phase 1 | Development of the narrative |
| Primary objective | To answer the question 'how did we get here?' |
| Tasks | Setting the narrative starting point |
| | Clarifying the narrative parameters and boundaries |
| | Establishing the sequence and timing |
| | Identifying plot points (people, things, events, situations) |
| | Completing the narrative line |
| | Assessing the narrative |
| Outcome | A detailed narrative that describes the history of the problem in question |
| | |
| Phase 2 | Structuring the current context |
| Objective | To establish a full description of current circumstances related to the problem |
| Tasks | Establish what is known, what is unclear, and what is presumed. |
| | Clarify what is the problem. |
| | Establish whose problem it is. |
| | Identify the desired outcomes. |
| | Set decision criteria. |
| | Assess the process. |
| Outcome | A description of the current situation including an impact assessment, the overall outcome objective and the basis for measuring progress towards that outcome |
| | |
| Phase 3 | Framing the decision |
| Objective | To systematise the analysis of options and to aid in decision-making |
| Tasks | List and describe available options/solutions. |
| | Develop/calculate probabilities and values. |
| | Evaluate uncertainty and subjective risk. |
| | Assess the decision process. |
| Outcome | Rational support for a decision related to a risk management problem or issue |

# TOOLS YOU CAN USE

## A simple risk management decision process

The decision process that is developed in this chapter offers a systematic way for public bodies to organise data for the purpose of making decisions about risk management projects. Undoubtedly, for very small public bodies, the capacity to undertake such a systematised method is limited, and the capacity to subject all decisions to such an analysis is virtually impossible. Thus this section introduces a simple, non-quantitative method for evaluating individual projects and for looking at a risk management programme as a whole. For purposes of introduction, this method is called the insurance method.

The insurance method involves four basic steps:

- risk identification
- insurance coverage identification
- risk and insurance coverage prioritisation
- consideration of alternatives and supplements.

## Risk identification

The first step is to undertake a risk identification process similar to the one Chapter 3 describes. Imagine that the small local authority has obtained a risk checklist from its agent or broker and has identified its risks by completing the checklist.

## Insurance coverage identification

After risks have been identified, the second step is to identify insurance coverages that correspond with the risks. For example, identification of the risk of fire to buildings would be matched against a standard property policy. The identification of errors and omissions risks would be matched against an officials' indemnity policy. Risks to boilers, heating and air conditioning equipment, and other machinery would be matched with a boiler and machinery policy.

## Risk and insurance coverage prioritisation

The product of the second step would be a side-by-side list of risks and coverages. Some risks will not have corresponding coverages, but this is not a bad thing necessarily. Such a finding simply indicates areas where risks exist but insurance coverage does not.

The third step is to prioritise the risks and corresponding coverages. The categories would be:

- *mandatory*: coverages/risks for which treatment is required
- *important*: coverages or risks that correspond with serious or catastrophic outcomes
- *useful*: coverages or risks that correspond with moderate or non-catastrophic outcomes
- *unimportant*: coverages or risks that are neither important or useful.

## Consideration of alternatives and supplements

The fourth step involves an evaluation of alternative methods and techniques that might be employed. For example, a manager might consider whether a loss control programme should be introduced in conjunction with important coverages. Or the manager might ponder whether a useful coverage might include a large deductible so the local government is paying for many of its small losses out of pocket (and thus reducing the premium dramatically). Or, in the case of risks where no insurance is available, the manager might consider whether an alternative financing mechanism might work best.

The result of the fourth step is a listing of the control and financing solutions that will be used by the local government.

Readers will realise that this process is highly flawed – at least from a theoretical perspective. It is heavily biased towards a decision to buy insurance. It does not contain decision rules (on what basis are deductible levels decided, or what is important). It also does not help sort out 'how much', that is, there is no guidance on how the programmes relate to the overall purposes of the local government.

And yet, the insurance method does accomplish a number of things not ordinarily seen in organisation management. First, it compels managers to systematically identify and think about risks. Second, it forces them to understand where coverages exist and where they do not. Third, it compels them to consider which are key problem areas, which are of moderate importance and which are unimportant. And fourth, it motivates managers to consider what other measures might be undertaken to help the risk management effort succeed. So, while the method is neither scientific nor theoretically rigorous, it does impose a systematic process of thinking about risk management, which is a significant improvement on most risk management practices found in smaller public bodies.

---

# READ MORE ABOUT IT

## Decision tools: an overview

Chapter 11 addresses the broad subject of risk management decision-making. In presenting an introductory discussion, the chapter offers an exposition of practical problems that risk managers encounter in organising data to analyse problems and make decisions. The chapter then develops an overall framework for approaching risk management problems and challenges – an approach that is not dependent on the availability of quantitative data. Finally, readers find a single quantitative method – cost/benefit analysis – in action and are given an exposure to the strengths and weaknesses of the cost/benefit approach.

Of course, there are numerous other decision-making methods or techniques that might be employed as well and the purpose of this discussion is to briefly highlight several commonly used techniques. Readers with a keen interest in the subject would do well to look at three recognised books on the subject of public sector decision-making:

1    John Bryson's *Strategic Planning for Public and Nonprofit Organizations* (Jossey-Bass, San Francisco, 1988).
2    K. J. Meier and J. L. Brudney's *Applied Statistics for Public Administration*, 3rd edn (Wadsworth, Belmont, CA, 1993).
3    E. S. Quade's *Analysis for Public Decisions*, 2nd edn (North-Holland, New York, 1989).

## Analytical techniques

While not exhaustive, the following listing and discussion of analytical techniques provides readers with a good overview of the types of approaches that might be used in framing and evaluating risk management projects.

## *1 The strategic planning framework*

This book develops the idea that risk management is 'mission driven' meaning the management of an organisation's risks is governed by the overall purposes, goals and objectives of the local authority. But, it also means the local authority risk manager can (must?) develop a strategic orientation to overall risk management efforts. In this light, the risk management function should be developed within a strategic planning framework. This framework is built around the following stages or steps:

a    *Mission statement development.* Just as the organisation has a mission statement, the risk management function should develop a guiding vision. Logically, that vision must link with the overall mission of the organisation, but often such a mission is too broad to provide clear guidance for risk management efforts.
b    *Environmental analysis.* Environmental scanning is a critical aspect of risk assessment, but here the framework is asking

the risk manager to consider the environment in which the risk management function exists. In other words, the risk manager is not seeking here to discover the organisation's risks per se but rather the specific risks of the risk management function (political support, internal communications, organisational culture, for example).

c    *SWOT (strengths, weaknesses, opportunities and threats) analysis.* Conventionally, strategic planning organises analysis around the internal evaluation of an organisation's strengths and weaknesses and an external analysis – culled from the environmental analysis – of the specific threats faced by the organisation and the opportunities available to it.

d    *Value analysis.* The stage may often be a part of mission development, but it stands alone here as a reminder that a clarification of managers' and employees' attitudes towards risk and their risk management 'value system' is important in designing the overall approach to risk management.

e    *Development of strategies.* The result of the first four steps is the creation of a strategic response or plan. Although the risk management strategy will incorporate use of the tools and techniques discussed elsewhere in the book (and will even be derived from techniques discussed in Chapter 11), the distinction to make here is that the risk management plan is viewed as an integrated, long-range and systematic effort to manage the organisation's risks in accordance with the overall mission.

## 2 Decision tree analysis

A common problem with many analytical techniques is that they do not necessarily factor risk into the equation – a rather ironic problem for risk managers. In light of this weakness, the use of decision tree schemes is understandable since they easily can address probabilistic outcomes. Decision trees involve the creation of a decision map or 'tree' that represents both the range of possible outcomes as well as the probabilities (or likelihoods) associated with each outcome. Often the outcomes can be quantified, but decision trees can also accommodate qualitative measurements (Exhibit 11.1).

Exhibit 11.1 here shows a very simple risk management problem – the decision to buy or forgo insurance. For purposes of introduction, some important elements of a sophisticated analysis are omitted. Most notably, the probabilities associated with each outcome are absent as are the actual cost of insurance and the cost of loss. Readers can easily see that such information matters a great deal.

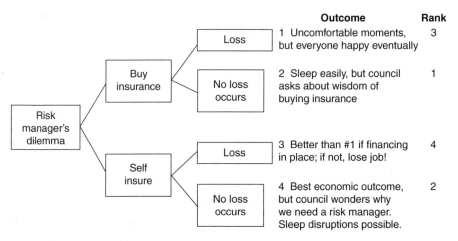

| | | | Outcome | Rank |
|---|---|---|---|---|
| | | Loss | 1 Uncomfortable moments, but everyone happy eventually | 3 |
| | Buy insurance | No loss occurs | 2 Sleep easily, but council asks about wisdom of buying insurance | 1 |
| Risk manager's dilemma | | Loss | 3 Better than #1 if financing in place; if not, lose job! | 4 |
| | Self insure | No loss occurs | 4 Best economic outcome, but council wonders why we need a risk manager. Sleep disruptions possible. | 2 |

**Exhibit 11.1**  Decision tree example

If, for example, the chance of loss virtually is nil then the self-insurance option appears more palatable. If the converse is true, insurance seems more compelling.

Still, despite the simplicity of this illustration, it does suggest the value in displaying complicated decisions in such a manner as it forces the risk manager to address each of the possible outcomes explicitly and to consider the consequences of the decisions.

## 3 Process or flow charting analysis

Unlike the more obvious decision-oriented method discussed previously, process/flow charting serves more of an analytical function. Charting involves the creation of a diagrammatic or pictorial representation of work or operational processes as a means of better understanding the nature of the risks in question. For example, part of a risk assessment of paperwork processing might include a simple flow chart as in Table 11.5.

From a risk management perspective, the key value of flow charting is the development of a clearer understanding of processes and where risks may come into play. As just a basic example deriving from the illustration, a risk manager might conclude that the transfer of documents from clerk to analyst and from analyst to chief clerk presents something of a 'security risk' inasmuch as it is an opportunity for documents to go missing and for confidential information to leak out of the process. This insight might lead to a more thorough examination of these steps in the process and a weighing of the possible measures that could address the risk.

**Table 11.5** Flow chart example

| Employee classification | | |
| Mail Clerk | Analyst | Chief Clerk |
| --- | --- | --- |
| Date-stamps mail, and Sorts for analyst, and Delivers to analyst, who | | |
| | Examines requests, and Conducts audit, and Confers with team, and Prepares draft opinion, and Delivers to Chief Clerk, who | |
| | | Reviews draft, and Prepares official response. |

## 4 PERT/CPM analysis

Two related and well-known analytical methods are the Programme Evaluation Review Technique (PERT) and the Critical Path Method (CPM).

The Programme Evaluation Review Technique is a system for organising and analysing projects where there are clear starting and ending points. The PERT approach uses diagrams (see Exhibit 11.2) to capture all the elements of a project and the sequence within which the elements must occur. Activities that are dependent on one another must be represented in a continuous sequence, whereas independent events are represented in parallel or separate sequences.

After the elements are identified and placed in sequence, timings must be assigned to represent the anticipated duration between steps in the sequence as well as the duration of the steps themselves.

The CPM actually builds from the PERT approach. Its distinction is that it focuses on the most time-consuming, complicated or 'critical path' in the scheme. Commonly, as the Exhibit 11.2 shows, this is the sequence upon which project success depends and so warrants the most intense managerial attention.

Exhibit 11.2 shows a project to develop and offer risk management training courses. Readers can easily imagine that real world projects quickly can become very complex and difficult to chart. And yet, the systematic mapping of such processes provides a useful perspective on familiar projects and activities. In this way PERT/CPM methods can help a risk manager identify risks and consider the more dynamic aspects of a particular project or endeavour.

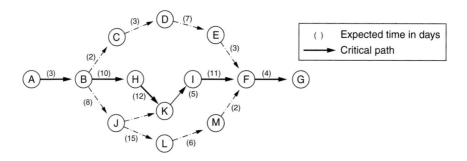

Key

(A) Decide to offer training          (F) Session registrations          (K) Contact educators/speakers

(B) Assemble training team          (G) Sessions begin          (L) Produce training materials

(C) Review logistics          (H) Programme budgeting          (M) Deliver training materials to site

(D) Secure facilities and services          (I) Advertise sessions

(E) Training room setup          (J) Develop curriculum

**Exhibit 11.2**  Planning for a risk management training programme

The PERT/CPM methods also can serve as a planning mechanism for risk management projects themselves (as the illustration shows), so PERT/CPM is not just an analytical tool but can serve as a management technique as well.

# *Index*